CRITICAL
INSIGHTS
The Awakening

CRITICAL INSIGHTS

The Awakening

Editor
Robert C. Evans
Auburn University at Montgomery

SALEM PRESS
A Division of EBSCO Information Services, Inc.
Ipswich, Massachusetts

GREY HOUSE PUBLISHING

∞ The paper used in these volumes conforms to the American National Standard for Permanence of Paper for Printed Library Materials, Z39.48-1992 (R1997).

Library of Congress Cataloging-in-Publication Data

The awakening / editor, Robert C. Evans. -- [1st ed.].
p. ; cm. -- (Critical insights)
Includes bibliographical references and index.
ISBN: 978-1-61925-228-8
1. Chopin, Kate, 1850-1904. Awakening. 2. Feminism in literature. 3. Sex role in literature. I. Evans, Robert C. II. Series: Critical insights.

PS1294.C63 A64352 2013
813/.4

PRINTED IN THE UNITED STATES OF AMERICA

Contents _____

Resources _____

Dedication

Respectfully dedicated to Per Seyersted and Emily Toth,
pioneering scholars of Kate Chopin's life and works.

About This Volume

Robert C. Evans

Fifty years ago, Kate Chopin's novel *The Awakening* was a relatively unknown work, purchased (if at all) by buyers of rare books. Today, it is one of the most widely read, most widely taught, and most widely available of all American literary "classics." Partly because of its brevity, but mainly because of a quality now generally recognized as superb, it appears in numerous anthologies of important texts, and separate editions also now abound. The relative "neglect" of *The Awakening* for over sixty years after it was first published in 1899 is one of the great embarrassments of American literature; the novel's eventual rediscovery and rehabilitation is one of the great achievements of recent literary criticism and scholarship. The present book, it is hoped, will further solidify the now-prominent place of *The Awakening* in the canon of great American literature.

Aside from offering a wide range of critical perspectives on the novel, this volume also provides much new and often surprising evidence about Chopin's life and works, including previously unpublished archival information suggesting that *The Awakening* was indeed banned—and even burned—by some libraries in the years following its initial publication. Also included is additional "new" evidence concerning the novel's initial reception, as well as "new" evidence of Chopin's opinions on a wide variety of topics, from the classic literature she recommended to young readers to her thoughts about women's clothing. A surprising amount of information about Chopin has never been reprinted since it first appeared in American newspapers in the late nineteenth century, and this book offers a first glimpse at some of the "new" data.

The present book begins with a brief essay by Courtney Rottgering that clearly surveys the major events of Chopin's life. This biographical introduction is then followed by a splendid essay by Bernard Koloski, one of a number of major Chopin scholars whose work appears in the present volume. Focusing on Edna Pontellier, the novel's protagonist, Koloski introduces readers to many of the most important debates about this character and provides a model of how to engage, thoughtfully and with an open mind, with the novel as a whole.

Koloski's essay is followed by an article by Julieann Veronica Ulin, the first of several "contextual" pieces designed to view Chopin's novel from particular perspectives. Ulin's essay, dealing with cultural and historical contexts, examines *The Awakening* in light of developments in "impressionist" painting in the late nineteenth century, showing how the novel resembles works by the impressionists, particularly in its use of light and imagery. My own article on *The Awakening* and Mark Twain's *Huckleberry Finn* is offered as a "comparison and contrast" essay. In this piece, I argue that Chopin would have admired Twain for many reasons, and in fact evidence presented later in the book—and discovered after my essay was written—provides explicit support for this claim.

The next "contextual" essay—by Stephen Paul Bray and Sarah Fredericks—offers a very detailed overview of critical reactions to the novel's main characters. Anyone reading this chapter will gain a quite solid sense of the kinds of debates the novel has provoked, as well as the kinds of consensus that sometimes exists in commentary about the book. Finally, another essay of mine rounds out the contextual section. This piece takes a basically "formalist" approach to the novel by arguing that ironies and juxtapositions of various sorts are crucial to the way the book is written, and to how it *reads*. *The Awakening* is an often surprising book, right down to the level of individual phrases and sentences.

The second major section of the present volume opens with the essay already mentioned—an essay in which I present the results of recent research in newspaper archives covering the later years of Chopin's life. As has already been suggested above, the results of this research have often been surprising, especially in the finding that *The Awakening* may actually have been banned (and even burned) by at least two libraries, one of them in Chopin's own hometown of St. Louis. Perhaps the other most interesting item in this chapter is an interview with Chopin, in which she discusses, in some detail, the classic literature she would recommend to younger readers, including the works of Mark Twain. This "archival" chapter presents just the tip of the proverbial iceberg of information about Chopin to be found in American newspapers of her period. Much of the rest of the iceberg will be visible soon in other venues.

The chapter on "new" archival information is followed by an excellent, deliberately "student-friendly" introduction to *The Awakening* by Joyce Dyer, another pioneering scholar of Chopin and author of one of the best book-length introductions to Chopin's most famous novel. In the present essay—written as a letter to students rather than as a standard piece of academic prose—Dyer reflects on her own involvement with *The Awakening* over many decades. Like Bernard Koloski earlier, she argues for an expansive, open-minded approach to a book that often can be (and often has been) read in fairly narrow terms. Dyer's "letter" should prove profitable not only to first-time readers of the novel but also to those who have read it repeatedly.

In two essays following Dyer's, I seek to do two things: first, defend *The Awakening* against the charge that its recent prominence is underserved, and, second, defend Robert Lebrun against the charge that he is a weak character unworthy of Edna's affections. The defense against the first charge is part of a larger effort to show how *The Awakening* is an admirably well-written book. While it is true that the novel is sometimes treated more as a sociological tract than as a great work of fiction, and while it is undeniable that renewed interest in the book coincided with a rebirth of feminism in the 1960s, I seek to show that *The Awakening* genuinely deserves its new status as a piece of great writing. In the second essay, I argue that Robert deserves far more respect than he usually receives. He is, I contend, a much more admirable person than he is usually given credit for being.

The next two essays—by Jeffrey Melton and Thomas Bonner, Jr.—examine *The Awakening* by relating it to issues of travel and leisure. Melton, who has published widely on Mark Twain and travel, here turns his attention to the ways Chopin's novel can profitably be read in light of developments in resort cultures, painting, and landscapes and seascapes in general in Chopin's time. Then Thomas Bonner, Jr.—another pioneering Chopin scholar— looks at *The Awakening* as a work affected by Chopin's familiarity with Louisiana in general and New Orleans in particular.

Another pair of essays—by two veteran scholars of Chopin— place *The Awakening* within the contexts of Chopin's reading. Mary E. Papke focuses her attention on "four novels from Chopin's 'time,' all of which are rarely discussed at length in Chopin scholarship though their affinity with *The Awakening* is striking." And then Robert D. Arner, one of the earliest contributors to the "Chopin revival" of the 1960s and 70s, examines how the idea of "folly" appears throughout the book and is often associated with allegedly foolish women, as is frequently also the case in the Bible. My own essay on humor in *The Awakening* deals less with folly (Arner's focus) than with the fact that Chopin's novel is often a very funny and/or wryly amusing book—an aspect of the text that has received far too little attention.

The three following essays—by Peter J. Ramos, David Z. Wehner, and Janet Beer paired with Helena Goodwyn—place the novel in a variety of fairly serious contexts. Ramos argues that Edna's tragedy results from her mistaken assumption that she can somehow transcend all conventional social roles. Wehner's stimulating piece argues that religion in general—and Catholicism in particular—is far more important to Chopin's thinking and writing than has hitherto been recognized. And, finally, Goodwyn and Beer (the latter the author of much previous work on Chopin) explore not only Edna's development as an artist, but also her ultimate refusal to continue that development.

THE BOOK AND AUTHOR

On *The Awakening*

Bernard Koloski

Is Edna Pontellier a wounded victim of her patriarchal society, or is she a triumphant pioneer in her search for freedom? Is she weak and emotionally troubled or strong and insightful? Would she be better off if she were living in our times, or is her struggle universal—true for women everywhere at all times, or true for women and men everywhere at all times? Should we pity her or admire her? And how are we to decide?

Questions like these have been a primary concern of readers in classes, book clubs, and other forums for decades, and there have been no answers that everyone accepts. But informed people agree that it may be helpful to make use of insights from the feminist movement, from social anthropologists, psychiatrists, historians, and scholars in additional fields, as well as from Kate Chopin's remaining fiction and that of other writers in her time. They agree also that, although we are all entitled to our own opinions, it's best to build those opinions on everything Kate Chopin reveals to us in *The Awakening*. So, it's worthwhile to gather together whatever it is we know about Edna.

Edna's Background

As the title tells us, the story is about a woman waking up and seeing what's going on around her. In a broader sense, it's about a woman becoming more aware of nature and her own character. It's about her understanding life in ways she had not understood it before. That is the heart of *The Awakening*, the principle theme through which Chopin reaches out to us and draws us into her imaginative world, the world of Edna Pontellier and the Creoles she vacations with on an island off the coast of Louisiana one balmy summer in the late nineteenth century.

Edna has a great deal to wake up to, in good part because of her childhood. Her mother had died when she was quite young, and she had problems with her coercive father. She says she once ran away from listening to him preach at a Presbyterian prayer service. When we meet him in chapter twenty-three, the former Confederate colonel sits rigidly while Edna makes a pencil sketch of him. As her children draw near, he chases them away with a motion of his foot. We might wonder how many times he chased away a young Edna in that manner.

At peace with neither an older sister who, we learn, "has all the Presbyterianism undiluted" (63)[1] nor with a vixen-like younger one, Edna turned inward. "Even as a child," the novel tells us, "she had lived her own small life all within herself. At a very early period she had apprehended instinctively the dual life—that outward existence which conforms, the inward life which questions" (14).

As a young adult, Edna fantasized about romantic men—a cavalry officer, a gentleman from a nearby plantation, a famous actor—before marrying Léonce Pontellier and moving with him to Louisiana. She is now twenty-eight years old. She is well off—with a nursemaid to take care of her children and servants to cook and clean—and she seems to have settled into a stable, if passive, life. Her husband is kind enough and generous enough in his own way, in the way his Creole upbringing had taught him. But he expects that Edna will be the loving mother of their sons and manage their home so that they can, as he phrases it, "get on and keep up with the procession" (49)—that is, maintain and enhance their position in New Orleans society.

Edna's Awakening

Edna's summer on Grand Isle affects her powerfully. The sultry air, the sunlight, the sandy beaches and fields of yellow chamomile reinforce her reclusive habits (Kate Chopin's original title for the novel was *A Solitary Soul*). Edna especially loves the sea. Chopin describes her experience in poetic passages: "The voice of the sea is seductive; never ceasing, whispering, clamoring, murmuring, inviting the soul to wander for a spell in abysses of solitude; to lose itself in mazes of inward contemplation" (14).

Yet the people around Edna on the island have the opposite effect on her. The Creoles draw her out of herself. Unlike the Presbyterians she grew up with, they are cosmopolitan, relaxed, warmhearted, open about their private lives, free from prudery, and in love with music, risqué stories, flirting, and good food and wine. They are more French than American, and they are a revelation for her.

Four of the Creoles are especially influential. The beautiful Adèle Ratignolle, whom Chopin calls a "mother-woman" (9) resembling a "sensuous Madonna" (12), subtly entices Edna out of her reserve and lures her to moments of self-revelation. The pianist Mademoiselle Reisz moves Edna powerfully with her music, understands her better than anyone else, and eventually becomes her confidant. Robert Lebrun, the older son of the woman who owns the summer resort, attaches himself to Edna, accompanying her on her daily routines—with the approval of her husband, who knows that Robert is a trustworthy man and will not violate Creole codes of honor. And Alcée Arobin, whom Edna meets after her return to New Orleans—and who is certainly not a trustworthy man—awakens Edna to her sexual nature.

Through her relationships, Edna is sensitized to the power of nature, to the richness of Creole life, to her emerging sexual longing for Robert—and, most important of all, to the reality of her tightly controlled life as a wealthy married woman in 1890s America. "A certain light was beginning to dawn dimly within her," Chopin tells us, "the light which, showing the way, forbids it. . . . In short, Mrs. Pontellier was beginning to realize her position in the universe as a human being, and to recognize her relations as an individual to the world within and about her" (14).

The world about her, she is coming to understand—her husband, her children, her social obligations—limits her from being the woman she would like to be, prevents her from uniting her outward and inward lives.

Back in the city with the summer over, driven by forces she neither fully understands nor seeks to resist, she finds herself unable to return to the life she had known before. She first abandons her required social duties. Then, with her husband in New York and her children visiting family in the country, she moves to a smaller house, begins an affair with Arobin, and declares her love for Robert. She is despondent when she learns that he cannot accept the love she offers him, and she soon heads toward her death in the sea.

Students of literature often describe Kate Chopin's book as a *Bildungsroman*—a story of development, of education, of maturation—a narrative about the psychological growth of a sensitive character, who seeks to understand the world and discover the meaning of life. Johann Wolfgang von Goethe's *Wilhelm Meister's Apprenticeship* is such a narrative, as is Charlotte Brontë's *Jane Eyre*, Mark Twain's *Huckleberry Finn*, and countless popular books and films of our own times. Fairy tales are often maturation stories, and many center on women—the "Little Mermaid," "Cinderella," and "Snow White," among others.

Characters in a *Bildungsroman* sometimes find their way to enlightenment and a fuller, more satisfying life. But sometimes they do not. Sometimes their awakenings are more than they can handle. As Chopin tells us, "the beginning of things, of a world especially, is necessarily vague, tangled, chaotic, and exceedingly disturbing. How few of us ever emerge from such beginning! How many souls perish in its tumult!" (14).

Whether or not Edna Pontellier is one of the souls who perish depends upon how we see her. Comments by influential scholars may help us sort through our thoughts.

A Triumphant Edna

From the year *The Awakening* appeared, people have regarded Edna in vastly different ways. In 1899, most critics saw her in an especially negative light. They condemned her for neglecting her duties to her husband and children. They denounced her sexual behavior and suicide. They called her selfish and weak.

When the novel finally became famous six decades later, a new feminist wave was sweeping the Western world, and people were much more sympathetic toward Edna. In our own times, in the twenty-first century, most critics and scholars see her as a strong woman struggling for selfhood and individual freedom in a social environment that demands she conform, that belabors the importance of her role as mother and homemaker, that regards her as one of her husband's treasured objects.

The Norwegian scholar Per Seyersted, who gathered together all of Chopin's stories, writes in *Kate Chopin: A Critical Biography* that Edna's death "is not so much a result of outer forces crowding her in as a triumphant assertion of her inner liberty." Edna, he adds, "is defeated in the sense that she cannot meaningfully relate herself to the people around her and in some way integrate her demands with those of society, a society, to be sure, which is responsible for the fact that emancipation is her goal rather than her birthright" (149).

Feminist scholars have written hundreds of articles building upon Seyersted's point of view, employing a host of critical approaches and finding evidence to support their arguments from the first sentence in the novel to the last. They write about Edna's search for integrity and autonomy and about her breaking sexual taboos. They write also about pregnancy, gender relations, and suicide, as well as—especially in the work of recent biographer Emily Toth— about how Chopin came to write the novel.[2]

There is no question that Kate Chopin's reputation today is founded on feminist insights into the importance of her work. Among the best-known feminist arguments is that of Sandra M. Gilbert, who, drawing on the work of social anthropologists, looks at archetypes in *The Awakening* and at myths, the ancient patterns of thought in the collective unconscious of people everywhere. Chopin, Gilbert writes, set out "to create a narrative structure in which she might coherently dramatize the female struggle for identity that was her central subject." She would have been aware of "the theology of feminist contemporaries who were revising traditional religious ideas to create woman-centered creeds" (18).

"Abandoning both formal Catholicism and conventional 'morality,'" Gilbert adds, "Chopin must have understood her own desire to tell a new kind of story about a woman's life, a story that would revitalize and vindicate the pagan presence of the goddess of love" (19). In a widely discussed sentence, Gilbert writes, "I want to suggest that *The Awakening* is a female fiction that both draws upon and revises *fin de siècle* [that is, end of nineteenth-century] hedonism to propose a feminist myth of Aphrodite/Venus as an alternative to the patriarchal myth of Jesus" (20).

The novel, she continues, "is organized by Kate Chopin's half-secret (and perhaps only half-conscious) fantasy of the second coming of Aphrodite" (21). In support of her thesis, Gilbert focuses on what she sees as symbolic objects, activities, people, places, and relationships (22). She finds influences in French and British writers—as do many other scholars—and she details, at length, the importance of Edna's learning to swim and her visit with Robert to the *Chênière Caminada*. She concludes with a discussion of the dinner party Edna arranges to celebrate her leaving what she thinks of as her husband's house and moving instead to her little pigeon-house.

At the dinner party, Gilbert argues, Edna "plays the part of the person she has metaphorically become," quoting the novel—"the regal woman, the one who rules, who looks on, who stands alone." The dinner party is for Gilbert "in a sense a Last Supper, a final transformation of will and desire into bread and wine, flesh and blood, before the 'regal woman's' inevitable betrayal by a culture in which her regenerated Aphrodite has no meaningful role" (30). The novel's close, she tells us, depicts Edna "journeying not just toward rebirth but toward an imaginary world beyond the restrictive culture of the nineteenth century, a world in which women might be as free as the mythic Aphrodite was" (32).

Gilbert's essay, reprinted in the widely distributed Penguin Classics edition of the novel, has had a readership around the world. Many people have been struck by the Aphrodite-in-place-of-Jesus argument and have responded to its mythic power.

A Wounded Edna

But there are other ways of reading *The Awakening*. Cynthia Griffin Wolff, writing in an influential *American Quarterly* article, understands the attraction of seeing Edna as a victim of an oppressive patriarchal society that offers her no viable options for living the life that her nature demands. She acknowledges "the power of the novel as growing out of an existential confrontation between the heroine and some external, repressive force. Thus, one might say that it is the woman against stifling sexual standards or that it is the woman against the tedium of a provincial marriage" (449).

But she rejects the argument. "The importance of Chopin's work," she writes, "derives from its ruthless fidelity to the disintegration of Edna's character. Edna, in turn, interests us not because she is 'a woman,' the implication being that her experience is principally important because it might stand for that of any other woman. Quite the contrary: she interests us because she is human— because she fails in ways which beckon seductively to all of us" (450).

Wolff draws on the work of Sigmund Freud and R. D. Laing. Edna, she says, lives with her fantasies and "is very little open to sustained emotional relationships because those elements of character which she might want to call her 'real' self must remain hidden, revealed only to herself." She exists with an "apparent terror" of deep emotional attachment. She marries Léonce Pontellier as a "defensive maneuver designed to maintain the integrity of the two 'selves' that formed her character. . . . An intuitive man, a sensitive husband, might threaten [her inner self]; a husband who evoked passion from her might lure the hidden self into the open, tempting Edna to attach her emotions to flesh and blood rather than phantoms" (451–52).

Wolff quotes R. D. Laing to explain why a "schizoid" personality like Edna understands interpersonal relationships as dangerous: "There is a constant dread and resentment at being turned into someone else's thing, of being penetrated by him, and a sense of being in someone else's power and control" (453).

Many readers sympathize with Edna's refusal to be her husband's possession, with her sense that she is imprisoned in her husband's house. But for Wolff, such feelings are Edna's "projections of her own attitudes and fears" (454). Wolff notes that Robert, however, is safe for Edna because he is much like her, almost a part of her. She cannot envisage that he has an existence separate from hers. Until after he leaves for Mexico, she does not imagine herself in an adult relationship with him (455).

And Alcée Arobin, Wolff writes, is also safe. Edna "can respond sensually to the kiss which initiates their relationship precisely because she has no feeling for him" (455). With Arobin, Edna can separate sex from love. Instead, the great crisis for her comes when Robert returns, responds to her kiss, and declares his love for her. But she cannot "yield her 'self' to the insistence of his passionate plea to stay; and his own subsequent flight destroys the fantasy lover as well. Both of Edna's selves are truly betrayed and barren, and she retrenches in the only manner familiar to her, that of a final and ultimate withdrawal" (456).

A Nineteenth-Century Edna

Sandra Gilbert and Cynthia Griffin Wolff take note of the times and the place in which Edna lives, but that is not their primary interest. Other scholars, however, do look closely at Edna's environment and approach her as governed by the nineteenth-century culture in which Chopin places her.

For much of the twentieth century, Kate Chopin was understood not as a writer focused on women's concerns—as she is understood today—but as a regional writer, a "local color" writer describing a way of life that was being transformed by modernization. Throughout the United States when Chopin was writing fiction in the 1890s, people were leaving farms and small towns and moving to cities where they sought higher-paying jobs and the promise of a better quality of life. And the farms and small towns themselves were being transformed by the appearance of railroads connecting every region to every other region and bringing outside products—factory-made clothing, for example, bicycles, or farm equipment—and outside people into communities that had been self-sufficient and isolated.

Chopin was well aware of such social disruption. Eight years before she wrote *The Awakening*, she had published a novel called *At Fault*, in which a fortyish widow tries to cope with powerful natural and economic changes affecting the plantation she inherited when her husband died.

Like other local color writers, Kate Chopin sought in her fiction to capture and preserve a way of life she understood was disappearing. As Nina Baym notes in the introduction to the Modern Library edition of the novel, "the story of Edna Pontellier could have been set anywhere in the world that allowed some freedoms to women without giving them complete freedom. That is to say, it could have been set *anywhere* in the world. But to be appreciated by readers, it had to be set *somewhere*, and this is how local color enters, and immeasurably strengthens, the novel" (xxviii–xxix).

In nineteenth-century America, Baym points out, "the elite woman's role demanded that she be devoted to home and children in spirit, even though no actual labor was demanded of her; and that she serve, so far as her husband was concerned, as the means by which he might display his wealth and social standing" (xxxvi). Edna has severe social pressures on her, pressures that greatly restrict her freedom and control her daily life. Readers today who are struggling with economic worries are sometimes less than sympathetic toward Edna because they see her as a rich woman free from many of the practical problems they face themselves. But Edna has other problems.

One that Nina Baym discusses at length is sex. It may take some effort for people in Western nations today to recognize how sex was understood when Kate Chopin was writing *The Awakening*. As Baym phrases it, "a contemporary reader may well be inclined to understand Edna's sexual emancipation as a feminist issue. But such a reading would be somewhat anachronistic." In the nineteenth century, Baym write s, progressive women thinking about sex "were more likely to perceive sexual freedom as being freedom *from* sex rather than freedom *through* sex. What they wanted for women was the right to say no, rather than the right to say yes whenever and wherever they pleased" (xxxvii).

The reason for that is complicated. "Much of the difference" Baym tells us, "derives from the relatively crude forms of birth control and the enormous risks of childbearing of those days—

every act of sexual intercourse was, for a woman, a literally life-endangering act" (xxxvii).

The truth of what Baym writes is clearly evident near the close of *The Awakening*, when Edna sees the agony attending the birth of Adèle's child. She is distraught by the experience: "She was seized with a vague dread," the novel tells us. "Her own like experiences seemed far away, unreal, and only half remembered. She recalled faintly an ecstasy of pain, the heavy odor of chloroform, a stupor which had deadened sensation. . . . With an inward agony, with a flaming, outspoken revolt against the ways of Nature, she witnessed the scene [of] torture" (104).

Scholars today often speak with admiration of how openly Chopin deals with sex, especially in *The Awakening* and in her famous short story, "The Storm." Baym agrees that "sexuality is portrayed with unusual frankness for the time and place," although readers used to sexual depictions in contemporary fiction may need to reread chapter twenty-seven to realize that Edna does actually have sex with Alcée Arobin. But, Baym argues, "that frankness does not derive from any conviction that more honest or open sexual behavior will lead to socially or personally desirable goals for women. Edna is really no better off as a result of her extended sexual consciousness" (xxxvii–xxxviii).

So, Baym concludes, "the treatment of Edna's sexual nature and experience is thus eccentric both for its own time and for our time. It is too frank for an earlier age, and too traditional for a later one, in its insistence that sex is not the gateway to freedom" (xxxviii).

Approaching Edna

Per Seyersted, Sandra Gilbert, Cynthia Griffin Wolff, and Nina Baym show us possible ways to understand Edna Pontellier by looking at the details of the novel through ideas growing out of the feminist movement or several academic disciplines. Along with other scholars, they raise people's sensitivity to Edna's struggles. Men as well as women today are likely to sympathize with Edna's feeling of oppression and to recognize the reality of paternalism and its relationship with the religiosity of the times. Of course, not

---

everyone will be comfortable with Gilbert's contrasting Aphrodite with Jesus. Not all people will accept Wolff's emphasis on Edna's emotional troubles. And some readers may be startled by Baym's description of the sexual concerns of women in the nineteenth century. Each of us will take what we can from what others have written about Edna Pontellier.

There are, to be sure, ways for us to approach an understanding of Edna without turning to scholarship. We might, for example, look at Chopin's other fiction, at her early novel and her hundred or so short stories. Reading some of those works makes clear that Kate Chopin is not a pessimistic author focused only on, or even especially on, people's difficulty in finding satisfaction in their lives. Her early novel At Fault and many of her strongest short stories— "Athénaïse" and "A Respectable Woman," among them—are, in fact, rather hopeful narratives. They are realistic, not romantic, but they are imbued with the conviction that people have a reasonable chance to find happiness.

Her fiction reveals, too, that Chopin is not focused only on narratives about strong, sensitive women and oppressive or inconsequential men. In "A No-Account Creole," At Fault, "Charlie," and other works, she offers us resourceful men quite deserving of partnerships with her attractive women. Positioning Edna among some of the other characters in Chopin's imaginative universe may help us gain perspective on her struggles.

We might acquire further understanding of Edna by looking into the historical moment, at which *The Awakening* appeared. Kate Chopin published the novel in 1899, at the cusp of the twentieth century, at the birth of modernist literature, with its emphasis on individuals gaining wide-ranging freedom and taking on major responsibility for their lives. Yet many individuals in early twentieth-century fiction find such freedom to be a great burden. They find themselves beset with despair and loneliness because they have lost their connections to their communities and to the accepted truths passed from one generation to the next by families and religion.

Through her awakening, through her striving for freedom, Edna turns away from her religion, her family, and many of the values she grew up with. She resembles a representative woman in a modernist novel.

Truth and Empathy

For some of us, however, Edna Pontellier does not feel like a character in a novel. She feels more like someone we know, like a real human being. We are left with the question of how we are to approach her.

Chopin offers us guidance through her comments about writing fiction and through her presentation of Edna. She is clear about what she wants to accomplish as a writer—and what she doesn't.

She emphatically does not want to teach people how to live. She finds Émile Zola to be interesting, but in her 1894 review of his novel *Lourdes*, she complains about "the disagreeable fact that his design is to instruct us" (697).[3] *The Awakening*, we are sure to notice, has no message, no lesson, no moral instruction.

And she does not want to change the world, to bring about social reform. In another review, she writes that the Norwegian dramatist Henrik Ibsen "will not be true in some remote to-morrow, however forcible and representative he may be for the hour, because he takes for his themes social problems which by their very nature are mutable." Her objections to him show us what she does not want to do in her own writing. "Social problems, social environments," she argues, "local color and the rest of it are not *of themselves* motives to insure the survival of a writer who employs them" (693).

Chopin admires not the novels of Émile Zola or the plays of Henrik Ibsen, but the short stories of her contemporary Guy de Maupassant, which she read in their original French. When she came upon his stories, she says, she:

> marveled at them. Here was life, not fiction. . . . Here was a man who had escaped from tradition and authority, who had entered into himself and looked out upon life through his own being and with his own eyes; and who, in a direct and simple way, told us what he saw. When a man does this, he gives us the best that he can. (700–01)

Kate Chopin, too, offers us the best that she can. She wants, she says in her first public comment about her work, to describe "human existence in its subtle, complex, true meaning, stripped of the veil with which ethical and conventional standards have draped it" (691).

Chopin wants us to see the truth about Edna. In presenting her to us, she sets aside the ethical and conventional standards of late nineteenth-century America. Her portrait is subtle. We may, in fact, need to reread parts of the novel to grasp what she is saying. And to be true to human existence, she tells us, she needs to capture its complexity. Anything less will not show us the truth—although she understands, as she phrases it in her Zola essay, that "truth rests upon a shifting basis and is apt to be kaleidoscopic" (697), that each of us is likely to reach different conclusions about the truth, based upon what we have learned from our own experiences.

Yet, through her example, through her treatment of Edna, she shows us that we can search for our truth with empathy. Chopin makes no moral judgments about Edna Pontellier. She neither praises her nor condemns her. She looks out upon Edna's life through her own being and tells us what she sees.

Drawing, then, upon everything we know today about Kate Chopin and her work, we can propose answers to the questions we began with:

- Yes, Edna Pontellier is damaged by her patriarchal society, as almost any woman would have been in her times. And yes, she is courageous in her search for freedom.
- Yes, it's true that, given her childhood, Edna is emotionally troubled in adulthood. She is, nevertheless, an insightful, extraordinary nineteenth-century woman.
- Yes, of course, she would be better off if she were living in our times. Her outward and inward struggle might be the same, although Presbyterianism in the twenty-first century is not what it was in parts of the American South over a hundred years ago. However, she would have access to opportunities and support not available in her times. And she could have sex without a fear of fatal consequences. Yet, in different degrees, the coercive power of patriarchy continues al-

most everywhere today, as it has for millennia. Like other forms of oppression and other environments, in which one group of people has disproportionate power over another group, a patriarchal culture damages everybody. It damages men as well as women, although certainly not equally. In the novel, we can see its effects on Edna's husband, on Robert Lebrun, and on Alcée Arobin.

- Finally, we might best approach Edna with neither pity nor admiration, but with the empathy that Kate Chopin employs in presenting her to us.

Notes

1. Kate Chopin, *The Awakening: An Authoritative Text, Biographical and Historical Contexts, Criticism.* Ed. Margo Culley. 2nd ed. New York: Norton, 1994. Quotations from *The Awakening* are cited in the text as page numbers.

2. Up-to-date listings of books and articles, along with extensive information about Kate Chopin and her work, is available at *KateChopin.org*, the website of the Kate Chopin International Society.

3. Kate Chopin, *The Complete Works of Kate Chopin.* Ed. Per Seyersted. Baton Rouge: Louisiana State UP, 1969. Quotations from Chopin's essays are cited in the text as page numbers.

Works Cited

ABaym, Nina. Introduction. *The Awakening and Selected Stories by Kate Chopin.* Ed. Nina Baym. New York: Modern Library, 1981. vii–xl.

Chopin, Kate. *The Awakening: An Authoritative Text, Biographical and Historical Contexts, Criticism.* Ed. Margo Culley. 2nd ed. New York: Norton, 1994.

_____. *The Complete Works of Kate Chopin.* Ed. Per Seyersted. Baton Rouge: Louisiana State UP, 1969.

Gilbert, Sandra, ed. "The Second Coming of Aphrodite." Introduction. *The Awakening and Selected Stories.* By Kate Chopin. New York: Penguin, 1984. 7–33.

Koloski, Bernard, ed. *KateChopin*.org. Kate Chopin International Society. Web. 23 Oct. 2013. <http://www.katechopin.org>.

Seyersted, Per. *Kate Chopin: A Critical Biography.* Baton Rouge: Louisiana State UP, 1969.

Wolff, Cynthia G. "Thanatos and Eros: *Kate Chopin's The Awakening.*" *American Quarterly* 25 (1973): 449–71.

Biography of Kate Chopin _____

Courtney Rottgering

The baby in the cradle was named Katherine O'Flaherty, daughter of Irish émigré-turned-businessman Thomas O'Flaherty and French Creole belle Elizabeth Faris. Born on February 8, 1850 in St. Louis, Missouri, the child would see the Civil War split her city and nation apart, her honeymoon abbreviated by the Franco-Prussian War, the birth of six children, the death of her husband, and an ascendant career in publishing under her married name of Kate Chopin. Her short stories and novels, though garnering uneven critical praise in her lifetime, have endured to become part of the canon of American local color and feminist writings. Her life has now been the subject of various biographies, including a pioneering early work by Daniel Rankin, a superb later work by Per Seyersted, and especially two recent, crucial works by Emily Toth (see "Works Cited" for details). These are all titles, on which all later biographies—including this one—must depend. Toth's works, for instance, are obviously the main sources for the superbly detailed chronology included in the Library of America's edition of Chopin's works.

Chopin was raised and educated as a Catholic, beginning her school career in 1855 at the Sacred Heart Academy in St. Louis. However, she was withdrawn, a short time into the term, after the death of her father in a freak railroad accident. Thomas O'Flaherty, along with other local dignitaries, was celebrating the opening of a line on the Pacific Railroad when a newly built bridge collapsed under the weight of the train and sent it plunging into a river.

Her father's death left Chopin immersed in a household of women, and strong women at that. Elizabeth Faris was now a wealthy widow, and her own mother and grandmother, who had joined the household, were unusually educated and liberated for women of the period. Chopin's great-grandmother, Victoire Verdon Charleville, undertook the girl's education before she returned to Sacred Heart in the fall of 1857, as a day student rather than a boarder. There, she developed a particularly close friendship with a girl named Kitty Garesché. Her friendship with Kitty and instruction by the Sacred Heart nuns continued and reinforced Chopin's female-dominated life (Toth, Kate Chopin 34-54).

After her father's death, there was one male figure who remained constant in Chopin's early life: her half-brother George. "Ten-year-old Kate had developed a case of hero worship for this big brother," says Cynthia Griffin Wolff. No doubt, this affection was enhanced by George's enlistment in the Confederate Army in 1861.

The Civil War years in St. Louis were turbulent, as most of the city's residents sympathized with the Southern cause, while the city itself was occupied by Union soldiers. The O'Flaherties were slave owners, and Chopin, even at her tender age, became an ardent anti-Unionist. Chafing under the Union regime, she was threatened with arrest for pulling down a Union flag and only escaped due to the intercession of a pro-Union neighbor. Her rebellion against the Union occupation was likely influenced by the 1862 capture and imprisonment of her half-brother George by Union forces.

Eighteen sixty-three saw the death of two of Chopin's early influences: her great-grandmother and early tutor, Victoire Verdon Charleville, in January, followed a month later by George's death from typhoid. Union occupation of St. Louis intensified after Southern defeats, and Chopin's family endured the forced raising of a Union flag over their home and the departure of the family slaves.

In the aftermath of the Civil War, Chopin resumed her Catolic education with a brief stint at Academy of the Visitation, before returning to Sacred Heart, from which she would graduate in 1868. While at school, she read voraciously and omnivorously: "She read not only Sir Walter Scott, Dickens, Jane Austen, and Charlotte and Emily Brontë, but also Dante, Cervantes, Pierre Corneille, Jean Racine, Molière, Madame de Staël, Chateaubriand, and Goethe. Being bilingual, she had an easy familiarity with, as well as a special affinity for, French literature" (Dimock; see also Seyersted 25). In her final high school years and for some time into her social debut,

Chopin began to fill a small book with various writings: the first hint of the renowned writer that she would become.

The St. Louis social scene grated on Chopin, with its emphasis on dancing, parties, and ladylike behavior. Although she would never ally herself with a particular cause or movement, Chopin was interested in the "woman question" and its application in real life. However, her social debut allowed her access to two things that would affect her for the rest of her life.

The first was a three-month trip to New Orleans with her mother, cousins, and friends. The city captivated Chopin; she wrote in her diary: "N. Orleans I liked immensely; it is so clean--so white and green. Although in April, we had profusions of flowers--strawberries and even black berries" (Seyersted and Toth 64). She took advantage of the permissive Creole culture by learning to smoke cigarettes, a dubious accomplishment for a lady in society. It was around this time that Chopin wrote her first short story, "Emancipation: A Life Fable," exploring themes of confinement and liberty. The story was not published.

Perhaps it was this trip that set the stage for the great romance of Chopin's life: her marriage to Oscar Chopin, whom she met at one of the society parties she loathed. Oscar was the scion of an old French Creole family, appropriately employed in cotton brokerage and with several farms under his control. The pair married on June 9, 1870 and spent their honeymoon abroad. Chopin continued her writing by way of a honeymoon diary, in which she records her impressions of the various sights the couple saw: zoos, mummies, museums, cathedrals, and natural scenery. The honeymoon was abbreviated, however, by the beginning of the Franco-Prussian War. The Chopins left Paris just days before the Germans invaded.

Settled into their home in New Orleans, Kate Chopin found herself pregnant with her first child. Her match with Oscar was a good one: "He respected his young wife as an intellectual equal, accepted her unconventional attire, put up with her cigarette smoking and beer drinking, and laughed it off when anxious relatives rebuked him for allowing her to forget her 'duty'" (Dimock). Oscar's relaxed attitude toward convention likely reflects his own rebellion against his father's rigidity and borderline abuse of his family.

For several years, the marriage was idyllic. Oscar's cotton brokerage thrived, and Kate gave birth to five sons: Jean Baptiste (1871), Oscar Chopin, Jr. (1873), George Francis (1874), Frederick (1876), and Felix Andrew (1878). Throughout this time, Kate made frequent trips to St. Louis to visit family, and the first three of the children were baptized there. The family also made summer trips to the resort island of Grand Isle. "This was certainly the happiest period of Kate Chopin's life. She was deeply and passionately in love with her husband; and as each of their six children arrived, she found motherhood to be profoundly moving as well" (Wolff).

Alas, the prosperity was not to last. Heavy rains in 1878 and 1879 ruined the cotton crop and, with it, Oscar's business. The family moved to Cloutierville, a small Creole village, where Oscar opened a general store and oversaw several small farms. Though she may not have realized it yet, Kate would never live in New Orleans again. Having lived her whole life in large cities, Kate found the small-town atmosphere both charming and stifling. Residents were scandalized by the worldly Mrs. Chopin's habits of smoking and dress. However, the December 31, 1879 birth of her daughter, Marie Laiza (called Lelia), went far toward turning the town's affection to her. "In 1880 the new Cane River packet was named after her newborn daughter, surely an eloquent testimony to her popularity" (Dimock).

Oscar had only a few short years to spend with his new daughter and the rest of his family. In fall 1882, he contracted malaria and died December 10, leaving his family in debt. For the next two years, Kate tried to run her late husband's businesses, focusing on the general store. During this period, she had a brief affair with a married man, Albert Sampite (*Toth, Kate Chopin* 164-72 and *Unveiling* 95-108).

In 1884, Kate gave up her husband's business ventures in Cloutierville and moved with her children back to St. Louis to attend to her mother, who died a year later. At a loss, Kate turned to her mother's doctor, Frederick Kolbenheyer, who encouraged her writing. Kolbenheyer encouraged her to explore the new studies of science, and soon she was reading Darwin, Huxley, and Spencer. At the same time—and perhaps even more significantly—she was read to as well. Her own letters, sent to Kolbenheyer from Louisiana, were now recited aloud by him, so that she might notice their literary merits. With such earnest promptings, she finally took up writing when she was thirty-eight years old and a mother of six (Dimock).

In 1888, Chopin made her first tentative steps toward writing for publication. She wrote her first poem, began the short story "Euphraisie," and actually published a polka. Under Dr. Kolbenheyer's tutelage, she read and much admired Guy de Maupassant. The next year, Chopin published a poem ("If It Might Be") and two stories—"Wiser Than a God" and "A Point at Issue." Realizing that she would never live in Louisiana again, she had Oscar's body brought to St. Louis for reburial.

Chopin's first novel, *At Fault*, was rejected for publication in 1890, but she paid to have a thousand copies printed. She began a second novel, Young Dr. Gosse, and joined the "Wednesday Club," an intellectual women's organization founded by T.S. Eliot's mother. However, as in her debutante years, Chopin disliked organizations and clubs and resigned her membership in 1892.

Her writing career, slowly but surely, began to thrive. She published several stories for children, and with the novel *Young Dr. Gosse* rejected ten times, she turned to writing her first stories set in Louisiana. In 1893, "Désirée's Baby" was published by *Vogue*, which would continue to be an outlet for Chopin's stories. In May of that year, Chopin traveled to New York and Boston to meet with various publishers and editors. In these meetings, she learned that her short stories were more marketable than her poetry. Houghton Mifflin accepted a collection of short stories called *Bayou Folk*, which came out in March 1894.

The year *Bayou Folk* came out was something of a banner year for Chopin. She began translating stories by de Maupassant with an eye toward publication. In June 1894, she attended a writers' conference, but true to her nature, disliked the experience and the importance placed on conventional writing. The experience was ameliorated by a profile of her placed in a national writers' magazine.

Throughout the year, she published more stories in prominent national venues, including "The Dream of an Hour" (later renamed "The Story of an Hour").

Despite several rejections from Houghton Mifflin, in 1897, her second story collection, *Nights* in *Acadie*, saw print. The next year, her new novel, *The Awakening*, and a third collection of short stories, *A Vocation and a Voice*, were both accepted for publication.

The 1899 publication of *The Awakening* stirred up a storm of controversy and mainly negative reviews. However, Chopin was buoyed by a series of positive, though anonymous, letters about the book, and she was well-received in St. Louis, speaking to several hundred women interested in local authors. She was also profiled in the local paper. Nevertheless, the mostly negative reception of *The Awakening* permanently damaged her career.

From 1900 until her death in 1904, Chopin's critical acclaim and publishing prowess waned. Although she was included in the first *Who's Who in America*, her story collection *A Vocation and a Voice* would not be published after all. In 1901, she wrote only a single story, and in 1902, the last tale she would see in print was published. Perhaps in anticipation or fear of her own death, Chopin made out her will.

In August 1904, Chopin—having seen both the Civil War and the turn of a new century—attended the St. Louis World's Fair. "Chopin was so entranced by it that she fell into the habit of strolling through it each day" (Wolff). After attending on August 20, the writer suffered a cerebral hemorrhage, from which she died on August 22. She was buried in St. Louis's Calvary Cemetery, under a headstone that listed only her name and dates, with no idea that her controversial works would eventually see rebirth into the American literary canon of cultural and feminist literature.

Works Cited

BChopin, Kate. *Complete Novels and Stories*. Ed. Sandra M. Gilbert. New York: Library of America, 2002.

Dimock, Wai-chee. "Katherine Chopin." *Modern American Women Writers*. Ed. Elaine Showalter, Lea Baechler, and A. Walton Litz. New York: Charles Scribner's Sons, 1991.

Rankin, Daniel. *Kate Chopin and Her Creole Stories*. Philadelphia: U of Pennsylvania P, 1932.

Seyersted, Per. *Kate Chopin: A Critical Biography*. Baton Rouge: Louisiana State UP, 1969.

Seyersted, Per and Emily Toth, eds. *A Kate Chopin Miscellany*. Natchitoches, LA: Northwestern State UP, 1979). 47-88.

Skaggs, Peggy. *Kate Chopin*. Twayne's United States Authors Series 485. Boston: Twayne Publishers, 1985.

Toth, Emily. *Kate Chopin*. New York: William Morrow, 1990.

____. *Unveiling Kate* Chopin. Jackson: U of Mississippi P, 1999.

Wolff, Cynthia Griffin. "Katherine Chopin." Ed. Leonard Unger. New York: Charles Scribner's Sons, 1979.

CRITICAL
CONTEXTS

"Oh! To be able to paint in color rather than in words!": Kate Chopin's *The Awakening* and Impressionism

Julieann Veronica Ulin

In a late conversation in Kate Chopin's *The Awakening*, Edna Pontellier asks Robert Lebrun to tell her of his experience in Mexico and particularly of the women there: "I should like to know and hear about the people you met, and the impressions they made on you" (96). Edna's question is motivated less by a desire to better understand the women in Mexico than to better understand Robert through his perception of them. Robert's reply is significant for its emphasis on the subjective nature of impressions. "There are some people," Robert tells her, "who leave impressions not so lasting as the imprint of an oar upon the water." Robert's use of water imagery here underscores the fluidity and the flux of impressions. When Alcée Arobin joins their conversation, he points out that impressions reveal the difference in perception. When he was in Mexico, he tells Edna and Robert, the girls "made more of an impression on me than I on them" (96). The discussion among the three participants in the novel's erotic triangle foregrounds the multi-perspectival nature of subjectivity, an assumption at the core of the artistic movement known as impressionism.

In *Unveiling Kate Chopin* (1999), Emily Toth locates the inception of the novel that would become *The Awakening* in Kate Chopin's conversations with the French artist Edgar Degas. Prior to his visit to New Orleans in 1872, Degas regularly attended the weekly soirées in Paris hosted by two artistic sisters, Berthe and Edma Morisot (Pfeiffer and Hollein 290). The Morisot sisters were trained by Geoffroy-Alphonse Chocarne, Joseph Guichard, and Camille Corot, and the sisters went on *enplein air* (open air) painting expeditions with Corot. While Berthe Morisot would become a well-known impressionist painter, an ambitious artist who would be among the first French women to make a career in art, Edma's 1869 marriage to Adolphe Pontillon "occasioned the end of her artistic career." Edma would later write to her sister that "[I] wish that I could escape, if only for a quarter of an hour, to breathe that air in which we lived for many long years." In 1872, Degas spent five months in New Orleans, living in the city of his mother's birth with his uncle on Esplanade Street at the edge of the French Quarter, and Toth speculates on his meeting with Chopin:

> There are more than a few clues that Degas met Kate Chopin—also a solitary stroller—during that short time. Both his uncle and his brother, René De Gas, belonged to the Cotton Exchange with Oscar [Chopin], and his uncle's office was next door to Oscar's on Carondelet Street. But certain other factors make it apparent that Edgar Degas gossiped with Oscar's wife with some depth and intensity. (Toth 73)

These "clues," Toth claims, may be found in the names of *The Awakening*'s Léonce and Edna Pontellier:

> In her New Orleans years, [Chopin] learned from Edgar Degas about his friend Berthe Morisot and her sister Edma, the painter who gave up her art when she married Adolphe Pontillon in 1869, a year before the Chopins arrived in New Orleans. Edma Morisot Pontillon regretted that sacrifice for the rest of her life. (215)

Toth links Degas's circle to the character name of Léonce in *The Awakening* as well. On April 13, 1878 his brother René De Gas ran off with América Durrive Olivier, the wife of Léonce Olivier (Benfey 252-257). According to Toth, Chopin chose the name for the abandoned husband of *The Awakening* based on this New Orleans scandal, just as she adapted the name of the female artist silenced in marriage for Edna Pontellier. "For the mismated spouses in *The Awakening*, then, Kate Chopin combined the real-life names that she must have heard, first, from Edgar Degas: (Edma) Pontillon and (Léonce) Olivier . . . Enda and Léonce Pontellier" (Toth 75). The similarities between the names, Toth argues, "cannot possibly be coincidental" (74).

In addition to the influence of Degas, Toth suggests that Chopin's style was influenced by his fellow impressionist painter Mary Cassatt, whose controversial *Modern Woman* mural adorned the Hall of Honor in the Women's Building of the World's Columbian Exposition in Chicago in 1893. Toth singles out Chopin's short story, "A Lady of Bayou St. John," and Madame Ratignolle in *The Awakening* as influenced by Chopin seeing Cassatt's work at the World's Fair:

> By 1893, for the Chicago fair, the Impressionist painter Mary Cassatt had produced 'Modern Woman,' a gorgeous mural with madonnalike female figures—much like the form of Madame Ratignolle in *The Awakening* . . . When she came back from the fair, Kate Chopin wrote a story using the shimmering colors and sunny pastels of the Impressionists. (Toth 138)

In her analysis of Cassatt's use of an impressionist garden scene as the setting for her mural, Griselda Pollock writes that the mural altered the representation of women through presenting an alternative perspective that challenged the representation in Genesis:

> To superimpose, therefore, a joyful and celebratory plucking of the Fruits of Knowledge and Science on the modernist landscape of suburban pleasure, country holidays, and recreation associated with Impressionist new painting is at once to find a way to signify the 'new' women's guilt-free claims to education and intellectuality as well as to propose modernity's supersession of the age-old definitions of Women created in the Biblical condemnation of Eve. (Pollock 43)

Despite these connections between the impressionists and the author of *The Awakening*, there have been few attempts to consider the result of these intersections between Chopin and the impressionists beyond matters of biographical interest. Despite its title, Christopher Benfey's *Degas in New Orleans: Encounters in the Creole World of Kate Chopin and George Washington Cable* keeps the three title figures with "interwoven lives" largely separated in his study (Benfrey 5). His discussion of *The Awakening* focuses primarily on illuminating the textual presence of the Civil War. Whether the nominal correspondences between the names of Chopin's artist-woman constrained by her marriage and of her abandoned husband come from Chopin's encounter with Degas (if such an encounter ever occurred) or if the portrait of Madame Ratignolle is indebted to Cassatt, there can be little doubt that the revolutionary impressionist aesthetic with which Morisot, Cassatt, and Degas are associated pervades Chopin's 1899 novel.

The world of Kate Chopin's *The Awakening* is one of fading light, softening focus, and melting instability; when Edna Pontellier awakens, it is to an impressionist landscape with all of its attendant possibilities and perils. *The Awakening* presents settings in which there are no clear demarcations, a fact that Edna will gradually perceive to offer possibilities for change. In choosing impressionism as the artistic palette for her novel, Chopin foregrounds perception to depict a self and the concept of identity in flux. While the descriptive language of the novel locates us in the impressionist aesthetic from the opening, Edna's own artistic endeavors begin in her unsatisfactory participation in the realist tradition before surrendering mimetic art in favor of a more revolutionary style. Ultimately, the impressionist realm of consistent change and unfixed contours proves too overwhelming for Edna, offering not only aesthetic possibility, but personal inconstancy. With the return to a world of strict lines finally impossible, she sees no choice other than to submerge herself within sensory perception in the novel's final scene. Though Edna Pontellier's aesthetic journey toward impressionism—not unlike her possible namesake's—is incomplete when compared to the journeys ofEdgar Degas, Berthe Morisot, or Mary Cassat, Chopin's use of impressionist techniques throughout the novel fulfills the artistic promise that her protagonist leaves unfinished.

In her study of literary impressionism, Maria Elisabeth Kronegger writes that "Life exists for the impressionists only where there are colors, sounds, the outdoors, and the sun" (Kronegger 39). At the heart of impressionism is the "erosion of contours, the fragmentation of form and matter" (26). From the opening of her novel, Chopin immerses the reader in an impressionist landscape of bathers carrying "sunshades," gardens, and mother and child figures (4, 5). Edna first appears as a blur through the cigar smoke and sun glare of a Grand Isle summer. Her husband watches her "white sunshade . . . advancing at a snail's pace from the beach" (4). From the start, Chopin's depictions of mental and physical spaces are awash in the language of impressionism, in descriptions that highlight the irresolute blending of forms and colors: "the gulf looked far away, *melting hazily* into the blue of the horizon" (emphasis mine, Chopin 4). Chopin describes the path to the beach on Grand Isle as an intrusion of growth and intoxicating scents:

> The walk to the beach was no inconsiderable one, consisting as it did of a long, sandy path upon which a sporadic and tangled growth that bordered it on either side made frequent and unexpected inroads. There were acres of yellow chamomile reaching out on either hand. Further away still, vegetable gardens abounded, with frequent small plantations of orange or lemon trees intervening. The dark green clusters glistened from afar in the sun. (15)

As Edna walks toward her first solitary swim after hearing the music of Mademoiselle Reisz, she is greeted by "a *tangle* of the sea smell and of weeds and damp, new-plowed earth, *mingled* with the heavy perfume of a field of white blossoms" (emphasis mine, 27). Chopin continually erases the lines of demarcation between sea and sky. "The night sat lightly upon the sea and the land" as Edna first swims alone in a sea of "broad billows that *melted* into one another and did not break" (emphasis mine, 27). Chopin designates this territory as *terra incognita*, a new and possibly dangerous world: "But the beginning of things, of a world especially, is necessarily vague, tangled, chaotic, and exceedingly disturbing. How few of us ever emerge from such a beginning!" (14). Edna's increasing willingness to submit herself to her impressions signals the start of a revolutionary awakening that Chopin emphasizes through the aesthetic revolution of impressionism.

In her repeated use of the word "impression," Chopin foregrounds subjective sensory perception over a fixed and solid presentation of reality. Kronegger writes that "impressionist artists started from perception. They rejected the traditional emphasis upon order, thought, and clearness. Through sensory experience, the impressionist opens a new relationship with the everyday world. Its stimulus affects the senses; the senses affect the mind" (Kronegger 35). Chopin uses the same language of melting and fading to depict shifts in Edna's mental landscape, emphasizing how the same aesthetic techniques apply to memory and perception. Chopin repeatedly shows Edna's vulnerability to impressions in a manner that foregrounds her perception. The verbal absence of prudery among the Creoles is "a characteristic which distinguished them and which *impressed* Mrs. Ponteller most forcibly" (emphasis mine, 10). Edna's troubled dreams leave "only an *impression* upon her half-awakened senses" (emphasis mine, 31-32), but the more she awakens, the more she becomes subject to impressions. In her first solitary swim, Edna chooses to alter her gaze, in order to achieve an alternative perspective:

> She turned her face seaward to gather in an *impression* of space and solitude, which the vast expanse of water, *meeting and melting* with the moonlit sky, conveyed to her excited fancy. As she swam she seemed to be reaching out for the unlimited in which to lose herself. (emphasis mine, 28)

The passage not only creates an impressionist landscape, in which clear limits and solid boundaries give way to a "meeting and melting" fluidity, but indicates that Edna is "reaching out" to lose herself in "an impression." After leaving the sanctuary of domestic bliss at the Ratignolles, Edna feels not envy but:

> a pity for that colorless existence which never uplifted its possessor beyond the region of blind contentment, in which no moment of anguish ever visited the soul, in which she would never have the taste of life's delirium. Edna vaguely wondered what she meant by 'life's delirium.' It had crossed her thought like some unsought, extraneous impression. (54)

This new Edna, subject to each "unsought, extraneous impression," is a departure from her past self. Edna has always been "self-contained" (17). The lines of her body "were long, clean and symmetrical" (15). In her growing rejection of the mimetic art for a revolutionary aesthetic that encompasses change and movement, Edna transcends not only the hard lines of her body, but the Gender, Race, and Region in the Writings of Grace King, Ruth McEnery Stuart, and Kate Chopined expectation that she produce decorative art that copies. Her growing voice and power intoxicate her and change her composition. As she talks with Madame Ratignolle on the beach, the sound of her own voice "muddled her like wine, or like a first breath of freedom" (19). She begins to feel the very opposite of self-contained: "her whole being seemed to be one with the sunlight, the color, the odors, the luxuriant warmth of some perfect Southern day" (56). But it is in the novel's final use of the word "impression" that Chopin underscores Edna as uniquely subject to the influence of impressions. In the penultimate chapter, Doctor Mandelet criticizes Adèle for allowing Edna to witness the childbirth: "There were a dozen women she might have had with her, unimpressionable women" (38). The Edna who returns to Grand Isle to swim into "the unlimited" has been medically diagnosed as impressionable (28).

While the descriptive relationship between Edna and impressionism would seem to indicate her potential as an artist, Chopin regularly uses the techniques of impressionism to suggest the instability of Edna's fortitude. As a child, Edna was enamored of a cavalry officer until he "melted imperceptibly out of her existence" (18). As for Robert, Edna's love for him ebbs and flows in a manner that Chopin describes in the language of impressionism:

> It was not that she dwelt upon the details of their acquaintance, or recalled in any special or peculiar way his personality; it was his being, his existence, which dominated her thought, *fading sometimes as if it would melt into the mist* of the forgotten, reviving again with an intensity which filled her with an incomprehensible longing. (emphasis mine, 52)

She grows "melting and affectionate" toward her husband though she loves Robert (69). Edna's resolve to behave indifferently to Robert "melted when she saw him" (100). This technique, in which Edna's mental landscape is rendered in the identical terms used to depict the surrounding land and seascape, unites the aesthetic of impressionism with Edna's development as an individual and as an artist, while simultaneously warning of the threat posed to her aesthetic potential by her irresolute character.

Edna's growing immersion—one might say submersion—into the realm of impressionism follows her experience listening to the music of Mademoiselle Reisz and is aligned with the loss of "material pictures" (26). Of this moment, Chopin writes "perhaps it was the first time she was ready, perhaps the first time her being was tempered *to take an impress* of the abiding truth. She waited for the *material pictures* which she thought would gather and blaze before her imagination. She waited in vain" (emphasis mine, 26). What follows this "impress" of truth is no easily categorized painting of a still-life, a demure woman with a cat, or the mythic Daedalus and Icarus, but instead a solitary immersion within a sensory and emotional experience: "the very passions themselves were aroused within her soul, swaying it, lashing it, as the waves daily beat upon her splendid body." Chopin's language here unites Edna's new state (her awakening to impressions) with the loss of the conventional "material pictures."

Edna Pontellier's rejection of the rigid constraints of social custom in favor of "becoming an artist" parallels the impressionists' subversion of the established schools of painting, and Edna's art in the novel shifts closer toward impressionism with each painting. Edna is attracted to images and mental pictures, in which the lines are blurred, movement is captured, and space is not fully resolved. Remembering a walk in a meadow in Kentucky when she was a girl, Edna recalls the "meadow that seemed as big as the ocean to the very little girl walking through the grass, which was higher than her waist. She threw out her arms as if swimming when she walked, beating the tall grass as one strikes out in the water. Oh, I see the connection now!" (17). On the one hand, Edna here "sees the connection" between the seascape she is looking at and the Kentucky memory, which she experiences. But on the other hand, we might interpret this recognition of a connection as the reason that impressionism, rather than mimetic or realist art, attracts Edna: it allows for recognition of the connection between disputed spaces. Edna's "self-contained" character begins to break down in a growing recognition of "her relations as an individual to the world within and around her" (17, 14).

As she develops an increasing individuality as an artist, Edna faces a number of the same critiques that the "savage, irreverent, undisciplined and heretical" impressionists did (Pfeiffer 145). In her study of the reception of women impressionist painters, Ingrid Pfeiffer notes that "impressionist art was accused of being *capricious*, nervous, irresolute, superficial, imitative, unfinished, naïve, weak, ephemeral, and of no lasting value—all attributes that were generally reserved for women" (emphasis mine, Pfeiffer and Hollein 15). In his 1880 criticism of the impressionist Berthe Morisot, whose sister Edma (Toth argues) is the inspiration for Edna, Paul de Charry asked: "Why, given her undeniable talent, does she not take the trouble to finish her pictures? . . . *Morisot is a woman and therefore capricious*. Unfortunately, she is like Eve, who bites the apple and then gives up on it too soon. Too bad, since she bites so well" (emphasis mine, Pfeiffer and Hollein 16). When she abandons the others on the beach following her first solitary successful swim, Edna elects to command her own path. This leads to an exchange that resonates with the language used above:

> She started to walk away alone. They called to her and shouted to her. She waved a dissenting hand, and went on, paying no further heed to their renewed cries which sought to detain her. "Sometimes I am tempted to think that Mrs. Pontellier is capricious" said Madame Lebrun. . . . "I know she is," assented Mr. Pontellier; "sometimes, not often." (Chopin 28)

As Edna begins to take her art more seriously, she progresses from a mimetic and domestic style, so often associated with females in art history, to a more imaginative form of creation. The first artistic endeavor that we witness Edna undertaking is Adèle's portrait on Grand Isle. In her opposing descriptions of Edna and Adèle, Chopin signals the division between the traditional portrait and the impressionist portrait. Adèle cannot be described except by "the old [words] that have served so often" (9). She has "nothing hidden or subtle about her charms," and her features are easily described and categorized: for example, her "spun-gold hair," her "blue eyes that were like nothing but sapphires," and her two lips "so red one could only think of cherries" (9). Even when she claims to feel faint, the "rose tint" does not fade from her cheeks (13). Adèle Ratognolle not only functions as the epitome of the "mother-woman," but she can be described in a portrait style that limits and controls interpretation and preserves conventions. Fittingly, we meet Adèle as she is sewing an "impervious" Eskimo-like garment designed to protect her children from the intrusion of the outside world into the sacred space of the home: "They were designed for winter wear, when treacherous drafts came down chimneys and insidious currents of deadly cold found their way through key-holes" (10). Edna, by contrast, will actively invite the outside world into the private space of the house. She herself is a blend, an "American, with a small infusion of French which seemed to have been lost in dilution" (6). She has eyes and hair of a "yellowish-brown," a merger of two colors that aligns her with the melting colors of impressionism (5).

Prior to beginning Adèle's portrait, the narrator tells us that Edna "dabbled with [art] in an unprofessional way" (12). Edna is drawn to paint Adèle less because of her appeal as a subject than because of the specific way that she is transformed through light: "Never had that lady seemed a more tempting subject than at that moment, seated there like some sensuous Madonna, with the gleam of the fading day enriching her splendid color" (12). At the moment when Edna desires to paint her, Adèle is in a transitional phase; both sensuous woman and Madonna figure, her easily identifiable features now enriched by "the fading day." As Kronegger notes, light is "the soul of impressionist paintings" (Kronegger 42). In *The Awakening*, there are over forty references to light sources and Chopin depicts the effect of changing light not only on seascape and landscape, but on mood and personality. Edna is "tempted" to paint Adèle because of how Adèle's conventional figure is transformed by light. Edna's effort, in so far as she wishes to create a likeness to Adèle, is a failure, and Adèle, who continually identifies with traditional representative art, shows her disappointment:

> The picture completed bore no resemblance to Madame Ratignolle. She was greatly disappointed to find that it did not look like her. But it was a fair enough piece of work, and in many respects satisfying. Mrs. Pontellier evidently did not think so. After surveying the sketch critically she drew a broad smudge of paint across its surface and crumbled the paper between her hands (13).

However, the narrator flags Edna's technique in a manner that suggests why her painting is a disappointment as a copy. As a painter, Edna "handled her brushes with a certain ease and freedom which came . . . from a natural aptitude" (12). This characterization of how Edna holds her tools suggests a more fluid style and may serve to explain the distinction between the narrator and Adèle's assessment of the work. In terms of achieving "invisible execution and the dominance of line over color," Edna's art seems to have failed (House 146). The ease with which Edna holds her brushes, however, suggests that her aptitude lies in more subversive art forms: "the visible colored *touche* was a marker of the rejection of academic shackles and demonstrated the painter's concern to translate personal visual experiences into paint" (House 146). Edna's strength does not lie in producing mimetic art in its historically "female" forms. Nonetheless, the narrator emphasizes her talent. As Edna begins to think of her art as "work," she moves from realistic to more imaginative art, thus abandoning the constraints of the traditional form.

After her return to New Orleans, Edna looks upon her art with an entirely new degree of professionalism and gradually forsakes copying for more imaginative subjects. Chopin tells the reader that "Edna spent an hour or two in looking over some of her old sketches. She could see their shortcomings and defects" (Chopin 52). Nonetheless, she takes them to Adèle's house and announces, "I believe I ought to work again. I feel as if I wanted to be doing something" (53). Edna once again wishes to paint Adèle, this time because of her "rich, melting curves," yet Edna's first paintings include a Bavarian peasant, likely copied from another painting, and a basket of apples (53). Adèle exclaims over the apples in a manner that suggests the temptation posed by such a realistic style: "Never have I seen anything more lifelike! One might almost be tempted to reach out a hand and take one." If still life tempts Edna, she successfully avoids giving in, instead donating the mimetic art to the Ratignolles.

In aligning Edna with the impressionist school, Chopin casts her as a rebel against tradition, a role that seems all the more promising as Edna's art improves. Soon after she announces to Mademoiselle Reisz that "I am becoming an artist," she becomes more attuned to the instability of light and form, characteristics of the impressionist movement as well as a clear revolt from her realistic art (61). Significantly, Edna's artistic mentor Mademoiselle Reisz is also associated with a breakdown of clear lines and the blending of musical forms: "She sat low at her instrument, and the lines of her body settled into ungraceful curves and angles that gave it an appearance of deformity. Gradually and imperceptibly, the interlude *melted* into the soft opening minor chords of the Chopin impromptu." Even Robert is described in a manner that suggests his affront to clean, classical lines. Edna's reasons for being in love with Robert include his inability to fit the classical ideal; his hair grows out from his temples, his nose is "out of drawing," and he has a "little finger which he can't straighten" (78). Edna is impressed with figures that shift, melt and bleed, and it is these forms and this music that inspires her.

As Edna becomes more independent, walking alone and neglecting her Tuesday callers, her art acquires more power, and she gradually abandons mimetic representations. Initially, Edna remains focused on portraits, painting her sons, the quadroon, and the housemaid. The quadroon sits for hours, indicating that Edna wishes to copy her likeness exactly, and Edna paints the housemaid because she "perceived that the young woman's back and shoulders were modeled on classic lines, and that her hair, loosened from its confining cap, became an inspiration" (55). Edna's work still recalls the classical and the traditional, but there is also a stronger element of sensuality in her depiction of the housemaid, and the tension appears in this portrait. When she paints her father, however, her artistic tools are equated with weaponry: "Before her pencil [her father] sat rigid and unflinching, as he had faced the canon's mouth in days gone by" (65). This description indicates a shift in control. If Edna appears to be transitioning from mimetic art to an art form that creates a space for the subjective, her abandonment of photographs, on which to base her paintings, suggests that she wants to inhabit the realm of the imaginative and the subjective. When Robert questions a picture of Alcée Arobin in Edna's new home, and she remarks, "I tried to make a sketch of his head one day . . . I have a great many such photographs . . . They don't amount to anything," we may well believe that she has abandoned such mimetic art altogether (94).

Edna's final painting is never finished, and its promise and its incompleteness align it with the impressionist aesthetic. Edna "had worked at her canvas—a young Italian character study—all the morning, completing the work *without the model*; but there had been many interruptions" (emphasis mine, 91). This appears to be Edna's most advanced piece, the first time she works primarily from imagination. Robert's return to New Orleans, and the events that follow, interrupt the painting. One of the chief criticisms leveled at impressionist painting was that the finished work looked incomplete. The impressionist vision is one "in which everything stable and coherent is dissolved and assumes the character of the unfinished, the fragmentary" (Kronegger 39). Contrasting impressionism with what preceded it, Ortega y Gasset writes:

> Nonimpressionistic painting, superior though it may be in other respects, suffers from one shortcoming: that it represents its objects altogether finished, mummified and, as it were past. That actuality, that existence in the present tense, which things possess in impressionistic pictures is irremediably missing. (Kronegger 52)

Fitting, then, that Edna's painting remains unfinished, and therefore present.

If Chopin's literary impressionism offers validation of the individual's sensory experience, it likewise retains the movement's alignment with formlessness and chaos; Edna's artistic development moves simultaneously toward new possibilities and the breakdown of structures. In the individual's, in this case Edna's, rejection of the solid and fixed world for the fluid and liminal world, she experiences some of the unmooring that Kronegger attributes to the total immersion characteristic of impressionism:

> With impressionism, faith in an absolute has disappeared, the world has been relativized. The Cartesian tendency to divide up the world, to fix and determine it, to comprehend and classify, to recognize in the world things we already know, this world is for the impressionist writer and artist . . . a reality with no possibility of growth, a dead world (87).

It is the recognition of the instability—and her eventual resolution to go into the instability—that precedes her death. When Robert leaves Grand Isle for Mexico, the effect on Edna is rendered in terms of color and light. After Robert leaves her, and she is faced with the reality of her solitude, "the lamp sputtered and went out," leaving Edna in an artistic and aesthetic darkness, from which she will not emerge (106). Later, the narrator explains that "Robert's going had taken the brightness, the color, the meaning out of everything. The conditions of her life were in no way changed, but her whole existence was dulled, like a faded garment which seems to be no longer worth wearing" (44). After his second leave-taking, the image of the faded color returns in Edna's "old bathing suit still hanging, faded, upon its accustomed peg" (108).

Edna's despair is caused less by the disappearance of Robert than by the knowledge that even her perceived love for him is not a fixed reality: "she even realized that the day would come when [Robert], too, and the thought of him would *melt* out of her existence, leaving her alone" (108). As Kronegger notes, in impressionist literature, "the individual's urge to live life at its fullest, paradoxically, ends in emptiness and destruction of the self. He cannot cope with the demands of a society which he feels demands that he wear masks and assume artificial poses in the presence of others" (Kronegger 89). Unwilling to live any longer pretending to fit within societal confines, Edna swims into the gulf and toward complete sensory immersion. In impressionistic novels,

> the states of the protagonist's consciousness find reflection in the images of drowning, sinking, intoxication, immobility, silence, dissolution, and decay. . . . This allurement of nothingness and this yearning for annihilation are in harmony with the breakdown of the surrounding world (61-62).

Here we do well to remember both the book's title and Edna's declaration to Mademoiselle Reisz ("I am becoming an artist"), which rely on the use of the present participle and might be the grammatical equivalent of the impressionist painting (61). In our own final impression of Edna, we imagine her swimming because we do not witness her drowning. The choice to suspend the novel in the fluidity of this moment is a choice to remain in the seemingly incomplete and unfinished space of indeterminacy and to allow for the novel to end in the impressionist aesthetic of suspension rather than resolution. Our failure to resolve Edna's character and the meaning of her death speaks finally to the success of Chopin's novel in eliminating the fixed contours of Edna's character. At Edna's final dinner party, Miss Mayblunt cries, "Oh! To be able to paint in color rather than words!" (85). Kate Chopin's novel closes with a verbal impressionist *ebauché* that answers this lament with a description that rivals its visual counterparts.

Works Cited

Benfey, Christopher. *Degas in New Orleans: Encounters in the Creole World of Kate Chopin and George Washington Cable*. New York: Knopf, 1997.

Chopin, Kate. *The Awakening*. Ed. Margot Culley. 2nd ed. New York: Norton, 1994.

House, John. *Impressionism: Paint and Politics*. New Haven, Yale UP, 2004.

Kronegger, Maria. *Literary Impressionism*. Lanham, MD: Rowman and Littlefield Publishers, 1973.

Pfeiffer, Ingrid and Max Hollein. *Women Impressionists*. Frankfurt: Hatje Cantz, 2008.

Pollock, Griselda. *Mary Cassatt: Painter of Modern Women*. London: Thames and Hudson, 1998.

Toth, Emily. *Unveiling Kate Chopin*. Jackson: UP of Mississippi, 1999.

Reactions to the Chief Characters in Kate Chopin's *The Awakening*: Positive, Negative, and Miscellaneous

Stephen Paul Bray
and Sarah Fredericks

Serious academic attention to Kate Chopin's *The Awakening* really began to build in the late 1960s and has proliferated ever since. But even though the main critical "tradition" is not yet fifty years old, an astonishing amount has been written about the novel in that time, including scores of books and hundreds of essays and articles. Perhaps the simplest way to provide a brief, basically chronological overview of the criticism is to focus on reactions (positive, negative, or miscellaneous) to the chief characters. Doing so will also suggest important themes, as well as the ways the novel is phrased and structured. In what follows, survey, articles, essays, and essay collections are the main focus of attention, as are books not solely about Chopin, since the contents of many such sources tend not to be indexed already, or seem obviously pertinent.[1]

Edna Pontellier

Many critics discuss Edna in positive terms. For instance, Eble in 1964 claimed that she personifies feminine harmony with one's body and exhibits the authenticity, force, and worthiness of a protagonist in a great tragedy (xii–xiii). In 1973, Wolff found her appealing because she falls in a way with which any reader could identify (450). Cantarow, in 1978, asserted that Edna possesses the internal fortitude to achieve, on her own, a new consciousness (31), and Huf, in 1983, celebrated her imagination and self-assertion (61). In 1987, Elfenbein saw her as the only woman in the novel who recognizes the gender and sexual realities of her time (312). Jacobs, in 1992, believed that Edna wins readers' admiration because of her self-respect, attractiveness, and gravity (82), and in 1996, Tuttleton asserted that even her isolation and boredom make her appealing (205).

However, not all critics praise Edna; some see her in a fairly negative light. In 1936, for example, Quinn found her narcissism unappealing (357). Several critics, such as Cantarow in 1978 (30), Elfenbein in 1989 (143–144, 148), Maguire in 2002 (135), and Kileen in 2003 (422–423) have thought that Edna sometimes overlooks or exploits the women of color who work for her. In 1978, Justus argued that Edna indulges in ruinous fantasizing, abject self-centeredness, and muddled thinking (112–119). In 1981, Portales argued that Edna thinks haphazardly and thus is not as insightful as Chopin implies (431–433). Walker in 1983 claimed that Edna has no capacity for introspection and is aimless (89, 147), and many critics, such as Girgus (173) and Gremillion in 1990 (173), Daigrepont in 1991 (8–9), Dawson in 1994 (6, 16–17), and Ward et al. in 2002 (11), have found Edna immature and egotistical. Numerous critics have seen her as emotionally and psychologically childish.

Some critics connect Edna to classical figures. Batten in 1985 (83), St. Andrews in 1986 (38), Franklin in 1988 (143–46), and Wheeler in 1994 (75) argued that she resembles both Venus and Psyche. In 1995, Vevaina compared her to both Persephone and Aphrodite (83–88), and Giorcelli, in 1988, asserted that she resembled such Greek goddesses as Persephone, Aphrodite, Athena, and Artemis (129-134). In 1988, Thornton saw her as an Icarus figure (138).

Other critics discuss Edna in light of more recent literary characters. For instance, Thornton in 1980 (50), Batten in 1985 (88), Witherow in 1997 (28–35), and too many others to list have associated her with Emma from Flaubert's novel *Madame Bovary*. Cantarow in 1978 connected her to the heroine of Zora Neale Hurston's *Their Eyes Were Watching God* (32), and Jones in 1981 (157–58) and Ewell in 1992 (163–64) argued that Edna resembles Huck Finn. Both Foster, in 1986 (163), and Wershoven, in 1987 (32–36), compared Edna to the heroine of Wharton's novel *The House of Mirth* (163). Mosely, in 1986, contrasted her self-disclosure with that of Tolstoy's Anna Karenina (367). In 1987, Bloom (among others) connected her to the speaker in Walt Whitman's *Song of Myself* (2). Rosowski, in 1988, compared her to the heroine of Willa Cather's *My Mortal Enemy* (31), and in 1992, Bonifer connected her to Ibsen's Hedda Gabler (2). In 1993, Emmitt drew parallels between Edna and characters created by Margaret Drabble and George Eliot (326–329). Griffith, in 1993, connected Edna and Robert's love affair to the one in Wagner's opera *Tristan and Isolde* (150). Benfey, in 1997, argued that Edna resembles the protagonist of *The Red Badge of Courage* (249). And in 2000, Treu compared her to the hero of Goethe's novel *The Sorrows of Young Werther* (31–32).

Many critics find it useful to analyze Edna by using literary, philosophical, or psychological theories. For example, in 1988, Bauer, drawing on Bakhtin's ideas, discussed Edna's connection with her culture (11, 138, and 162), and Jacobs, in the same year, analyzed her maturity by using the philosophy of Rollo May (109–112). In 1989, Kouidis using Emersonian terms, explored her perception of existence as illusory (121–124). Wyatt, in 1990, asserted that Edna, divided between culturally prescribed roles and a yearning for freedom, is relevant to the theories of both Lacan and Kristeva (5, 68–69). Bender, in 1991, used Darwinian ideas to conclude that Edna is a female animal who becomes aware of her ability to make her own sexual selections (464–468). Both Bande, in 1995 (158–165), and Paris, in 1997 (216–232), claimed that it was useful to examine Edna using the psychological terms of Karen Horney. Bharathi, in 1995, used existentialist language to discuss Edna's character (94–97), while Lewis, in 1997, drew on the writings of feminist theorist Luce Irigaray (51). In 1998, Ryan used modern psychoanalysis to conclude that Edna seems afflicted with Bipolar II Disorder (255–256), and in 2002, Petruzzi used Heidegger's work to analyze Edna and her need to confront "nothingness" (289–308). Countless critics have also utilized Freudian psychoanalysis to discuss Edna's lack of a maternal figure, her awakening sexuality, and her emotional and psychological development. Edna is, by far, the character critics most often discuss, and so the preceding overview can do little more than skim the surface of the many responses she has provoked.

Léonce Pontellier

Some critics discuss Léonce's positive characteristics. Arner, in 1975, argued that he is not oppressive (107), and Justus, in 1978, found him not particularly unkind (117). St. Andrews, in 1986, called Léonce not foolish or abusive but complex and truthful when unexpectedly presented with conflict (44). Likewise, Wolff, in 1973, contended that he is a normal man of his time, not malicious or spiteful (452–454). In 1997, Benfey concluded that Léonce is not a tyrant (244), and Papke, in 1990, argued that he is a responsible husband and father (71) and a talented businessman (69). Finally, Tuttleton, in 1996, argued that Léonce embodies positive characteristics of husbands in his day (201), and Paris, in 1997, asserted that he demonstrates remarkable tolerance toward Edna and affords her a respected lifestyle (223).

Other critics discuss Léonce's negative aspects. Arner, in 1975 (107), and Davis, in 1992 (146), contended that Léonce is materialistic (107), while Wade, in 1999, called him egotistical (99), and Morton, in 1997, saw him as an absentee father and husband (65-66). Similarly, Battawalla, in 1995, argued that Léonce cannot see his own immaturity and inconsistency (198), and Roller, in 1986, thought him often confused and inconsiderate (9). Franklin, in 1984, called Léonce passive (513) and Collins, in 1984, termed him superficial (180). Likewise, in 1988, Bauer argued that Léonce failed to perceive his own conformity (162). Finally, Showalter, in 1991, suggested that Léonce probably visits prostitutes in New Orleans (78), while Woolf, in 1996, argued that Léonce was likely unfaithful (11).

Almost all critics discuss Léonce's relationship to Edna. Wolff, in 1973 (453), and Anastasopoulou in 1991 (20–21) argued that Léonce ignores Edna. Arner, in 1975, asserted that he is unable to understand Edna's desires (107), while Menke, in 1997, contended that Léonce's suppression of Edna's rebellion actually encourages it (75). Furthermore, Ward et al., in 2002, claimed that Léonce expects Edna to treat him better than he treats her (71), while Jones in 2003 (275), Showalter in 1991 (77), and Taylor and Fineman in 1996 (40) saw Léonce as a father figure to Edna (275). Candela, in

1980, emphasized Léonce's lack of authority over Edna (6), while George, in 1988, and many other critics have contended that he treats Edna as property (53). Girgus, in 1990, suggested that Léonce later regrets his early triumphs over Edna (139), and Schweitzer, in 1990, felt that Léonce is doomed to see Edna escape (167). In 1988, Bauer asserted that Léonce derives his identity from Edna's submissiveness (139). Seidel, in 1996, contended that Léonce believes he should control Edna's body (230), and Wyatt, in 1990, said that his patience with Edna ironically reveals that he does not take her seriously (66). Finally, Paul, in 1995, asserted that Léonce's gifts to Edna actually suggest his autocratic nature (49), while Kileen, in 2003, proposed that Edna's awakening began when she embraced Léonce's Catholicism (426–27).

Various critics have compared Léonce to other characters in the book. Wade, in 1999, argued that unlike Adèle Ratignolle, Léonce lives for himself in the peaceful ignorance of routine (98–99). In 1988, Goldman argued that Léonce considers Robert a man like himself (160), while Biggs, in 2004, contended that Léonce thinks Robert is gay (158). In 1997, Lewis found that Léonce's insignificance allows Robert to take control of Edna (59), while Papke, in 1990, claimed that both men ultimately abandon Edna (82). In 1992, Harrison contended that, unlike Doctor Mandelet, Léonce is materialistic and patriarchal (192–193). Finally, Fox-Genovese, in 1979, emphasized similarities between Léonce and Edna's father (269–270), but Girgus, in 1990, claimed that Léonce, unlike the Colonel, treats Edna with relative clemency (145).

Some critics examine the various ways Chopin employs Léonce in constructing *The Awakening*. For example, Toth, in 1990 (288), and Dressler, in 1992 (61), stressed her choice to begin the novel by emphasizing his perspective. Paul, in 1995, claimed that Chopin does not villainize Léonce (49), and Stein, in 1980, contended that Chopin refuses to pass simple judgment on him (198–199). Battiwalla, in 1995, claimed that Chopin depicts Léonce in mostly negative ways (199), and Huf, in 1983, contended that Chopin presents Léonce as dull, unobservant, and egocentric (64–67). Finally, Leary, in 1968, argued that Léonce resembles a male in Chopin's first novel (72), while Kileen, in 2003, argued that Léonce is an ineffective character (419).

Many critics—including St. Andrews in 1986 (45), Jones in 1981 (173), and Hoder-Salmon in 1992 (135)—discussed symbolism associated with Léonce and how he resembles other men of his era. Bonifer, in 1992, compared Léonce to the husband in Ibsen's *Hedda Gabler* (2). Black, in 1992, contended that Léonce functions much like a typical husband-businessman described by G.B. Shaw (103), while Mikolchak, in 2004, claimed that he resembles the decent but dull husbands in novels by Fontane, Flaubert, and Tolstoy (31–32). Rowe, in 1990, and Boone, in 1998 (84–85), found that Léonce symbolizes advanced capitalism (7), while Harrison, in 1992, thought he embodies not only capitalism but also patriarchy and materialism (185). In 1988, Matchie argued that Chopin often links him to economic motives and economic language (8).

Robert Lebrun

Most critics see Robert in negative terms. Woolf, for instance, argued in 1973 that Robert resembles Edna in the shallowness of his emotions and in his avoidance of erotic contact (460). Fox-Genovese suggested in 1979 that he flirts with women at Grand Isle partly to promote his mother's vacation resort (277). Thornton, in 1980, saw him as not especially or genuinely interested in Edna's feelings (56), while Jones, in 1981, suggested that when Robert leaves for Mexico, he begins behaving like a typical male of his era and never achieves real independence (180). Lant, in 1984, was particularly critical, arguing that that the note he leaves Edna at the end of the book is insensitive and that, in general, he seems shallow and weak, partly because Edna's sexuality scares him (173). St. Andrews, in 1986, also saw Robert as weak, boring, and unworthy (53–54), while the next year, Wershoven described him as unfortunately conventional (30, 34). His conventionality was also stressed by Gilbert and Gubar in 1989 (107), and in 1990, Papke found him even more romantic (and thus less realistic) than Edna (78). Shaw, in 1990, was especially hard on Robert, calling him a limited character who doesn't deserve Edna's love because he is immature, sentimental, self-pitying, and almost infantile (65–67). Indeed, a very common charge against Robert is that he fails to behave maturely but instead acts like a shy, unassertive boy. His alleged weakness is a point made repeatedly by critics too numerous to mention.

A few critics, however, have discussed Robert's positive characteristics. Quinn, in 1936 (356), and Cantwell, in 1956 (492), thought him so moral and proper that he is willing to leave Edna alone to protect her reputation. Additionally, Stone, in 1986 (30), and others have credited his encouraging nature and passion with Edna's discovery of and love for the arts.

Several critics discuss the connection between Robert and other characters in the novel. For example, George, in 1988, argued that he, Léonce, and Arobin share the same patriarchal values (54), and Harrison, in 1992, asserted that the three men all represent assumptions associated with capitalism (193). Additionally, Rowe, in 1990, argued that Robert and Arobin each represent different aspects of Léonce (9). In 1990, Shaw claimed that Robert acted immaturely when responding to Arobin's photograph (218–219), and Wheeler, in 1994, thought Robert's first name and resembled Arobin's last name, implying that they have more in common than Edna realizes (68–69). Wade, in 1999 (101), like others, asserted that Robert attracts Edna spiritually while Arobin excites her erotically. In 1997, Lewis argued that, when Robert returns from Mexico, he begins competing with Arobin for male dominance over Edna (59). In 2002, Berg argued that Robert and Arobin both induce a passiveness in Edna that often undermines her assertiveness (68). Davis, in 1992, claimed that Edna lusts after Robert partly because he is not as materialistic as Léonce (147), while Wade, in 1999, argued that Robert is just as materialistic as Léonce and that both men often submit to social pressures (100). Biggs, in 2004, asserted that Léonce is not bothered by Robert's relationship with Edna because he believes Robert may be homosexual (158). Wheeler, in 1994, claimed that Robert's brother Victor symbolically reveals Robert's own shallowness (68–69), and in 1997, Menke argued that both Victor and Robert each see women as either off-limits, marginal, or ready for sexual intercourse (76) and that neither minds having sex with women of color (17). Rankin, in 1988, contended that Robert and Edna are bound, in part, by mutual love of reading (150), while Bender, in 1992, claimed that Robert and Edna treat each other as owned property (203). Finally, Biggs, in 2004, claimed that Robert's mother is the only character to whom he remains undoubtedly loyal (164).

Some critics discuss symbolism associated with Robert. For example, Franklin, in 1984, argued that Robert can be interpreted as one aspect of Eros, the god from the Psychemyth (513). Similarly, Franklin, in 1988 (147), and Batiwalla, in 1995 (193-94), claimed that Robert resembles Cupid. Batiwalla also suggested that Robert resembles Jesus because he inspires Edna's self-confidence (195), while Vevaina, in 1995, argued that Robert resembles Hermes, the love object of Aphrodite (117–18). Griffith, in 1993, saw Robert as comparable to Tristan from Wagner's *Tristan and Isolde* (150), while Mikolchak argued, in 2004, that Robert acts like the main male lover in Tolstoy's *Anna Karenina* (37). Similarly, Wershoven, in 1987, claimed that Robert resembles a male lover in an Edith Wharton novel (29–30). Finally, Delbanco, in 1994, thought he typified the dreary, powerless young men often found in nineteenth-century American fiction (117–18), and Ward et al. asserted in 2002 that he resembles lovers often portrayed in medieval literature (26–27).

Several critics examine Chopin's treatment of Robert in other ways. For example, Shaw, in 1990, claimed that Chopin may have realized Robert was unworthy of Edna (67), while Jones, in 1981, argued that Chopin uses the relationship between Robert and Edna to explore the idea that humans can achieve various types and degrees of harmony (178). Wheeler, in 1994, argued that Chopin mocks the relationship of Edna and Robert by having them speak like characters in a fairy-tale (64). In 2004, Biggs claimed that Robert was based on a young man Chopin knew in St. Louis (148–149) and that Chopin often speaks of Robert using the words "gay" and "queer" (150). Finally, Toth argued in 1999 that Robert's name resembles that of a man with whom Chopin had an affair (47), a claim Tuttleton doubted in 1996 (189).

Adèle Ratignolle

Several critics have seen Adèle as a positive influence on Edna. For example, Justus in 1978 (109), Fox-Genovese in 1979 (280), Amin in 1995 (72), and Ward et al. in 2002 (7–8, 13–14) all argued that Adèle is largely responsible for igniting Edna's transformation. In 1996, Taylor and Fineman contended that Adèle shows the most concern for Edna's wellbeing (42). Stone, in 1986, asserted that Adèle helps Edna develop psychologically, emotionally, and artistically (25–26). Many critics, such as Fox-Genovese in 1979 (280), Girgus in 1990 (140–141), Seidel in 1990 (98), and Anastasopoulou in 1991 (24) saw Adèle as a mother figure for Edna.

However, not all critics view Adèle positively. In 1981, for instance, Portales asserted that her self-interest makes her dismiss Edna's problems (435). Lant, in 1984, argued that she is a temptress who, like the ocean, ultimately helps cause Edna's death (167). Elfenbein, in 1989, argued that her social position interferes with her ability to sympathize with Edna (146). Both Ward et al. in 2002 (13) and Larrabee, in 2003 (69), claimed that Adèle is a static character (13).

Many critics discuss Adèle in connection to Mlle. Reisz. Seeing the two women as opposites, for instance, Fox-Genovese argued in 1979 that, unlike Mlle. Reisz, Adèle is depicted as fair-haired, sexually attractive, and maternal (285). Likewise, Jones, in 1981, contended that while Reisz is socially aloof, Adèle represents the standards of conventional society and religion (172). Other critics, however, see similarities between the two women. In 1979, Fox-Genovese asserted that both women make concessions to survive in a patriarchal society (287), and Shaw, in 1990, claimed that both women experience more freedom than Edna (222).

Some critics connect Adèle to other characters within the novel as well as in classic literature. In 1992, Black saw parallels in the ways both Adèle and Madame Lebrun are defined by their children (112), and in 2002, Ward et al. connected Adèle's coquetry to that of Mariequita (10). Franklin, in 1984, associated Adèle with the myth of Pysche (525) and Vevaina, in 1995, argued that she resembles the mythical figure Demeter (83, 88).

Another topic of great concern to many critics is Adèle's role as a mother. Numerous critics, such as Schweitzer in 1990 (169), Barker in 1992 (64, 72), and Gray in 2004 (57-59), argued that she embodies traditional patriarchal views of women and mothers. Nevertheless, other critics have claimed that she, in some ways, complicates or subverts these roles. For instance, Bauer, in 1988, asserted that Adèle feigns illness because maternity is not entirely satisfying (156), and Elfenbein, in 1989, suggested that she enjoys motherhood because it makes her the object of male attention (153). Other critics, such as Shaw in 1990 (64) and Kileen in 2003 (431), have pointed to Edna's erotic attraction to Adèle as complicating Adèle's supposed conventionality.

Mademoiselle Reisz

Frequently, critics emphasize Mademoiselle Reisz's positive influence on Edna. For instance, Vevaina in 1995 (87) argued that Reisz alone comprehends and encourages Edna's transformation and autonomy. Portales, in 1981, saw Mademoiselle Reisz as Edna's confidant (435), and in 1984, Franklin saw her as a maternal figure or guardian spirit (522). Several critics, such as Roller in 1986 (13-14), St. Andrews in the same year (53), Elfenbein in 1989 (145), and Papke in 1990 (81), also discussed Reisz's role as someone who anticipates (and cautions Edna against) the dangers of involvement with Robert. Wolff, in 1973, argued that she is assertive, but has a realistic sense of limits (466), while in 1979, Fox-Genovese saw her as a symbol of female autonomy (285). Daigrepont, in 1991, suggested that she symbolizes Teutonic Romanticism, which emphasizes courage and freedom (7).

However, not all critics see Reisz positively; some have criticized her alleged egotism and her supposedly negative effects on Edna. In 1980, for example, Thornton saw her as harsh and self-centered (55), and Papke, in 1990, suggested that she is immature (84). Likewise, Daigrepont, in 1991, connected her with narcissism, self-deception, and weakness (7). In 1992, Boren suggested that she is an almost demonic figure who seduces and enslaves Edna (194), and Dressler, in the same year, argued that she seems impotent and unappealing (64).

Numerous critics see Reisz and Adèle as opposites. For example, Fox-Genovese, in 1979, contrasted their physical appearance and their attitudes toward motherhood (285). Several critics, such as Jones in 1981 (171–172), Collins in 1984 (180), Martin in 1988 (21), and Paul in 1995 (59), argued that, unlike Adèle, Reisz symbolizes art, social isolation, and artificiality (171–172). Benfey, in 1997, argued that Adèle represents physical courage and Reisz artistic courage (249). Many critics contrast the women in terms of eroticism, femininity, and emotional expression.

Other critics tend to define Reisz in connection to various characters within the novel or even in classic literature. Fox-Genovese, in 1979, likened Reisz to a menacing shadow and to the lady in black (285). Davis, in 1992, suggested that, like Madame Lebrun, Reisz exemplifies the financial hardships of unmarried females (151). Several critics, such as Franklin in 1984 (51), Giorcelli in 1988 (136), Horner and Zlosnik in 1990 (52), Boren in 1992 (189–190), and Battawalla in 1995 (190), argued that she resembles a witch. Connecting her to classical mythology, Thornton, in 1988, contended that Reisz resembles Daedalus from the myth of Icarus (141), and Vevaina, in 1995, connected her to Artemis and, to a lesser degree, Aphrodite (87).

Several critics have also focused on her sexuality. For instance, Seidel, in 1990, drew parallels between Reisz and lesbians (89–90), and Showalter, in 1991, suggested romantic overtones in her relationship with Edna (75). Dawson, in 1992, found her interest in the two lovers voyeuristic (92), and in 1994, Dawson suggested sadomasochistic overtones in her relationship with Edna (13).

Alcée Arobin

Many critics emphasize the negative aspects of Arobin's character. For example, in 1980, Stein argued that Chopin's masterful use of Arobin far exceeds Arobin's own complexity (201). Horner and Zlosnik argued in 1990 that Arobin is good-looking and stylish, but shallow (47), while Collins, in 1984, suggested that he profits from deception (188). George, in 1988, claimed that he often ironically speaks in a feminine way, emphasizing emotion, when he wants to deceive women (55).

Many critics discuss the symbolism associated with Arobin. For example, in 1984, Franklin argued that he represents the darker, sinister side of Eros from the Psyche legend (513), a point she reiterated in 1988 (147). Battawalla, in 1995, contended that Arobin and Dionysius share a common bond by pragmatically pursuing sexual pleasure (197). Rowe, in 1990 (23), and Harrison, in 1992 (193), both associated Arobin with the malicious side of capitalism and male authority. Thornton, in 1980 (63), and Gilbert and Gubar, in 1989 (107), both claimed Arobin resembles Emma Bovary's lover. Toth in 1999 (47), Menke in 1997 (77-78), and Larrabee in 2003 (60) all argued that Arobin resembles a man with whom Chopin had an affair, partly because the two men resembled one another physically and shared similar names. However, in 1996, Tuttleton questioned this claim (189). In 1997, Benfey argued that Arobin largely resembles Edna's father (366); and Boone, in 1998, asserted that he shares many of Robert's characteristics (87).

Most critics discuss Arobin's involvement with Edna. For example, Wolff in 1973 (455), Huf in 1983 (68), Matchie in 1988 (9), Taylor and Fineman in 1996 (42), Delbanco in 1997 (121, 129), and Ward et al. in 2002 (54–55) all argued that Edna's desire for Arobin is strictly sexual. Hoder-Salmon, in 1992, argued that Arobin's deviation from social norms encouraged Edna's own deviation (135–36). Similarly, Menke in 1994–95 (96), Gilbert and Gubar in 1989 (108), Thornton in 1988 (141), and Amin in 1995 (73–74) argued that Edna's assertiveness toward Arobin reflects her desire for freedom and erotic knowledge, while Stone, in 1986, similarly suggested that Edna's affair with Arobin helps her realize sexual freedom (25). Webb, in 1982, asserted that Arobin conquers Edna (150), while Jacobs, in 1992, claimed that his control over her is limited because she is married (85). Davis, in 1992, argued that Arobin is like a drug to Edna (204), and George, in 1998, argued that he wants to control Edna sexually (54). Paris, in 1997 (232-233), and Wade, in 1999 (101), argued that Arobin cannot provide

Edna the spiritual pleasure Robert provides, but offers only sensual pleasure instead.

The sheer variety of comments critics have offered about Chopin's major characters over the past four and a half decades suggests something—but *only* something—of the richness of *The Awakening*, a novel whose complex dimensions remain to be even more fully explored.

Note

1. This chapter draws heavily on the unpublished work of Robert C. Evans, who is in the final stages of preparing a critical variorum edition of *The Awakening*. The standard bibliographies of works about Chopin are (1) Stringer and (2) Green and Caudle.

Works Cited

Amin, Amina. "Kate Chopin's *The Awakening*: Sex-role Liberation or Sexual Liberation?" *Chopin's The Awakening: Critical Essays*. Ed. Iqbal Kaur. New Delhi: Deep and Deep, 1995. 68–79.

Anastasopoulou, Maria. "Rites of Passage in Kate Chopin's *The Awakening*." *Southern Literary Journal* 23.2 (1991): 19–30.

Arner, Robert. "Kate Chopin." *Louisiana Studies* 14.1 (1975): 11–139.

Ballenger, Grady, et al., eds. *Perspectives on Kate Chopin: Proceedings from the Kate Chopin International Conference, April 6, 7, 8, 1989*. Natchitoches, LA: Northwestern State U, 1992.

Bande, Usha. "From Conflict to Suicide—A Feminist Approach to Kate Chopin's *The Awakening*." *Chopin's The Awakening: Critical Essays*. Ed. Iqbal Kaur. New Delhi: Deep and Deep, 1995. 157–69.

Barker, Deborah E. "The Awakening of Female Artistry." *Kate Chopin Reconsidered: Beyond the Bayou*. Eds. Lynda S. Boren and Sarah deSaussure Davis. Baton Rouge: Louisiana State UP, 1992. 61–79.

Batten, Wayne. "Illusion and Archetype: The Curious Story of Edna Pontellier." *Southern Literary Journal* 18.1 (1985): 73–88.

Battawala, Zareen. "The Long and Winding Road: An Analysis of Kate Chopin's *The Awakening*." *Chopin's The Awakening: Critical Essays*. Ed. Iqbal Kaur. New Delhi: Deep and Deep, 1995. 187–203.

Bauer, Dale. *Feminist Dialogics: A Theory of Failed Community*. Albany: State U of New York P, 1988.

Bender, Bert. "The Teeth of Desire: *The Awakening* and the Descent of Man." *American Literature* 63.3 (1991): 459–73.

_____. "Kate Chopin's Quarrel with Darwin before *The Awakening*." *Journal of American Studies* 26 (1992): 185–204.

Benfey, Christopher. *Degas in New Orleans: Encounters in the Creole World of Kate Chopin and George Washington Cable*. New York: Knopf, 1997.

Berg, Allison.*Mothering the Race: Women's Narratives of Reproduction, 1890– 1930*. Urbana: U of Illinois P, 2002.

Biggs, Mary. "'Si Tu Savais': The Gay/Transgendered Sensibility of Kate Chopin's *The Awakening*." *Women's Studies: An Interdisciplinary Journal* 33.2 (2004): 145–81.

Black, Martha Fodaski. "The Quintessence of Chopinism." *Kate Chopin Reconsidered: Beyond the Bayou*. Eds. Lynda S. Boren and Sarah deSaussure Davis. Baton Rouge: Louisiana State UP, 1992. 95–113.

Bloom, Harold, ed. *Kate Chopin*. New York: Chelsea House, 1987.

Bonifer, M. Susan. "Hedda and Edna: Writing the Future." *Bulletin of the West Virginia Association of College English Teachers* 14 (1992): 1–11.

Boone, Joseph Allen. *Libidinal Currents: Sexuality and the Shaping of Modernism*. Chicago: U of Chicago P, 1998.

Boren, Lynda S. "Taming the Sirens: Self-Possession and the Strategies of Art in Kate Chopin's *The Awakening*." *Kate Chopin Reconsidered: Beyond the Bayou*. Eds. Lynda S. Boren and Sarah deSaussure Davis. Baton Rouge: Louisiana State UP, 1992. 180–96.

Boren, Lynda S. and Sarah deSaussure Davis, eds. *Kate Chopin Reconsidered: Beyond the Bayou*. Baton Rouge: Louisiana State UP, 1992.

Candela, Joseph L., Jr. "Domestic Orientation of American Novels, 1893–1913." *American Literary Realism* 13 (1980): 1–18.

Cantarow, Ellen. "Sex, Race and Criticism: Thoughts of a White Feminist on Kate Chopin and Zora Neale Hurston." *Radical Teacher* 9 (1978): 30–33.

Cantwell, Robert. "*The Awakening* by Kate Chopin." *Georgia Review* 10 (1956): 489–94.

Collins, Robert. "The Dismantling of Edna Pontellier: Garment Imagery in Kate Chopin's *The Awakening*." *Southern Studies* 23.2 (1984): 176–97.

Daigrepont, Lloyd M. "Edna Pontellier and the Myth of Passion." *New Orleans Review* 18.3 (1991): 5–13.

Davis, Sarah deSaussure. "Chopin's Movement Toward Universal Myth." *Kate Chopin Reconsidered: Beyond the Bayou*. Eds. Lynda S. Boren and Sarah deSaussure Davis. Baton Rouge: Louisiana State UP, 1992. 199–206.

Dawson, Melanie. "Edna and the Tradition of Listening: The Role of Romantic Music in *The Awakening*." *Southern Studies* 3 (1992): 87–98.

Dawson, Hugh J. "Kate Chopin's *The Awakening*: A Dissenting Opinion." *American Literary Realism* 26.2 (1994): 1–18.

Delbanco, Andrew. "The Half-Life of Edna Pontellier." *New Essays on* The Awakening. Ed. Wendy Martin. New York: Cambridge UP, 1988. 89–107.

_____. *Required Reading: Why Our American Classics Matter Now*. New York: Farrar, Straus, & Giroux, 1997.

Dressler, Mylène. "Edna Under the Sun: Throwing Light in the Subject of *The Awakening*." *Arizona Quarterly* 48.3 (1992): 59–75.

Eble, Kenneth, ed. *The Awakening*. New York: Capricorn, 1964.

Elfenbein, Anna Shannon. "Kate Chopin's *The Awakening*: An Assault on American Racial and Sexual Mythology." *Southern Studies* 26.4 (1987): 304–12.

_____. *Women on the Color Line: Evolving Stereotypes and the Writings of George Washington Cable, Grace King, Kate Chopin*. Charlottesville: U of Virginia P, 1989.

Emmitt, Helen V. "'Drowned in a Willing Sea': Freedom and Drowning in Eliot, Chopin and Drabble." *Tulsa Studies in Women's Literature* 12 (1993): 315–32.

Ewell, Barbara C. "Kate Chopin and the Dream of Female Selfhood." *Kate Chopin Reconsidered: Beyond the Bayou*. Eds. Lynda S. Boren and Sarah deSaussure Davis. Baton Rouge: Louisiana State UP, 1992. 157–65.

Foster, Shirley. "The Open Cage: Freedom, Marriage and the Heroine in Early Twentieth-Century American Women's Novels." *Women's Writing: A Challenge to Theory*. Ed. Moira Monteith. New York: St. Martin's, 1986. 154–74.

Fox-Genovese, Elizabeth. "Kate Chopin's Awakening." *Southern Studies* 18 (1979): 261–90.

Franklin, Rosemary F. "*The Awakening* and the Failure of Psyche." *American Literature* 56.4 (1984): 510–26.

_____. "Edna as Psyche: The Self and the Unconscious." Ed. Bernard Koloski. *Approaches to Teaching Chopin's* The Awakening. Modern Language Association. 1988.144–49.

George, E. Laurie. "Women's Language in *The Awakening*." Ed. Bernard Koloski. *Approaches to Teaching Chopin's* The Awakening. Modern Language Association. 1988. 53–59.

Gilbert, Sandra M. and Susan Gubar. *No Man's Land: Sexchanges*. New Haven: Yale UP, 1989.

Giorcelli, Cristina. "Edna's Wisdom: A Transitional and Numinous Merging." *New Essays on* The Awakening. Ed. Wendy Martin. New York: Cambridge UP, 1988. 109–48.

Girgus, Sam B. *Desire and the Political Unconscious in American Literature: Eros and Ideology*. New York: St. Martin's, 1990.

Goldman, Arnold. "Life and Death in New Orleans." *The American City: Literary and Cultural Perspectives*. Ed. Graham Clarke. New York: St. Martin's, 1988. 146–78.

Gray, Jennifer B. "The Escape of the 'Sea': Ideology and *The Awakening*." *Southern Literary Journal* 37.1 (2004): 53–73.

Green, Suzanne Disherron and David J. Caudle. *Kate Chopin: An Annotated Bibliography of Critical Works*. Westport, CT: Greenwood, 1999.

Greer, John Thomas. "Dialogue across the Pacific: Kate Chopin's Awakening and the Short Fiction of Zhang Jie." *Perspectives on Kate Chopin: Proceedings from the Kate Chopin International Conference, April 6, 7, 8, 1989*. Eds. Ballenger, Grady, et al. Natchitoches, LA: Northwestern State Univ., 1992. 47–58.

Gremillion, Michelle. "Edna's Awakening: A Return to Childhood." *Perspectives on Kate Chopin: Proceedings from the Kate Chopin International Conference, April 6, 7, 8, 1989*. Eds. Ballenger, Grady, et al. Natchitoches, LA: Northwestern State Univ., 1992. 169–76.

Griffith, Kelley. "Wagnerian Romanticism in Kate Chopin's *The Awakening*." *English Romanticism: Preludes and Postludes*. Ed. Donald Schoonmaker and John A. Alford. East Lansing: Colleague's, 1993. 145–53.

Harrison, Antony H. "Swinburne and the Critique of Ideology in *The Awakening*." *Gender and Discourse in Victorian Literature and Art*. Ed. Antony H. Harrison and Beverly Taylor. Dekalb: Northern Illinois UP, 1992. 185–203.

Hoder-Salmon, Marilyn. *Kate Chopin's The Awakening: Screenplay as Interpretation*. Gainesville: U of Florida P, 1992.

Horner, Avril and Sue Zlosnik. *Landscapes of Desire: Metaphors in Modern Women's Fiction*. New York: Harvester Wheatsheaf, 1990.

Huf, Linda. *A Portrait of the Artist as a Young Woman: The Writer as Heroine in American Literature*. New York: Ungar, 1983.

Jacobs, Jo Ellen. "*The Awakening* in a Course on Philosophical Ideas in Literature." *Approaches to Teaching World Literature*. Ed. Bernard Koloski. New York: Modern Language Association, 1988. 107–13.

Jacobs, Dorothy H. "The Awakening: A Recognition of Confinement." *Southern Literary Studies (Southern Literary Studies)*. Eds. Lynda S. Boren, Sarah deSaussure Davis, and Cathy N. Davidson. Baton Rouge: Louisiana State UP, 1992. 80–94.

Jones, Anne Goodwyn. *Tomorrow Is Another Day: The Woman Writer in the South, 1859–1936*. Baton Rouge: Louisiana State UP, 1981.

Justus, James H. "The Unawakening of Edna Pontellier." *Southern Literary Journal* 10 2 (1978): 107–22.

Kaur, Iqbal, ed. *Chopin's The Awakening: Critical Essays*. New Delhi: Deep and Deep, 1995.

Kileen, Jalath. "Mother and Child: Realism, Maternity, and Catholicism in Kate Chopin's *The Awakening*." *Religion and the Arts* 7.4 (2003): 413–38.

Koloski, Bernard. *Approaches to Teaching Chopin's* The Awakening. New York: Modern Language Association, 1988.

Kouidis, Virginia M. "Prism into Prism: Emerson's Many Colored Lenses and the Woman Writer of Early Modernism." *The Green American Tradition*. Ed. H. Daniel Peck. Baton Rouge: Louisiana State UP, 1989. 115–134.

Lant, Kathleen Margaret. "The Siren of Grand Isle: Adèle's Role in *The Awakening*." *Southern Studies* 23.2 (1984): 167–75.

Larrabee, Denise. "Kate Chopin 1850–1904." *American* Writers. Ed. Jay Parini. New York, NY: Scribner's, 2003.

Leary, Lewis. "Kate Chopin's Other Novel." *Southern Literary Journal* 1.1 (1968): 60–74.

Lewis, Jenene. "Women as Commodity: Confronting Female Sexuality in *Quicksand* and *The Awakening*." *MAWA Review* 12.2 (1997): 51–62.

Maguire, Roberta S. "Kate Chopin and Anna Julia Cooper: Critiquing Kentucky and the South." *Southern Literary Journal* 35.1 (2002): 123–37.

Martin, Wendy, ed. *New Essays on* The Awakening. New York: Cambridge UP, 1988.

Matchie, Thomas. "The Land of the Free: Or, the Home of the Brave." *Journal of American Culture* 11.4 (1988): 7–13.

Menke, Pamela Glenn. "Chopin's Sensual Sea and Cable's Ravished Land: Texts, Signs, and Gender Narrative." *Crossroads: A Journal of Southern Culture* 1994: 78–102.

_____. "'I Almost Live Here': Gender and Ethnicity in *The Awakening* and 'The Storm.'" *Southern Studies: An Interdisciplinary Journal of the South* 8 1-2 (1997): 73–81.

Mikolchak, Maria. "Kate Chopin's *The Awakening* as Part of the Nineteenth-Century American Literary Tradition." *Interdisciplinary Literary Studies* 5.2 (2004): 29–49.

Morton, Mary L. "The Semiotics of Food in *The Awakening*." *Southern Studies* 8.1-2 (1997): 65–72.

Moseley, Merritt. "Chopin and Mysticism." *Southern Studies: An Interdisciplinary Journal of the South* 25.4 (1986): 367–74.

Papke, Mary Elizabeth. *Verging on the Abyss: The Social Fiction of Kate Chopin and Edith Wharton*. New York: Greenwood, 1990.

Paris, Bernard J. *Imagined Human Beings: A Psychological Approach to Character and Conflict in Literature*. New York: New York UP, 1997.

Paul, Premilla. "The Sea Holds No Terrors: Search and Beyond in *The Awakening*." *Chopin's The Awakening: Critical Essays*. Ed. Iqbal Kaur. New Delhi: Deep and Deep, 1995. 42–67.

Petruzzi, Anthony P. "Two Modes of Disclosure in Kate Chopin's *The Awakening*." *Lit: Literature Interpretation Theory* 13 4 (2002): 287–316.

Petry, Alice Hall, ed. *Critical Essays on Kate Chopin*. New York: G.K. Hall, 1996.

Portales, Marco A. "The Characterization of Edna Pontellier and the Conclusion of Kate Chopin's *The Awakening*." *Southern Studies* 20.4 (1981): 427–36.

Quinn, Arthur Hobson. *American Fiction: An Historical and Critical Survey*. New York: Appleton-Century, 1936.

Rankin, Elizabeth. "A Reader-Response Approach." *Approaches to Teaching World Literature*. Ed. Bernard Koloski. Modern Language Association, 1988. 150–155.

Roller, Judi M. *The Politics of the Feminist Novel*. New York: Greenwood, 1986.

Rowe, John Carlos. "The Economics of the Body in Kate Chopin's *The Awakening*." *Southern Literary Studies (Southern Literary Studies)*. Eds. Lynda S. Boren, Sara deSaussure Davis, and Cathy N. Davidson. Baton Rouge: Louisiana State UP, 1992. 1–24.

Ryan, Steven T. "Depression and Chopin's *The Awakening*." *Mississippi Quarterly* 51 2 (1998): 253–73.

St. Andrews, Bonnie. *Forbidden Fruit: On the Relationship Between Women and Knowledge in Doris Lessing, Lagerlöf, Kate Chopin, Margaret Atwood*. Troy, NY: Whitson, 1986.

Schweitzer, Ivy. "Maternal Discourse and the Romance of Self-Possession in Kate Chopin's *The Awakening*." *Boundary 2: An International Journal of Literature and Culture* 17.1 (1990): 158–86.

Seidel, Kathryn Lee. "Art is an Unnatural Act: Homoeroticism, Art, and Mademoiselle Reisz in *The Awakening*." Grady Ballenger, et al., eds. *Perspectives on Kate Chopin: Proceedings from the Kate Chopin International Conference, April 6, 7, 8, 1989*. Natchitoches, LA: Northwestern State U, 1992. 85–100.

_____. "Picture Perfect: Painting in *The Awakening*." *Critical Essays on Kate Chopin*. Ed. Alice Hall Petry. New York: G.K. Hall, 1996. 227–36.

Shaw, Pat. "Putting Audience in Its Place: Psychosexuality and Prospective Shifts in *The Awakening*." *American Literary Realism* 23.1 (1990): 61–69.

Showalter, Elaine. *Sister's Choice: Tradition and Change in American Women's Writing*. New York: Oxford UP, 1991.

Springer, Marlene. *Edith Wharton and Kate Chopin: A Reference Guide*. Boston: Hall, 1976.

Stein, Allen F. "Kate Chopin's *The Awakening* and the Limits of Moral Judgment." *A Fair Day in the Affections: Literary Essays in Honor of Robert B. White, Jr.* Ed. Jack M. Durant et al. Raleigh: Winston, 1980. 159–69.

Stone, Carole. "The Female Artist in Kate Chopin's *The Awakening*: Birth and Creativity." *Women's Studies: An Interdisciplinary Journal* 13.1-2 (1986): 23–32.

Taylor, Walter and Jo Ann B. Fineman. "Kate Chopin: Pre-Freudian Freudian." *Southern Literary Journal* 29.1 (1996): 35–45.

Thornton, Lawrence. "*The Awakening*: A Political Romance." *American Literature* 52.1 (1980): 50–66.

Thornton, Lawrence. "Edna as Icarus: A Mythic Issue." *Approaches to Teaching World Literature*. Ed. Bernard Koloski. New York: Modern Language Association, 1988.,*Approaches* 138–43.

Toth, Emily. "The Shadow of the First Biographer: The Case of Kate Chopin." *The Southern Review* 26: 2 (1990): 285–92.

_____. *Unveiling Kate Chopin*. Jackson: U of Mississippi P, 1999.

Treu, Robert. "Surviving Edna: A Reading of the Ending of *The Awakening*." *College Literature* 27.2 (2000): 21–36.

Tuttleton, James W. *Vital Signs: Essays on American Literature and Criticism*. Chicago: Dee, 1996.

Vevaina, Coomi S. "Puppets Must Perform or Perish: A Feminist Archetypal Analysis of Kate Chopin's *The Awakening*." *Chopin's The Awakening: Critical Essays*. Ed. Iqbal Kaur. New Delhi: Deep and Deep, 1995. 80–92.

Wade, Carol A. "Conformity, Resistance, and the Search for Selfhood in Kate Chopin's *The Awakening*." *Southern Quarterly* 37.2 (1999): 92–104.

Walker, Nancy. "Women Drifting: Drabble's The Waterfall and Chopin's *The Awakening*." *Denver Quarterly* 17.4 (1983): 88–96.

Ward, Selena et al. The Awakening: *Kate Chopin. Sparknotes*. New York: Spark, 2002.

Wershoven, C. J. "*The Awakening* and *the House of Mirth*: Studies of Arrested Development." *American Literary Realism* 19.3 (1987): 27–41.

Wheeler, Kathleen. *"Modernist" Women Writers and Narrative Art*. New York: New York UP, 1994.

Wolff, Cynthia G. "Thanatos and Eros: Kate Chopin's *The Awakening*." *American Quarterly* 25 (1973): 449–71.

Wyatt, Jean. *Reconstructing Desire: The Role of the Unconscious in Women's Reading and Writing*. Chapel Hill: U of North Carolina P, 1990.

Surprises, Complications, Unexpected Shifts, and Ironic Juxtapositions in Kate Chopin's *The Awakening*

Robert C. Evans

Kate Chopin's *The Awakening* has so often been read for its themes and "meanings" that it is easy to lose sight of its style and structure. The book is often splendid in its frequently subtle phrasing and is often intriguing in its artful design. One trait typical of both the style and the structure of the novel might be called "ironic juxtaposition." By this phrase I mean Chopin's tendency to place striking differences, contrasts, or even opposites side-by-side, often in surprising ways. One clue to her interest in such contrasts appears in the very opening paragraph of the work, where she juxtaposes a colorful, exotic, and self-assertive parrot with a rather drab, familiar, and imitative mockingbird. Later, in the same chapter, she juxtaposes the youthful, charming, good-humored Robert Lebrun with the older, more reserved, somewhat humorless Léonce Pontellier, just as Edna Pontellier is later contrasted with Adèle Ratignolle. Perhaps the most obvious evidence of Chopin's interest in ironic juxtaposition, however, is the way she repeatedly pairs a somber, religious, older "lady in black" with a pair of romantic young lovers. Rarely do we see the lady without seeing the lovers, and *vice versa*. In this way as in many others, Chopin reveals a pervasive interest in meaningful contrasts.

In this essay, I plan to explore a number of such contrasts to show how they add to the sheer narrative interest of the book. Often, Chopin uses "ironic juxtapositions" within or between sentences in ways that keep the novel continually surprising and unpredictable. If one role of a good novelist is to keep her readers from feeling bored, and if one function of a skilled writer is to prevent her prose from seeming predictable, then Chopin succeeds on both counts. Her use of ironic juxtaposition, however, is evident not only at the level of individual sentences but also in the placement of adjacent chapters, especially in the ways the conclusion of one chapter "sets up" an ironic contrast with the beginning of the next chapter.[1]

* * *

One of the earliest ironic juxtapositions in the novel occurs in the first four paragraphs, which juxtapose lively, noisy birds (a parrot and mockingbird) with the stodgy, frustrated Léonce, who quickly abandons the birds in search of peace and quiet (3). Clearly, his behavior is symbolic: just as he leaves the chatty birds behind, so he will leave the equally chatty Edna and Robert behind at the end of the chapter. *The Awakening* is full of these kinds of contrasts and parallels. Some are blatant (such as the juxtaposition of the lovers with the lady in black). Many, however, are far more subtle.

Often—astonishingly often—the juxtapositions involve the placement of white and black characters side-by-side. Anyone who reads the book with these racial juxtapositions in mind will be surprised by their frequency. The first example such contrasts occurs already in Chapter I, where the narrator first mentions the Pontellier children ("sturdy little fellows of four and five") and then immediately mentions their mature, thoughtful black attendant: "A quadroon nurse followed them about with a far-away, meditative air" (Chopin 4). Here, and even more clearly later in the book, the effect of such juxtapositions is to contrast the comfortable, privileged, relatively carefree life of the novel's white characters with the status of most of its black characters as workers, who must cater to the whims of the whites. Often, the black characters emerge from such contrasts (as in the one just quoted) as enchantingly mysterious and intriguing. What is the "quadroon nurse" thinking about or meditating? The narrator doesn't say, but here and elsewhere Chopin suggests that the black characters have lives, thoughts, and feelings of their own. The white characters may ignore the existence of these black people *as people*, but the narrator doesn't. Instead, she repeatedly implies that there is more to these "servants" than that title implies.

However, Chopin's treatment of her black characters has been the subject of so much recent discussion that there seems no point in expanding it here. Instead, it seems worth paying attention, for a while, to Chopin as a stylist of sentences and sentence placement. Consider, for example, the following passage from chapter three, which describes Léonce's disappointment in Edna's neglectfulness:

> He thought it very discouraging that his wife, who was the sole object of his existence, evinced so little interest in things which concerned him, and valued so little his conversation. // Mr. Pontellier had forgotten the bonbons and peanuts for the boys. (Chopin 7)

I have inserted "//" marks (here and elsewhere) to make the ironic shift even more obvious than it already is. No sooner does Léonce find fault with Edna's negligence than the narrator immediately, but subtly, reminds us that Léonce himself is often neglectful: he failed to remember an explicit promise to his sons. This moment of implied neglect is then ironically followed by his decision to check on his sons while they are sleeping (is he motivated partly by guilt?), to make sure that they are "resting comfortably." This act, in turn, is followed by the fact that he ironically awakens them, which, in turn, is ironically followed by his suggestion that Edna has neglected the boys' health. This, in turn, is ironically followed by his decision to go out onto the porch to smoke while letting Edna attend alone to the disturbance Léonce has created. This string of ironies is then capped by an especially ironic moment, when the narrator paraphrases Léonce's point-of-view: "He reproached his wife with her inattention, her habitual neglect of the children. If it was not a mother's place to look after children, whose on earth was it?" (Chopin 7).

This cascade of ironies, ending in an unintentionally ironic accusation and an unintentionally ironic rhetorical question, is typical of Chopin's methods throughout the book. She loves to pile irony upon irony, saying nothing explicitly herself but allowing readers to draw their own amused and/or appalled conclusions. If the narrator had openly reproached Léonce here, the episode would have been far less effective. Instead, she shows us how insensitively he behaves even as he accuses Edna of insensitivity. Having unleashed the chaos of two little, wide-awake boys, Léonce soon falls asleep, and in the very next sentence, the narrator informs us that "Mrs. Pontellier was by that time thoroughly awake" (Chopin 7).

Such juxtapositions are typical of Chopin's style throughout the novel. They imply, for one thing, that she credits her readers with enough intelligence to notice ironies without having to have them pointed out or over-emphasized. They also imply the intelligence, wisdom, good humor, and restraint of the narrator, who can perceive her characters' foibles without feeling any need to preach about them. The narrator of *The Awakening* usually "shows" rather than "tells," and she frequently uses ironies and ironic juxtapositions to imply points without having to state them explicitly. Given the fact that the novel is often read as a book intended to promote a particular "message," the narrator's restraint is especially impressive. She is the understated narrator of a subtle novel, not the excited spokesperson in a blatant political tract.

Chopin's use of ironic juxtapositions also implies that life and relationships are complex and cannot be reduced to simple truisms. Consider, for example, these sentences, where the inserted "//" marks again indicate the moments of ironic juxtaposition:

> A certain light was beginning to dawn dimly within [Edna], -- the light which, showing the way, // forbids it.

> At that early period it served but to bewilder her. It moved her to dreams, to thoughtfulness, // to the shadowy anguish which had overcome her the midnight when she had abandoned herself to tears. (Chopin 15)

The juxtapositions here typify Chopin's narrative method. Just when the narrator seems to be moving in one direction, she veers off in an entirely unexpected and often completely opposite direction. A light shows a way but then forbids passage; dreams and thoughtfulness are juxtaposed with shadowy anguish. Such phrasing not only suggests the sheer complexities of the subjects discussed, but it also provokes and holds our readerly interests. We can never confidently predict how a sentence by Chopin will end. Her prose is rarely monotonous in the true sense of that word. The pages of *The Awakening* brim with constant surprises, often resulting from ironic juxtapositions of the sort just illustrated.

Ironic juxtapositions are especially useful when the narrator is describing Edna, the book's most complex character. Here is a typical passage, with the juxtapositions once again marked:

> [Edna] was fond of her children // in an uneven, impulsive way. She would sometimes gather them passionately to her heart; // she would sometimes forget them. The year before they had spent part of the summer with their grandmother Pontellier in Iberville. Feeling secure regarding their happiness and welfare, // she did not miss them // except with an occasional intense longing. //Their absence was a sort of relief, // though she did not admit this, // even to herself. (Chopin 19)

Edna is complicated and unpredictable, and so she is often described in a complicated, style—a style that darts back and forth from one position to another and then back and forth again. It would have been easy—too easy—for Chopin to make Edna a far less ambiguous, ambivalent character than she is, but *The Awakening* is so fascinating partly because it often evokes reactions that are as complex as Edna herself and as the phrasing used to describe her. Edna often doesn't know exactly *what* she thinks or feels, and we are often unsure exactly *how* to respond to Edna. Such uncertainties are both reflected in Chopin's style and created by it.

Chopin's use of ironic juxtapositions implies an alert narrator, alive to the complexities of her episodes and characters. But the juxtapositions also encourage alertness in readers, leading us (with typical irony) to expect the unexpected.

Yet, ironic juxtapositions are also especially appropriate not only to descriptions of Edna, but to any description of the Pontelliers' marriage, especially as it becomes more entangled in tensions and complications. The more the marriage begins to break down and become unpredictable, the more suitable ironies are when the narrator depicts it. Here, for instance, Léonce tells Edna that even though she is a musician, Adèle doesn't neglect her domestic duties:

". . . she doesn't let everything else go to chaos. And she's more of a musician than you are a painter."

// "She isn't a musician, and I'm // not a painter. It isn't on account of painting that I let things go."

"On account of what, then?"

"Oh! // I don't know. Let me alone; you bother me."

It sometimes entered Mr. Pontellier's mind to wonder if his wife were not growing a little unbalanced mentally. He could see plainly that she was not herself. That is, // he could not see that she was // becoming herself and daily casting aside that fictitious self which we assume like a garment with which to appear before the world. (Chopin 55)

This passage overflows with ironic surprises, both for Léonce and for us as readers. Thus, Edna's response that Adèle is not a musician might have been predicted and might initially seem catty and self-defensive. But her frank admission that she herself is not a painter makes her seem the opposite of self-defensive; it makes her seem honest and self-aware. Next, she implies that there may be a definite reason that she is letting "things go," but then she says that she doesn't know what that reason might be (suggesting, perhaps, that she *does* know but is reluctant to say, or suggesting, perhaps, that she really and simply doesn't know). Léonce's assumption that Edna may be losing her mind is obviously ironic, although in another sense there, may be some truth to his suspicion. But then what he *can* see is ironically juxtaposed with what he *can't* see. The Pontellier marriage has become enormously complicated, and Chopin's phrasing both reflects and creates that sense of complication.

In fact, the more one probes many of Chopin's passages, the more complex they seem. In the one just quoted, for instance, Léonce thinks that Edna is "not herself." Then the narrator counters by commenting that she was in fact "becoming herself." But then the narrator can define this process of becoming only as a stripping away of a "fictitious self" without plainly saying what her new self is. Edna herself is unsure *what* her new self is, and so are we, and so, apparently, is the narrator. To call attention to all these uncertainties, however, is by no means to criticize Chopin; it is, in fact, to compliment her for refusing to make things neat, tidy, and obvious. Edna is a compelling character partly because no one—not readers, not the narrator, and definitely not Edna herself—can ever quite figure her out. An ironic style is a perfect style for attempting to describe such a character and her marriage to Léonce.

Sometimes Chopin uses ironic juxtapositions to suggest the brutal honesty of some of her characters as well as the ability of other characters to appreciate such frankness. Thus, at one point, Edna pays a visit to Mademoiselle Reisz:

> "So you remembered me at last," said Mademoiselle. "I had said to myself, 'Ah, bah! she will never come.'"
>
> "Did you want me to come?" asked Edna with a smile.
>
> // "I had not thought much about it," answered Mademoiselle. . . . And how is *la belle dame*? Always handsome! always healthy! // always contented!" . . . "Yes," she went on; "I sometimes thought: 'She will never come. She promised as those women in society always do, without meaning it. She will not come.' //For I really don't believe you like me, Mrs. Pontellier."
>
> // "I don't know whether I like you or not," replied Edna, gazing down at the little woman with a quizzical look.
>
> The candor of Mrs. Pontellier's admission // greatly pleased Mademoiselle Reisz. (Chopin 59-60)

The ironic juxtapositions here typify the ways Chopin keeps both her narrative *and* her dialogue lively and unpredictable. Mademoiselle Reisz obviously desired a visit from Edna but then claims that she didn't think much about it. But then she is clearly glad that Edna has come, but then implies unwittingly (or not?) that the discontented Edna is content. She surprisingly suggests that Edna may not like her, and Edna just as surprisingly admits that this may be true, but then Mademoiselle Reisz, rather than being offended by Edna's admission, seems greatly pleased by it. Both characters (here at least) seem remarkably honest and willing to face life and other people as they truly are. The exchange thus contributes to the novel's thematic contrast between the false and the real. Edna seems more mature and admirable here than she does at other times, and her relationship with Mademoiselle Reisz seems especially valuable because it is rooted in utter frankness (unlike some of her other relationships, especially her marriage to Léonce).

Many of the passages most filled with ironic juxtapositions, however, are ones that suggest the essential ambivalence and complexity of Edna. She is full of divisions, complications, uncertainties, and indecisions, and so Chopin often describes her in a style that makes readers realize, and experience for themselves, just how much she feels pulled in opposite directions. In chapter twenty-five, for instance, she is meditating on her adulterous relationship with Alcée Arobin, who is himself described with an especially effective bit of ironic juxtaposition: "Arobin's manner was so genuine //that it often deceived even himself" (Chopin 74). This is Chopin at her ironic best: the shift catches us by surprise, seems witty and even humorous, and thus implicitly characterizes the narrator while explicitly characterizing Arobin.

In any case, when the narrative turns, a few sentences later, to Edna's own thoughts about Arobin and their developing relationship, the ironic juxtapositions effectively convey the complexities of her situation:

> She felt somewhat like a woman who in a moment of passion is betrayed into an act of infidelity, and realizes the significance of the act // without being wholly awakened from its glamour. The thought was passing vaguely through her mind, "What would he think?"
>
> She did not mean // her husband; she was thinking // of Robert Lebrun. Her husband seemed to her now like a person whom she had married without love as an excuse.

She lit a candle and went up to her room. Alcée Arobin was absolutely nothing to her. // Yet his presence, his manners, the warmth of his glances, and above all the touch of his lips upon her hand had acted like a narcotic upon her.

She slept a languorous sleep, interwoven with // vanishing dreams. (Chopin 74)

Anyone who has ever had ambivalent thoughts and feelings will recognize, and perhaps even sympathize with, the ways Edna is thinking and feeling here. The phrasing is even more complex than the marked ironic juxtapositions already suggest. Thus, the simple word "somewhat" in the first quoted sentence is itself uncertain and contributes to the uncertainty of Edna's thoughts and to our own uncertainty in evaluating them. Remove that single word, and the sentence is far more definite and precise. Keep that word—that simple "somewhat" —and the sentence is far more ambiguous.

Next, notice the careful balancing here, which itself suggests ambivalence and division. The phrase "moment of passion" is balanced against the phrase "act of infidelity," while the word "significance" is set against (and balanced by) the word "glamour." In both cases, the balanced terms are ironically juxtaposed. A "moment of passion" might seem a good thing, but can it be justified if it leads to an "act of infidelity"? Realizing the "significance" of something seems wise and mature, but being under the allure of "glamour" can seem superficial and childish. As Chopin's prose shifts back and forth from one alternative to another, we as readers almost experience for ourselves how it feels to be inside Edna's complicated, divided mind.

Yet the phrasing of this passage is effective in other ways as well and involves other kinds of juxtaposition. Consider, for instance, this splendidly constructed sentence, in which each new noun is increasingly more intense: "Yet his presence, // his manners, // the warmth of his glances, // and above all the touch of his lips // upon her hand had acted like a narcotic upon her" (74). Mere physical "presence" means almost nothing: a table or lamp can be physically present. The word "manners," however, already suggests a *human* presence and a cultivated human presence, at that. Warm glances imply much greater intimacy and interest than mere manners, but they do not imply physical contact. Finally, however, the "touch" of "lips" suggests not merely physical contact but *erotic* physical contact, while the reference to a "narcotic" suggests a movement from erotic contact to intense psychological possession. In a single sentence, then (and there are thousands like it in this book), Chopin shows an understated mastery not only of style but of syntax (that is, sentence structure). Anyone who thinks Chopin's skills as a writer were amateurish or immature (one thinks of Robert Dawson) has given insufficient attention to sentences—and passages—such as this. The passage concludes with yet another example of ironic juxtaposition, in which "languorous sleep" (suggesting peaceful, undisturbed relaxation) is juxtaposed with "vanished dreams" (suggesting ephemeral disturbances, with perhaps a hint of dark foreshadowing, especially of the novel's conclusion).

This passage is just one of many in the book's final section that display Chopin's use of ironic juxtapositions to underscore the complexity of Edna's thoughts and moods. In chapter twenty-seven, for example, Edna, speaking to Arobin, says, "By all the codes which I am acquainted with, I am a devilishly wicked specimen" of womanhood. Then, however, she immediately adds: "But some way I can't convince myself that I am" (79). Later, she thinks of life as a "monster, made up of // beauty // and brutality" (80). One doesn't normally think of a monster as beautiful, but then, no sooner is its beauty mentioned than life's brutality is also asserted. Later still, in a bid to assert her independence, Edna decides to move into a small, modest house of her own. But no sooner does she indicate her desire to simplify her life than she announces her plans to throw a lavish party: "Oh! it will be very fine; all *my best* [emphasis added] of everything—crystal, silver and gold, Sevres, flowers, music, and champagne to swim in. // I'll let Léonce pay the bills. // I wonder what he'll say when he sees the bills" (81). She will display all of *her* best, but Léonce will pay the bills, and then she wonders about his reaction to the bills. Is she feeling malicious or vindictive when she decides that Léonce will pay the bills? And is she feeling vindictive—or guilty —when she wonders how he will react to the party's cost? In both cases, the questions are hard to answer. Edna is an exceedingly complex character. Sometimes she seems sympathetic; sometimes she seems self-centered; often, she seems both at once. Edna is conflicted, and ironic juxtapositions are one way for Chopin to keep reminding us of that fact.

There are times when the ironic juxtapositions seem especially ironic—times when they become almost subtly satirical. Interestingly, Edna, the book's apparent heroine, often seems the target of this understated satire. At one point, for example, she explains why she plans to move out of her big house: "It's too much trouble. // I have to keep too many servants. // I am tired // bothering with them" (76). Only a naïve and privileged person (some would say) could speak this way. And in this case the privileged person is a wealthy white woman dependent on black servants, many of them themselves female. It is difficult to feel enormous sympathy for Edna when we realize just how relatively easy her life is, especially when that life is compared with the lives of the black people who serve her. (Some of them, apparently, will become unemployed because Edna is "tired" of "bothering with them." Nothing is mentioned about Edna trying to find them good new jobs.)

Sometimes ironic juxtapositions suggest not only Edna's shortcomings in dealing with other people, but also some other limitations she may not wish to think about. Thus, in chapter twenty-six, Mademoiselle Reisz asks Edna if she loves Robert: "'Yes,' said Edna. It was the first time she had admitted it, and a glow overspread her face, // blotching it with red spots" (Chopin 78). No sooner does the narrator seem to be indulging in facile romanticism (when describing the the "glow" of Edna's face) than she immediately complicates any such impression by mentioning "blotching . . . red spots." Any simple romanticism is immediately muddied, if not altogether obscured. Something similar happens later, when Arobin caresses Edna: "His fingers strayed occasionally down to her warm, smooth cheeks and firm chin, which was // growing a little full // and double" (Chopin 79). The ironic juxtapositions here remind us that although Arobin values Edna primarily as a sex object, she will never be as physically attractive to him as she is right now; inevitably, in Arobin's eyes, her appeal will lessen as she ages. If Edna is wise (always an intriguing question), she will realize that she should not build her hopes on relations with men like Arobin. As this sentence and the others already quoted illustrate, Chopin doesn't hesitate to gently mock Edna. But mocking Edna is one way of keeping her human and credible and thus adding credibility to the novel as a whole.

Mockery, however, is just one of the many ways in which ironic juxtapositions are used in *The Awakening*, as this essay so far has tried to show. Instead, juxtapositions are key devices Chopin uses for organizing her paragraphs and sentences. By placing opposites (or other kinds of differences) side-by-side, she contributes to our sense of the complexity of her narrative, her characters, her themes, and life itself. It should not surprise us, then, that the final passage of *The Awakening* is full of abrupt, unexpected, unexplained, and therefore thought-provoking shifts. As Edna moves out into the waters of the Gulf of Mexico, we are taken inside her extremely complex and constantly oscillating consciousness:

> She thought of Léonce and the children. They were a part of her life. // But they need not have thought that they could possess her, body and soul. // How Mademoiselle Reisz would have laughed, // perhaps sneered, if she knew! "And you call yourself an artist! What pretensions, Madame! The artist must possess the courageous soul that dares and defies."

> // Exhaustion was pressing upon and overpowering her.

> // "Goodby—because I love you." He did not know; he did not understand.

> He would never understand. // Perhaps Doctor Mandelet would have understood if she had seen him—// but it was too late; the shore was far behind her, and her strength was gone.

She looked into the distance, and the old terror flamed up for an instant, // then sank again. // Edna heard her father's voice and her sister Margaret's. // She heard the barking of an old dog that was chained to the sycamore tree. // The spurs of the cavalry officer clanged as he walked across the porch. // There was the hum of bees, and the musky odor of pinks filled the air. (Chopin 109)

Inevitably (and appropriately), Edna in her final seconds is confused. This passage, indeed, epitomizes the ways she has been torn in different directions throughout the novel—the ways her thoughts and feelings throughout the book have been chaotic, unfocused, and unpredictable. One second, she is thinking of "Léonce and the children," then the next second she is dismissing them, then the next second she thinks of Mademoiselle Reisz and her insistence on spiritual strength, then the next second Edna's physical exhaustion is emphasized. The closing paragraphs are full of abrupt shifts, as befits a novel that is itself full of abrupt shifts. It is as if, in the book's final section, Edna's life flashes before her eyes even as Edna's story flashes before ours. Rather than bringing the book to any neat and tidy conclusion, however, these final paragraphs leave us (and Edna) pretty much where we have been all along: inside the consciousness of a character whose complexities are underscored by unpredictable alterations of thought and feeling.

Such alterations, however, not only typify the novel's style and structure at the level of individual phrases, clauses, sentences, and paragraphs; they also often typify its shifts from one chapter to another. Chopin is especially talented in creating surprises, or using ironic juxtapositions, when she moves from one chapter to the next—a talent she demonstrates almost from the very beginning. When she shifts from chapter two to chapter three, for instance, she shifts from a chapter dealing with Edna's increasingly close relationship with Robert to a chapter revealing unexpected conflicts in Edna's marriage with Léonce. The shift from chapter three to chapter four is especially ironic: chapter three ends with Edna publicly praising Léonce (perhaps because she feels obligated to do so), while chapter four opens with Léonce privately finding fault with Edna. Chapter five is long and frequently humorous; chapter six is extremely short and is deeply serious and meditative. Chapter seven, meanwhile, is especially long and deals in detail with Edna's past, while Chapter eight immediately shifts to Adèle's concerns about Edna's future—concerns rooted in her fear that Edna may be falling in love with Robert. Chapter eight ends with familiar chit-chat between Robert and his mother, who is operating a sewing machine (with the crucial help of a small black girl), but then Chapter nine shifts the book's emphasis to an elaborate party (much more elaborate than the one Edna throws in chapter thirty-four). The book, then, is built around a whole series of major shifts—shifts that alter the tones, moods, characters, themes, settings, and implications of the novel, helping to create a social world that seems rich and complex.

Just as one can never quite predict how Chopin will end a sentence or move from one paragraph to the next, so the same holds true of her juxtapositions of the book's various chapters. Other effective shifts take place between chapters twelve and thirteen, thirteen and fourteen, fifteen and sixteen, eighteen and nineteen, twenty-six and twenty-seven, thirty-one and thirty-two, thirty-four and thirty-five, and especially twenty-seven and twenty-eight, where the earlier chapter ends by describing how Arobin has aroused Edna's sexual passion and the later chapter begins by reporting that "Edna cried a little that night" (from sadness, not joy, about her relations with Arobin) "after Arobin left her" (Chopin 80).

As this last example suggests, some shifts from one chapter to the next are particularly striking. Thus, readers are just as surprised as Edna when she suddenly learns, near the start of chapter fifteen that Robert has abruptly decided to leave for Mexico. In the immediately preceding chapters, her relationship with Robert had grown increasingly intimate; now, without warning either to Edna or to Chopin's readers, he is suddenly heading off on a long and unexpected business trip. Another especially striking shift is the one from chapter sixteen to seventeen, when we suddenly move from an idyllic vacation at Grand Isle back to the normal, tedious routines of big-city life in New Orleans. Rather than making a smooth transition from one major setting to the other, Chopin once more catches us by surprise, and she does the same thing even more powerfully in the shift from chapter thirty-eight to chapter thirty-nine. Suddenly, Edna and the reader are back on Grand Isle again, and then, almost as suddenly, the tone has shifted from comic (in the first part of chapter thirty-nine) to tragic (in the final paragraphs). Edna abruptly shifts from apparently looking forward to a healthy supper to apparently committing suicide. Here, as so often happens throughout the book, Chopin uses unexpected shifts and ironic juxtapositions to enhance her novel's variety, interest, intrigue, and artistic effectiveness. The juxtaposed parrot and mockingbird at the very novel's beginning, like the juxtaposition of those birds with Léonce, provide our very first clues that *The Awakening* will skillfully employ juxtapositions. The varied juxtapositions of the final chapter bring that process full circle. From start to finish, *The Awakening* is an exceedingly ironic book.

Note

1.   For some earlier comments on Chopin's use of irony, see, for instance, Harmon (65), Rocks (which mainly deals with Chopin's short fiction), and Wheeler (52).

Works Cited

Chopin, Kate. *The Awakening*. Ed. Margot Culley. 2nd ed. New York: Norton, 1994.

Dawson, Hugh J. "Kate Chopin's *The Awakening*: A Dissenting Opinion." *American Literary Realism* 26.2 (1994): 1–18.

Harmon, Charles. "'Abysses of Solitude': Acting Naturally in *Vogue* and *The Awakening*." *College Literature* 25.3 (1998): 52–66.

Rocks, James E. "Kate Chopin's Ironic Vision." *Revue de Louisiane / Lousiana Review* 1 (1972): 110–119.

Wheeler, Kathleen M. *"Modernist" Women Writers and Narrative Art*. London: Palgrave Macmillan, 1994.

Mark Twain, Kate Chopin, *Huckleberry Finn*, and *The Awakening*

Robert C. Evans

In the final quarter of the nineteenth century, Mark Twain was widely considered one of the most talented of all the American authors. By the 1890s, his works had made him immensely popular, immensely wealthy, and even something of a national treasure. In 1884, he had published the *Adventures of Huckleberry Finn*, the book for which he is best known today, although he was at least as well known in his own period for his travel writings and other humorous non-fiction. In contrast, in the early 1890s, Kate Chopin was just beginning to build her career as a writer. By the end of that decade, however, she had established a respectable and growing reputation as a writer of short fiction, and in 1899, she published *The Awakening*, the novel today considered her masterwork. That book, after much immediate condemnation and a half-century of critical neglect, has now entered the canon of American literature as one of the most important and accomplished novels of its time. Today, *Huckleberry Finn* and *The Awakening* frequently appear together in large anthologies of the nation's literature. Did Chopin know of Twain? Was she consciously influenced by him? Are there any significant similarities in their writings?

The first question is easy to answer: Chopin definitely knew of Twain's works, because practically all literate Americans with any interest in good writing knew Twain's writings, or at least they knew *of* them. Whether Chopin was consciously *influenced* by Twain is more difficult to determine. We have strong evidence that she valued his work, because she tells us that she did. She put Twain at the very pinnacle of a whole catalogue of "western" American writers she listed in an essay published in late 1900 ("Development of the Literary West: A Review"). After briefly discussing, one by one, a long parade of worthy writers (including Bret Harte, Hamlin Garland, and Ambrose Bierce, to mention just a few), she concludes by arguing that people of the west would "still have enough to be proud of" if they had "only Mark Twain" ("Development" 225).

This is a remarkable comment—one that has perhaps received far too little attention from scholars. It suggests that Chopin had read Twain carefully and that she greatly valued what she had read. Yet, we have little other explicit evidence of her interest in his work. Nowhere else, apparently, does she mention his writings, but her high praise of Twain in 1900, however off-hand it seems, suggests that she genuinely admired his accomplishments. In the essay that follows, some of the reasons Chopin probably did admire Twain (and how she may have been influenced by him) will be explored. The essay will then turn, briefly, first to the short stories that most resemble Twain's writings and then, in more detail, to the many similarities, in theme, style, and probable purpose, between *Adventures of Huckleberry Finn* and *The Awakening*.

I.

In the essay by Chopin already mentioned, titled "Development of the Literary West: A Review," several comments suggest precisely *why* she may have admired Twain. Thus, she praises Bret Harte's story "Luck of Roaring Camp" for having:

> startled the Academists on the Atlantic coast, that is to say, in Boston. They opened their eyes and ears at the sound and awoke to the fact that there might some day [sic] be a literary West. Something different from the East, of course, and alien, but to be taken seriously, to be observed and considered. ("Development" 223)

One intriguing aspect of this comment is the reference to Eastern "Academists." That reference suggests Chopin's disdain for formulaic, conventional, rule-obeying art. It suggests an interest in innovations in both content and style—innovations of the sort for which both she and Twain are now famous. *The Awakening*, for instance, had offended many readers precisely because it was so boldly innovative, and perhaps Chopin's slighting reference to the "Academists" is partly a response to the poor reception her own novel had recently received from conventionally-minded critics.

Her novel was certainly something "different" from the norm and perhaps even "alien" from a traditional point of view, and it also takes place in a part of the country quite remote from the East, both geographically and culturally.

In these two senses, as well as in the others just mentioned, *The Awakening* resembles not only *Huckleberry Finn*, but also many of Twain's other writings. It therefore seems unsurprising that Chopin might consider Twain the best of all the "Western" writers, by which she means writers not of the far west (such as California), but of what we would today call the Midwest (such as Missouri). Twain, after all, was by far the most notable of all the writers of his day to hail from the Mississippi River Valley in general and from Missouri in particular. Chopin, of course, was herself born in, raised in, and for most of her life a resident of Missouri, and so she had yet another reason to take both a special interest and a special pride in Twain.

Having already used her essay to praise the writing of Bret Harte, Chopin next extols the work of a much less famous Western writer— "Father [Pierre-Jean] De Smet" ("Development" 223), an early Catholic missionary to the Indians of the Middle West. Chopin praises his writings for their "simplicity and directness" and for their local "atmosphere and color" (223). These, of course, are also traits of much of Twain's writing (especially when his work is contrasted with the work of someone like Henry James), and they are also traits of much of Chopin's own fiction, especially her short stories. She had another reason, then, to admire Twain: she was herself a prominent "local colorist," and no one had written more colorfully about various western, southern, and non-Bostonian locales than Twain. No wonder she praised him so highly: he had helped set various precedents, both in style and in subject matter, that had helped make possible her own early career as a writer of "regional" short fiction.

Although Chopin expressed disapproval of a "too obvious lack of reserve" in some recent "Western" writers (a somewhat surprising comment from the author of such works as *The Awakening* and "The Storm"), and although she disliked the "tawdriness" she found in some of these writers' works, she nevertheless praised the consistent "vigor" she found in even the less impressive examples of Western fiction. In all three of these additional respects, then, her admiration for Twain becomes even more comprehensible: rarely, if ever, are his works guilty of a "lack of reserve" or "tawdriness" (particularly in their treatment of sexual matters), but almost always his writings do display a genuinely healthy "vigor." It was, ironically, partly Chopin's own alleged "lack of reserve" and "tawdriness," especially in *The Awakening*, that caused her great novel to be initially condemned by many reviewers and then ignored for many years by most scholars and critics. Of course, even *Huckleberry Finn* was considered a poor influence on the young by some of its first readers, and so Chopin had yet another reason to admire Twain: his work had been subject to some of the same narrow-minded, moralistic condemnation as hers had been. Twain's offense, however, had not been to violate the sexual mores of his day but to describe free-spirited boys as they really often are.

Even when Chopin sometimes criticizes other "Western" writers, she implies additional reasons that she may have admired Twain. Thus she generally praises an author named Mary Hallock Foote, calling her work "excellent" and vaguely commending its "fine literary quality," but she regrets that Foote's work is sometimes damaged by "a too great conventional romanticism" ("Development" 224). Twain, of course, went to great pains to avoid such romanticism himself, and he often openly mocked it (especially in *Huckleberry Finn*). Chopin also tried to avoid seeming a mere romantic, and indeed one way to read *The Awakening* is as (in part, at least) a subtle send-up of Edna Pontellier's excessively romantic fantasies and behavior.

When it comes time for Chopin to praise Ambrose Bierce, she does so because "he has that peculiar faculty or privilege of genius which ignores subservience. He acknowledges no debt and pays no tribute" ("Development" 224). He is, in short, a literary independent, an original, who charts his own path. The same might easily be said of Twain, and the same might just as easily be said, in its own way, of Chopin, especially in the final phases of her career. Little wonder that the author of *The Awakening*, or of some of the stories collected in *A Vocation and a Voice*, would rank Twain so highly. Anyone who respected Bierce as much as Chopin did would almost be bound to feel even greater admiration for Twain.

In commenting, next, on Owen Wister, Chopin expresses discomfort with the "spectacular" elements of his writing, which, she thinks, give "the impression of a stagy fellow with an eye on his audience in the East" ("Development" 224). Wister, in other words, strikes her as possibly inauthentic, as a mere performer who, rather than rejecting conventional expectations, is playing up to others' stereotypes of what a "Western" writer is or should be. She admires Twain, presumably, because Twain seems genuine: he is what he is, makes no apologies for what he is, and does not dance to anyone else's tunes, especially if the tunes are cheap and cartoonish. Surely Chopin herself strove to be an independent without creating merely entertaining caricatures of the people and/or the writers of the West (and South). Twain managed to be appealing without being false or "stagy," and the same might be said of Chopin.

Indeed, when she praises the writings of Octave Thanet, she particularly praises Thanet's "[s]incerity":

> Her heart is essentially with the plain, everyday people. We meet her characters everywhere – crowding the department stores on bargain days, hurrying with bundles through the streets; thronging the lodge meetings and church sociables [sic]. She must walk about our Middle Western towns with her mental notebook open, chuckling to herself. ("Development" 224)

These comments on Thanet could just as easily be comments on Chopin, especially on much of her later short fiction, where the Louisiana "local color" elements recede and the depiction of life (and lives) in up-to-date urban centers becomes more prominent. One thinks, especially, of such stories as "The Blind Man" or "A Pair of Silk Stockings." Twain, of course, also shared an interest in "plain, everyday people," but just as significantly, he also possessed a very fine sense of humor. He could rarely contemplate people without feeling amused—without "chuckling to [him]self." And, of course, the same thing is true of much of Chopin's writing. *The Awakening*, in particular, is full of droll observations and phrasing, but gentle comedy is also often a main feature of much of Chopin's short fiction. Chopin's praise of Thanet, then, implies at least two more reasons why she admired Twain: his sense of humor and his interest in the lives of ordinary folks.

Another Western writer whose works Chopin valued was Hamlin Garland. Although she felt that he had sometimes "been guilty of inexcusable crudities in handling men and women," she also argued that when he was at "his best, he has not been surpassed in his field," especially in his depiction of nature, particularly the weather. One of his stories (she believed) "could only have been told by one whose soul was close to nature. He believes in himself and follows his own light. May he never he tempted to follow false gods" ("Development" 225). Twain and Chopin, of course, both often depict nature memorably, especially in *Huckleberry Finn* and *The Awakening*. But the note that aligns this praise of Garland with earlier praise of other writers is the emphasis on following one's own light. This, perhaps, was the keynote of Chopin's admiration for Twain.

Interestingly enough, the one kind of writing that Chopin most explicitly censures in her essay is writing she associates with the younger authors of Chicago,

> whose mental vision seems impaired by the city's skyscrapers, and who are apparently fascinated by the hideous complexities of life which so phenomenal and abnormal a growth has produced. Their work has its place in the great mosaic word-picture of the West, but it makes unpleasant reading. ("Development" 225)

Whom did Chopin have in mind when she wrote these words? Theodore Dreiser is one possibility: his notorious novel *Sister Carrie* had been published earlier in 1900, the year of Chopin's essay (which appeared in December). Frank Norris is another possible candidate, although his grim novel *McTeague* (1899) is set in San Francisco. Upton Sinclair's novel *The Jungle* (which is set in Chicago and which *certainly* "makes for unpleasant reading") would not appear until 1906. Ultimately, then, it is hard to know precisely which Chicago writers Chopin had in mind. But she clearly seems to have disliked depictions of "hideous complexities" in an urban setting that made for "unpleasant reading." Three more reasons, then, for her to admire Mark Twain, whose most famous works emphasized none of these features.

Chopin's essay on contemporary "Western" writers says remarkably little about Twain himself, but it says so much about other authors that we can reasonably infer why she admired Twain as highly as she did. If we total up the reasons that may have led her to rank Twain so highly, the list is remarkably long:

- he startled many Eastern "Academists"
- he wrote as an explicitly "Western" (i.e., non-Eastern) writer
- he charted his own path, breaking academic rules as he saw fit
- he was innovative both in content and in form
- his style was simple and direct
- he emphasized local atmosphere and color
- his writing was not tawdry but was full of vigor
- like Chopin herself, he had been censured by prudish critics
- he rejected conventional romanticism
- he did not seem "stagy" or "spectacular"
- he did not seek to ratify Eastern stereotypes about the West
- he had a sincere interest in "plain, everyday people"
- he had a wry but not malicious sense of humor
- he did not depict relations between the sexes crudely
- he memorably described nature

All these traits that Chopin probably admired in Twain are traits evident in much of her own writing, especially her short fiction. In focusing so much of our critical attention on her great novel *The Awakening*, we often forget that Chopin wrote scores of short stories and that it was these stories that established her fame. Of course, some of her most famous tales (particularly "The Story of an Hour") closely resemble *The Awakening* in subject matter, style, and tone. But many of her other works are much more obviously "Western" or "Southern" and thus seem much more obviously similar to works by Twain. This is especially the case because so many of her stories are humorous in tone, were written for young readers, and/or feature young people as central characters. In all these ways, many of Chopin's tales resemble the most famous works by Twain, especially *Huckleberry Finn* and *Tom Sawyer*.

Stories that exemplify some or all of these criteria include "Beyond the Bayou," "Boulôt and Boulotte," "The Lilies," "A Little Country Girl," "Mamouche," "A Matter of Prejudice," "Odalie Misses Mass," "Regret," "Ripe Figs," "A Turkey Hunt," and "With the Violin." In general, Chopin (who was, like Twain, a loving parent) presents children as appealingly rambunctious and funny. Certainly, this is how the Pontellier children, Raoul and Etienne, appear in *The Awakening*. Like Twain, Chopin seems to have had a soft spot for young people and to have found their antics highly amusing. It is often in the short stories, in fact, that she most resembles Twain in style, content, and themes.

And it is in several of her short stories (most notably "La Belle Zoraïde" and "Désirée's Baby") that Chopin comes closest to satirizing the evils of racism as powerfully as Twain does in *Huckleberry Finn*. It is hard to think of anything in Twain's novel that constitutes a more searing indictment of racism that "La Belle Zoraïde." Anyone who thinks that Chopin was indifferent to racial injustice need only read that story, which is intensely heartbreaking. The attitudes implied in that tale suggest that the many references to black people in *The Awakening* were put there deliberately and were clearly intended to seem highly ironic. Edna may largely overlook her black servants and be relatively indifferent to their plight, but "La Belle Zoraïde" suggests that the same thing was by no means true of Chopin herself. In her short fiction, especially (with its often rich emphasis on regional dialects), Chopin most resembles Twain. But what of Twain and *The Awakening*? Are there any significant similarities between Chopin's novel and Twain's work, especially his own greatest novel (*Huckleberry Finn*)?

At first glance, Chopin's *The Awakening* and Twain's *Adventures of Huckleberry Finn* might seem to have little in common. One is the story of a rich, sophisticated, urban woman who grows frustrated with her conventional marriage and her confining life and who apparently commits suicide; the other is the story of a poor, uneducated boy from a small village who, after a series of exciting exploits, while accompanied by an older black man and then another white boy, heads off West for what one hopes will be a long and happy life. The style of *The Awakening* is urbane and refined; the book's narrator is obviously cultured and shrewd. In contrast, the style of *Huckleberry Finn* is folksy and plain, as befits its innocent, wide-eyed narrator (Huck himself). The events of *The Awakening* are presented from a cultivated, omniscient point-of-view, while the story of Huck is a story told *by* Huck. Finally, to list just one more significant contrast, the narrative structures of the two books radically differ. *The Awakening* is a short, tightly constructed novel focused on a narrowly defined geographical area and a relatively small cast of characters, while *Huck Finn* rambles hither and yon and depicts a wide range of diverse persons and personalities.

Despite these obvious differences, however, the two books have much in common. Both, for instance, are set on or near major, iconic bodies of American water (the Gulf Coast and the Mississippi River). The central characters of both books feel confined and constricted and yearn for freedom. Both Edna and Huck resist being "sivilize[d]" (as Huck puts it [1]), and both reject efforts to control them, however well-intended those efforts may be. Both Edna and Huck have to deal with overbearing fathers (Leder 239), and both are attracted—and consoled—by the beauties of physical nature. Each character has a close companion, with whom he or she enjoys a special relationship (Robert Lebrun in Edna's case; Jim the slave in Huck's). Both books derive much of their appeal from their presentation of intriguing settings, distinctive subcultures, and fascinating "local color," and both major characters often feel isolated and lonesome. Both *The Awakening* and *Huckleberry Finn* were controversial (at least in some circles) when first published, and both provoked not only negative reactions but even some efforts at censorship. Finally, both books are major American treatments of the theme of freedom, and both books end on notes of intriguing ambiguity, with each major character heading off in a new and unknown direction.[1]

To say this, however, is to be reminded of some other important contrasts between the two novels. At the end of *The Awakening*, Edna heads toward her death; at the end of *Huckleberry Finn*, Huck heads (presumably) toward greater freedom and a richer life. The ending of one book is explicitly tragic; the ending of the other is just as explicitly comic and happy. Both books present black characters who are more confined and constricted than either book's central character, but issues of race and racial oppression are far more overtly important in *Huckleberry Finn* than in *The Awakening*. Huck, in fact, seems far more racially conscious, sensitive, and enlightened than Edna, but whereas Twain's satire of racism is explicit and is part of the main purpose of the book, Chopin's satire (if it exists at all, as I believe it does) is more muted and implicit. The oppression faced by Jim and other blacks in *Huckleberry Finn* is far worse than anything Edna faces in *The Awakening*, and Edna has many more opportunities to achieve genuine freedom than Jim does. (Her options may even be greater than Huck's simply because she is wealthy, although Huck has the advantage of being male.) Jim's love of his children seems deeper and more emotional than Edna's love for hers, and a case can be made that Huck matures far more in the course of his *Adventures* than Edna does during *The Awakening*. In some ways, Huck seems more sensitive to the needs and feelings of others than does Edna, and he is far more self-critical. To say this, however, is not to say that one book or one character is more admirable than the other; it is simply to say that the books explore issues that are intriguingly similar, but also decidedly distinct. Both richly deserve their status as classics of American literature.

III.

Some of the similarities between *The Awakening* and *Huckleberry Finn* are especially obvious when one reads the opening chapter of Twain's novel. Huck resists the widow Douglas's efforts to "sivilize" him in much the same way that Edna resists the similar efforts of Léonce (Twain 1; Chopin 49). Yet, Huck is willing to concede that the widow is "dismal regular and decent" (Twain 1) in much the same way that Edna concedes the basic decency of Léonce (Chopin 9). Neither the widow nor Léonce is especially oppressive in any conventional sense of the word; neither is a villain; and neither Huck nor Edna is suffering from any enormous lack of liberty. Many people would be more than happy to have Léonce as a husband or the widow as an adoptive parent. Neither Edna nor Huck, however, is satisfied with a merely "sivilized" life; each wants something more. Each wants to be "free and satisfied" (Twain 1).

Both Huck and Edna associate their lack of freedom with restrictive clothing. The widow puts Huck into "new clothes again, so that I couldn't do nothing but sweat and sweat, and feel all cramped up" (Twain 2). Edna also comes to consider clothes somewhat confining. In one memorable scene she feels free and relaxed when she disrobes: the narrator describes how Edna

> loosened her clothes, removing the greater part of them. She bathed her face, her neck and arms in the basin that stood between the windows. She took off her shoes and stockings and stretched herself in the very center of the high, white bed. (Chopin 35-36)

Later she wears an "ordinary house dress" when she should be wearing an elaborate "reception gown," and "Mr. Pontellier, who was observant about such things, noticed it" (Chopin 48). Likewise, when Edna is later preparing to move out of the Pontellier mansion and into her own little "pigeon house," Alcée Arobin finds her:

> with rolled sleeves, working in company with the housemaid . . . . She was splendid and robust, and had never appeared handsomer than in

the old blue gown, with a red silk handkerchief knotted at random around her head to protect her hair from the dust. (Chopin 80)

The less conventionally Edna dresses, the freer she feels—or perhaps it is just as accurate to say that the freer Edna feels, the less conventionally she dresses. In any case, by the end of the book, when she turns her back on all the various restrictions imposed on her life, she is completely naked as she wades into the Gulf. Even Huck never achieves that degree of freedom from clothing.

But Huck and Edna resemble each other in other ways, as well. Each, for instance, feels confined by conventional expectations about meals and dining. Huck regrets the fact that when the "widow rung a bell for supper, . . . you had to come to time" (Twain 2). Léonce also takes proper dining very seriously and becomes quite upset when his meals are not perfectly prepared (Chopin 49-50). Edna, in contrast, is far less concerned about what or how she eats (Chopin 50, 107), and even her elaborate dinner party is less a concession to conventional expectations than a way of celebrating her growing freedom (Chopin 77). Neither Huck nor Edna is especially interested in obeying others' rules or meeting others' expectations. Both would rather set their own agendas. Increasingly, neither of them wants to "try to behave" (Twain 3), as Miss Watson advises Huck. Huck, pondering this advice, says "All I wanted was to go somewhere; all I wanted was a change – I warn't particular" (Twain 4). Edna could not have said it better herself (although she might have phrased it differently). In response, Miss Watson tells Huck that he is "wicked" (Twain 4), just as Edna herself later tells Arobin that "By all the codes which I am acquainted with, I am a devilishly wicked specimen of the sex. But some way I can't convince myself that I am" (Chopin 79). Huck feels torn in much the same way: society tells him that his impulses are evil, but ultimately he decides to follow them anyway.

Neither Huck nor Edna seems especially interested in, or impressed by, conventional religion. Huck sees little advantage in going to heaven if Miss Watson will be there (Twain 4), and Edna feels ill oppressed and drowsy and develops a headache during her one visit in *The Awakening* to a church (Chopin 34-35). Huck feels so alienated from conventional society and its customs that he even comments, "I felt so lonesome I most wished I was dead" (Twain 4). For Huck, this is merely an exaggerated figure of speech, but for Edna—who feels far lonelier than Huck—it eventually becomes an actual fact. She, after all, apparently really does commit suicide. It is hard to imagine Huck, even in the direst circumstances, doing any such thing. He is too much a figure of vibrant vitality ever to really kill himself.

Both Huck and Edna take great solace in the beauty of physical nature. Huck's love of nature is already implied in chapter one, when he describes the beauty of shining stars (Twain 4), and throughout the novel, Huck pauses to appreciate the attractions of nature, as does Edna, especially in the first half of *The Awakening*. For both protagonists, nature symbolizes freedom and peace, although both are also aware of its dangers. Edna sees the Gulf as a symbol of beauty and liberty but also as a potential threat (to which she eventually succumbs), and the same might be said of Huck's attitude toward the Mississippi, whose charms he appreciates but whose overwhelming force he acknowledges and respects.

Yet, if Edna resembles Huck in many respects, she also resembles Tom Sawyer in various other ways. Both Edna and Tom are incurable Romantics in many of the worst senses of that word. Each lives, to a great degree, in a kind of fantasy world, in which each is the main center of his or her own attention. Each tends to think and behave unrealistically, and each can be accused of neglecting the best interests of people who deserve better. In Tom's case, the person whose needs and feelings he most neglects is Jim, especially in the notorious closing chapters of the novel, when Tom invents a wholly unnecessary, very elaborate, and very dangerous plot to free Jim from captivity when he knows that Jim is already technically free. In Edna's case, the persons whose needs and feelings she most neglects—as she herself seems to acknowledge just before the novel concludes—are her two small sons: "It makes no difference to me, it doesn't matter about Léonce Pontellier—but Raoul and Etienne!" (Chopin 108). In the end, Edna dies, whether deliberately or by accident, leaving her two little boys without a mother. The happy ending that Tom contrives for Jim is a happy ending that Edna and her children fail to achieve, which is just one of many reasons that *The Awakening* is a much darker book than *Huckleberry Finn*.

Both books, however, take the quest for freedom as major themes, and in both books, the central characters achieve memorable moments of self-reliance and self-definition in the face of real pressures to conform. This is especially true of Huck at the very end of his novel; whether it is also true of Edna at the very end of hers is, however, very much a matter open for debate.

Note

1. A search for "Chopin and Twain" in the comprehensive electronic bibliography of the Modern Language Association turns up nothing. For brief general comments on *The Awakening* and *Adventures of Huckleberry Finn*, see, for example, Leder (239); Wade (93); and, more whimsically, Toth and Fitzgibbons.

Works Cited

Chopin, Kate. *The Awakening*. Ed. Margot Culley. 2nd ed. New York: Norton, 1994.

_____. "Development of the Literary West: A Review." *Kate Chopin's Private Papers*. Ed. Emily Toth and Per Seyersted. Bloomington: Indiana UP, 1998. 223-25.

Ewell, Barbara C. "Kate Chopin and the Dream of Female Selfhood." *Kate Chopin Reconsidered: Beyond the Bayou*. Eds. Lynda S. Boren and Sara deSaussure Davis. Baton Rouge: Louisiana State UP, 1992. 157-65.

Leder, Priscilla. "Land's End: *The Awakening* and 19th Century Literary Tradition." *Critical Essays on Kate Chopin*. Ed. Alice Hall Petry. New York: G. K. Hall, 1996.

Toth, Emily and Dennis Fitzgibbons. "Kate Chopin Meets *The Harvard Lampoon*." *Kate Chopin Newsletter* 3.1 (1975-76): 28.

Twain, Mark. *Adventures of Huckleberry Finn*. Ed. Victor Fischer and Lin Salamo. Berkeley: U of California P, 2001.

Wade, Carol A. "Conformity, Resistance, and the Search for Selfhood in Kate Chopin's *The Awakening*." *Southern Quarterly* 37.2 (1999): 92-104.

CRITICAL
READINGS

Was *The Awakening* Banned or Burned? What Did Chopin Think Worth Reading? (And Other New Archival Evidence About Kate Chopin's Life and Writings)_____

Robert C. Evans

In the time since the "rediscovery" of Kate Chopin in the 1960s, scholars have unearthed more and more information about Chopin's life and writings. The major biographies—by Per Seyersted and especially by Emily Toth—resulted from much dedicated sleuthing and turned up (particularly in Toth's works) many fresh and intriguing results. More recently, however, it has become much easier to search the archives, and this article presents some recent archival findings. Much of this information has not been presented before, and even the data that have been noted by previous scholars have sometimes not been presented in as much detail as they are here.

Especially important is the discovery of much new evidence that *The Awakening* may indeed have been banned (and even burned)—a claim sometimes doubted. Also intriguing are "new" reviews of Chopin's works, "new" information about her life and career, and even "new" writings by her. What follows is just the tip of the proverbial iceberg of "new" information about Chopin.

To save space and respect copyright restrictions, much of the information below is, for the time being, paraphrased rather than reprinted.

Was *The Awakening* Banned or Even Burned?

For years, it was assumed that *The Awakening* was banned in various places, including St. Louis. Little evidence of such suppression could be found, however, and, therefore, recent scholarship has tended to doubt these claims (see, for example, Toth, *Kate Chopin*, 367-69, and Toth, *Unveiling Kate Chopin*, xx-xxi, 227, 243).

New evidence suggests, however, that there may be some truth in the claims that *The Awakening* was suppressed, not only in St. Louis but also in Evanston, Illinois.

Was *The Awakening* Banned in Evanston, Illinois?

An article published on page four of the Rockford, IL *Republic* on July 3, 1902 is headlined "'QUO VADIS' NOT FIT TO READ / So Says an Evanston Minister—Other Books Proscribed by the Librarian There." The article begins by quoting J. Scott Clark, head of the English department at Northwestern University, as saying that some books recently "excluded" from an Evanston library are not as bad as others left on the shelves, including works by Zola and Tolstoy. "I do not see," he says, "where the line is to be drawn." He then opines about which books are worth reading and which are not. He approves of *The Scarlet Letter* as fit reading for a typical "young girl" but says that he personally never wastes time reading modern fiction.

The article then mentions four works that have recently been added to the "proscribed list": *Foma Gordyeef* by Gorky; *Wild Rose* by Francis Francis; *McTeague* by Frank Norris; and *The Awakening*. A local Presbyterian pastor is quoted as saying that he has no time to read most of such books himself but that Hardy's *Jude the Obscure* is impure and *Quo Vadis* by Henryk Sienkiewicz "is not fit for the young to read." This last phrase, like the earlier reference to a "young girl," raises the possibility that only young people, not adults, were prohibited from borrowing the "proscribed" books.

Was *The Awakening* Banned—and Burned—in St. Louis?

A long article on the front page of the *St. Paul Globe* on September 3, 1902 has this headline: "'THE AWAKENING' OUT OF A LIBRARY / Regarded as Improper by the Mercantile, St. Louis, and Removed From Its Shelves." This is one of several reports suggesting that Chopin's novel was not only banned in her hometown, but actually burned.

[PARAPHRASE:] Dateline: St. Louis, Sept 2. *The Awakening* "has been placed under the ban with Zola, Balzac, Mark Twain, Walt Whitman and other noted writers by Horace Kephart, librarian of the Mercantile library, because it was objected to by some members of the governing board." Copies of the novel were burned in the library's furnace. Although the book was attacked by reviewers, everyone realizes its "artistic merits."

Various copies remain in the public library, and "Librarian Cruenden" has never thought of removing it.

> Kephart was unavailable for comment, but his assistant confirmed the report, saying that "some members of the library association" disliked the book and that Kephart simply did what they had asked. The assistant claimed to know Chopin personally and called her "a very fine woman, a gifted writer." The article ends with this unattributed statement (which perhaps continues to report the opinions of the assistant): "Mrs. Chopin is in no wise disturbed over the action taken by Librarian Kephart."

The same article appeared on page five of the September 4, 1902 edition of *The Denver Post* under the headline "LIBRARIAN'S BONFIRE: Radical Action Taken by Head of St. Louis Library."

On the front page of the September 3, 1902 edition of Indiana's *Fort Wayne News*, a much shorter version of the same story is printed under the following headline: "BURNS NOVEL AS IMPROPER. / St. Louis Librarian Destroys All Copies of 'The Awakening.'" This article quotes Kephart as saying that "members of the library have told him the book is improper. He does not undertake to pass on the subject himself." The article says that the novel, until recently, had "been considered harmless."

A somewhat puzzling brief report on page seven of the September 3, 1902 edition of *The St. Louis Republic* mentions a "sensational article" published "yesterday" in an unnamed newspaper (perhaps *The Denver Post*?). The *Republic* comments that the Mercantile Library supposedly burned copies of *The Awakening* "three years ago" because one member found the book unfit for circulation. *The St. Louis Republic's* brief report then closes with this mysterious sentence: "The incident then closed."

A one-sentence report on page seventeen of *The Minneapolis Journal* for September 3, 1902 simply sums up the earlier claims about *The Awakening*, also mentioning Zola, Balzac, Twain, and Whitman as other writers whose books have been "placed under the ban." Meanwhile, a slightly longer article on page eight of Canton, Ohio's *The Stark County Democrat*, dated September 5, 1902, repeated the same basic story while adding some additional information. This article is headlined "OBJECTIONABLE BOOKS / Were Burned by the Librarian—Clever Work Under the Ban" and is datelined "St. Louis, Sept. 4." The article repeats the claim that *The Awakening* was not only banned but actually burned. It comments that while the novel "has been sharply criticised [sic] by the reviewers, all agree as to the artistic merits of the work." The article notes that "Librarian Cruenden" of the St. Louis public library has never thought of withdrawing the book from that institution.

Finally, a one-sentence report on page four of Montana's *The Anaconda Standard* for September 8, 1902 is datelined "St. Louis, Sept. 7" and merely repeats the same basic claims, mentioning Kephart specifically.

Various elements of these claims seem especially intriguing. First and foremost, of course, is the repeated assertion that *The Awakening* was actually not only withdrawn from at least two libraries but was actually destroyed by one of them. Second is the widespread interest in the case. Apparently, the book was well enough known that editors thought their readers would be interested in stories that the novel had been banned. Almost certainly, similar stories of the book's alleged banning remain to be found in newspapers not yet easily searchable.

Interestingly enough, roughly a year after Kephart was accused of banning books, he resigned as head librarian at the Mercantile Library, claiming ill health (see *The St. Louis Republic*, November 25, 1903, front page). Even more interesting is the fact that not long after his resignation, he was committed to a local hospital because he had been acting strangely and was considered potentially suicidal (see *The St. Louis Republic*, March 27, 1904, part 3, page 9).

How Was *The Awakening* Initially Received?
Much evidence survives about the initial reception of *The Awakening*. Some of it has not been reported at all, or in any great detail, before.

For instance, an announcement on page 442 of *Publisher's Weekly*, dated March 11, 1899, notes the novel's impending publication and describes the book as "a story essentially for women, which studies the mental, emotional, and moral development of one woman in smallest detail." Since this description seems to have been provided by the publisher, it is possible that the ultimate source of the description is Chopin herself.

A brief review (almost a blurb) of the book was published in various newspapers, including on page six of the March 25, 1899 edition of *The St. Louis Republic*; page ten of the March 26, 1899 edition of the *Colorado Springs Gazette*; page two of the March 26, 1899 edition of the *Grand Rapids Herald*; and on page three of the April 4, 1899 edition of the *San Diego Evening Tribune*. Other newspapers, not yet traced, probably carried the same piece, and its appearance in various papers demonstrates how opinions expressed in one source could easily be disseminated throughout the country. The fact that this particular assessment is so highly positive seems significant, especially since this account of the book was so widely distributed. One even wonders if this piece may have been part of the publisher's publicity campaign. Emily Toth reprints the piece in its entirety in *Kate Chopin* (329).

The Awakening received a brief, but very complimentary, review on page four of the May 6, 1899 *St. Louis Post-Dispatch*:

[PARAPHRASE:] *The Awakening* shows deep insight into buried motives. Chopin unflinchingly reveals truth and assumes that truth is valuable. Edna is imperfect, and her imperfections lead to tragedy, implying that unconventional behavior exacts penalties. "There is much beauty . . . in the development of this beautiful, graceful, subtle character," and Chopin's artistry is exceptional. "There is no pose in her attitude; it is absolutely simple and sincere."

Far less positive was a brief assessment, published on page seven of the May 20, 1899 edition of *The New York Sun*. While praising Chopin's earlier "entertaining" local-color short fiction, this review regrets that she has now "taken herself seriously, and made a study of a woman's yielding without any excuse of passion to the impulses of her physical senses." Chopin resembles other women who "rush into fields" they should have avoided. She "tells some things more plainly than she probably imagined, which adds to the unpleasantness of a story repulsive enough in itself."

A much lengthier response, on page two of the Jersey City *Evening Journal* of June 16, 1899, begins by noting that a story by Tolstoy called "The Awakening" had been refused for publication by a French editor because of its offensive theme. The reviewer says that Chopin's novel is open to similar objections. The review praises the novel's phrasing and use of local color but finds its main plot or theme "revolting." Edna and her various involvements and decisions are not "an attractive picture." Chopin's tone is objective; she offers no moral. She simply describes Edna's transition from a contented if mundane life to one of "mental disturbance" and "physical pleasures." Edna is unappealing, but Chopin depicts her effectively. "The book is extremely interesting, but leaves a troubled impression."

A review on page three of part two in the June 17, 1899 edition of *The Minneapolis Journal*, titled "Love Among the Creoles," begins by describing Edna as a "brilliant and accomplished beauty" married to a man with whom she has little in common. If a woman like this lacks "deep and fixed principles," she risks a huge fall. Edna desperately wants love, tries to "feed her passionate nature on chaff," and ultimately suffers tragedy. "Out at sea far from the shore they find the body of a beautiful woman floating enmeshed in the golden hair which in her society days had called for the exclamations of admiration" [sic; an odd and inaccurate bit of plot summary]. Chopin writes well, by why do talented persons always depict "unhappy marriages and guilty loves" as well as "weak women and men who take advantage of their weakness"?

A paragraph on page eighteen of the *Saint Paul Globe,* dated June 18, 1899, is especially harsh, calling *The Awakening* "commonplace enough, as such stories go, albeit worthless, and not even possessing marked merit from a literary standpoint." After recounting the plot, the reviewer cannot understand the point of such books, or why writers even bother "to produce such tales of morbid life."

A lengthy review on page eighteen of part two in the District of Columbia's *Washington Times* was much more positive:

[PARAPHRASE:] Chopin has already won some fame for her stories of Louisiana. *Bayou Folks* was especially well done. *The Awakening* is, as a novel, more advanced and seems to have been written with some kind of intention.

Average readers will be uncertain of that intention, but clearly this novel was not intended for unsophisticated readers ("the Philistines"). Edna acts on impulse, follows her passions, and is partly egotistical. She married when still young, mainly because marriage seemed the thing to do. Robert awakens her but then, realizing "the nature of the situation," he goes away. Most puzzling is Edna's involvement with Arobin.

Readers will decide whether the book "was worth writing," although it is undeniably well-written. It depicts the mind of the kind of woman who now appears in court for divorce and who, two hundred years ago, "would have figured in grim and horrible" tragedy. "It is a psychological dissection of such a woman's soul; and most people will not understand it any more than they would understand the woman herself."

Mademoiselle Reisz and Adèle are depicted perfectly. Léonce is effective drawn, but the portrait of Robert seems "slightly vague." *The Awakening* suggests that Chopin may eventually "write a novel which will be an important addition to American literature."

On page thirty-five of *The Dial* magazine's July 1, 1899 issue, the publisher advertised *The Awakening* as "The story of the mental, moral, and emotional development of a woman."

A brief review on page thirty of the July 2, 1899 edition of *The San Francisco Call* quickly recounts the novel's plot and says that Léonce "grows jealous" of Edna "for cause." Edna "has married him to crush from her heart a fancied love of her girlhood, but she finds neither marriage nor motherhood cause enough in their holiness

---

to keep her in the paths of virtue." Never repenting, she commits suicide. "The story is vulgar, but the style in which it is handled refined and graceful."

A review on page thirty of the July 9, 1899 issue of Denver's *Rocky Mountain News* opened by calling the novel "a sad, a pitifully sad story." It would have been better if Edna had not "awakened" but had continued as a happy wife and mother. Edna's sudden emotions inevitably lead to tragedy. "The treatment of a difficult subject is delicately done," but the tone is oppressive and the characters seem futile.

Annette Crawford, in a syndicated column called "The Unquiet Sex," wrote in the summer of 1899 that *The Awakening* had caused "something of a sensation in the literary world," and she also gave a few details of Chopin's life. Her column appeared in various venues, including, for instance, on page seven of the August 31, 1899 edition of *The Janesville Daily Gazette*, based in Janesville, Wisconsin.

A review on page five of the October 17, 1899 edition of *The Boston Daily Globe* calls *The Awakening* the "story of a love-sick married woman" whose husband has always been kind to her. Robert goes to Mexico "to escape himself." Meanwhile, Edna's behavior makes readers doubt her morality. Just as she is about to "lose herself" with Robert, he leaves again, "and she discovering nothing further to live for goes to the beach and swims out. She never came back."

A full-page piece on Chopin, with a portrait and a drawing of her home, appeared on page thirty-five of the *St. Louis Post-Dispatch* on November 26, 1899 under the title "A ST. LOUIS WOMAN WHO HAS WON FAME IN LITERATURE." The article is sub-titled "Mrs. Kate Chopin, Whose Stories of Bayou Folk, of St. Louis and Louisiana and Whose Latest Novel Has Been Recommended by the Dutch Poet and Novelist, Maarten Maartens, for Translation into European Languages."

[PARAPHRASE:] *The Awakening* has not been as popular as fellow St. Louis writer Winston Churchill's *Richard Carvel*, but it has provoked more thought. Chopin is more concerned with art than with money and thus appeals to discerning readers. "Her style is clear, frank and terse, never a word too many or too few." Her effective plots seem effortless. Her art does not seem contrived but organic. Although she is called a Southern author, her appeal is not limited by region, nation, race, or dogma. Here is her own self-description. [The article then reprints an essay by Chopin beginning "On certain brisk, bright days . . . ."; see her *Complete Works* 2: 721-23.] A boxed insert briefly describes the development of Chopin's career, mentioning her first (unpublished) story, her artistic integrity, and the artistic success of her two collections of short fiction. The "perfection" of the art of *The Awakening* is recognized in Great Britain, and Maartens has urged that it be translated into continental languages.

New Information about Chopin's Life

In addition to containing commentary on Chopin's work, early newspapers also contain many references to her life. Sometimes, of course, the two categories are hard to separate, but listed in this section are reports that deal mainly with Chopin herself, rather than with her writings.

[1889]

A brief note on page ten of the March 3, 1889 edition of the *St. Louis Post-Dispatch* mentions Chopin's attendance at a lavish masked ball at the Germania Club and describes her attractive clothing.

[1891]

An article on page twenty-two in the *St. Louis Post-Dispatch* of March 15, 1891 briefly mentions Chopin. It is titled "Have Written Books: The Authors that St. Louis Can Call Her Own." Chopin is called "very clever," and her stories are said to imply her thoughtfulness. Her style always sparkles and holds one's attention. Her stories are all "bright" and intriguing, and *At Fault* is "clever" and has won her particular fame.

[1892]

A brief note on page nine of the June 23, 1892 edition of the *St. Louis Post-Dispatch* reports that Chopin is staying for the week with Mrs. Heister Clymer in the suburbs. Another article, on page thirty-five of the November 6, 1892 edition of the *St. Louis Post-Dispatch*, also praises Chopin's writings. Titled "The Book Table: Mrs. Chopin's Short Stories about the Southern Creoles," this article especially commends her shorter works:

> [PARAPHRASE]: Chopin is one of the nation's best authors of short fiction. When she decides to write a longer work, as seems likely, she will belatedly win the local appreciation she deserves. Having already published in many periodicals, well-known and obscure, she can now decide where she wants her work to appear. Much of her finest writing has been published in *Short Stories* and *Two Tales*, where new works have just appeared. One is "The Maid of San Filipe" (sic), about early St. Louis. "At the 'Cadian Ball" features warm, colorful, realistic characterization and effective dialect, as well as plotting so subtle that the outcome catches readers by surprise. Chopin rightly believes that her best work focuses on Creoles, and she effectively uses local color. Her depiction of the 'Cadian ball illustrates her success (a long excerpt follows).

[1893]

Chopin is leaving for New York, according to page nine of the *St. Louis Post-Dispatch* on April 13, 1893. Chopin and Miss McAllister are departing for a lengthy trip to the East, according to page thirty-eight of the *St. LouisPost-Dispatch*, dated April 30, 1892.

[1894]

A brief article, titled "A St. Louis Writer", appearing on page four of the January 14, 1894 edition of the *St. Louis Post-Dispatch* argues that, although magazine editors are often said to ignore original talent, they actually seek it out, as Chopin's rising career shows. She has been writing for less than three years, but she has already published in some of the best magazines in the country. She exemplifies the rise of the literary West; "her merit is acknowledged and her fame secure."

A brief article, titled "Petticoats in Literature," commends Chopin and Mary Wilkins for being (unlike most women authors) serious writers more concerned with being "true observers" than with merely making an impression. They, therefore, "do not have the vogue of their noisier and shallower sisters." Their realism makes them, like many male writers, less popular than they should be (*St. Louis Post-Dispatch*, September 30, 1894, p. 4).

[1895]

At a local party, Chopin read "one of her delightful little Creole stories" (*St. Louis Post-Dispatch*, February 14, 1895, p. 9).

A profile of Chopin on page twenty of the *St. Louis Post-Dispatch* for March 10, 1895 includes a large ink portrait:

> [PARAPHRASE]: Chopin has quickly joined the "front rank" of American writers and is as important to Southern literature as Mary Wilkins is to the literature of New England. *At Fault* contained her typical strengths in an imperfect form. When she turned to short fiction, she was immediately successful. National magazines welcomed her work as "original and not conventional." "Desirée's Baby" and "In and Out of Old Nachitoches" are "masterpieces of art and feeling unsurpassed" in strength, delicacy, and subtlety. *Bayou Folk* has been embraced everywhere as "literature of a very high rank." Although her early work dealt with Creoles, her more recent, wider work is even stronger. Chopin is quiet, confident, and unpretentious. She seems to manage her house and children as effortlessly as her career, and her children do credit to their mother, although she has no fixed ideas about child-rearing.

A brief, page-five reference to Chopin in the March 28, 1895 edition of the *St. Louis Post-Dispatch* calls her "the well-known writer" and says she is confined to her house because of "the grippe." It reports that she intends to go to Louisiana to recuperate. A note on page thirty-three of the April 14, 1895 edition of the *St. Louis Post-Dispatch* says that Chopin will receive visitors in connection with an art exhibit.

A profile on page twenty-eight of the August 11, 1895 edition of *The St. Louis Republic* calls Chopin "An Interesting Woman Who Has Made Fame with Her Pen."

[PARAPHRASE:] Chopin, from St. Louis, is now considered among the most popular writers of fascinating short stories. *Bayou Folk* quickly won wide attention. Chopin is "a creole" and has spent much time in Louisiana, which helps "explain her choice of style and faithful description of creole life." Before marrying, she was as famous in St. Louis for her beauty as she is now for her fiction. She graduated from Sacred Heart Convent and loves learning languages.

Chopin is still physically attractive. "Her soft gray hair is decidedly becoming, and her dark brown eyes and rarely [sic!] lovely complexion retain much of their youthful charm." Her personality is "charmingly cordial and easy." She does not try to be intimidating but rather exhibits "natural and unaffected conversation." She is not pretentious and is not a "reformer." Her stories are charming, strong, colorful, and vivid.

An article on page ten in the August 25, 1895 edition of Anaconda's *The Montana Standard* suggested that Southern writers had to publish initially in newspapers to help earn money and attention. Southern newspapers paid "reasonable prices" and thus offered aspiring writers a chance to publish without "directly competing with already successful authors in the magazines." Chopin is one such writer.

Chopin has gone to Chicago for a short stay, reported the *St. Louis Post-Dispatch* on page nine of the November 21, 1895 edition.

[1897]

An article called "Literary Children of St. Louis" by Ripley D. Saunders on page six of *The St. Louis Republic* of September 12, 1897 also praised Chopin:

[PARAPHRASE:] Chopin writes stories "of peculiar truth, dramatic value and faithfulness to their environment." Her depictions of Creole life are not distorted (like those of George W. Cable) but are more realistic, sympathetic, and credible. They are remarkable stories of "a remarkable people." Having lived in the South, Chopin knows the habits and peculiarities of the people she depicts. "I am told—but I must confess to a disposition to doubt the statement—that

Mrs. Chopin now chafes against the restriction of magazine editors" who want only more stories about Creoles. "I am given to understand that she is ambitious" for a broader field not confined to local color. Supposedly she proclaims that she will no longer restrict herself to Creole stories, but any change would be unfortunate: she has found her true niche and should "stick to it."

An article, titled "A Corner in Gossip," which appeared on page thirteen of *The St. Louis Republic* on November 21, 1897, reports that Chopin's favorite enjoyment is cards and that she is always ready to play. During almost every evening at her house, "duplicate whist" is played. It is the game she loves most. Typically, she plays "with her sons and their young men friends." She also enjoys solitaire and is often teased because of her extreme interest in it.

[1898]

Chopin, the "distinguished authoress," read "delightful selections from her new novel" [sic] at a Chart Club reception in her honor, according to page seven of the January 13, 1898 edition of the *St. Louis Post-Dispatch*. At a recent Chart Club meeting, Chopin read (in her "charming" manner) "A Night in Acadie" and "Polydore." A speaker praised Chopin for her talents as a writer of multicultural stories, which will give future readers a true idea of past lifestyles and cultures (*St. Louis Post-Dispatch*, February 20, 1898, p. 29).

Several articles refer to Chopin's attendance at the fourth biennial convention of the General Federation of Women's Clubs in Denver, including page eight of the *Kansas City Star* on June 28, 1898. Even before the conference began, one woman was excited about hearing both Chopin and other writers read ("Think what it will be," she said; see *Kansas City Star*, June 12, 1898, p. 13). The *Boston Sunday Herald* reported, on page thirty-four of their June 12, 1898 edition, a forthcoming session, in which Chopin and others would read. Page five of the Springfield, Massachusetts *Republican*, dated July 1, 1898, reported weeks afterwards that, although the readings took place in a hot room, they were "much enjoyed."

[1899]

Comment on Chopin in 1899, the year *The Awakening* was published, was generally brief, aside from reactions to the novel itself. Thus, an article titled "Discussing Some of the Prominent Southern Writers," on page thirteen of part four in *The St. Louis Republic* of January 1, 1899, Chopin's work is generally described as "delicate and strong." *The Sacramento Record-Union*, on page six of the July 31, 1899 edition, referred to a portrait of Chopin appearing in a section called "The Lounger" of a journal called *The Critic* (August 1899; no. 866; 677). A brief note, accompanying the photograph there, reports that "Mrs. Chopin was educated at the Sacred Heart Convent. She was an indifferent student with a mistaken belief that she possessed musical talent" (677). The same note also reports that "Mrs. Chopin is said to avoid the society of literary and 'bookish' people. She does not like to talk about her work. She writes seldom, but with great rapidity and little or no correction" (677; for the same information, see also *Public Opinion*, August 17, 1899, 223).

The *St. Louis Post-Dispatch* reported, on page thirty of their December 3, 1899 edition, that Chopin had recently read "Ti Demon" to the Wednesday Club.

[1900]

References to Chopin in 1900 ranged from minimal to substantial. Thus, *The St. Louis Republic* noted, on page twenty-six of the February 4, 1900 edition, that she attended the theater with her son and some ladies—a report that is one of many suggesting how prominent she was in St. Louis society. On September 9, 1900, the District of Columbia's *Washington Times* mentioned her briefly in a long article on "realist" writers. And H. B. Wandell called her, in a book on St. Louis, "a writer of charming stories of southern life" (16). Most interesting, however, is a lengthy piece titled "Two St. Louis Women Who Have Recently Achieved Considerable Success," published on page fifty-two of *The St. Louis Republic* on December 9, 1900. The author's chronology is unreliable, but the piece (excerpted briefly in Toth, *Unveiling* 233) is still valuable:

[PARAPHRASE:] Chopin and Mrs. Sheppard Stevens "rank well as popular authors." Chopin was "well known as a beauty and social favorite" before her marriage. Today her gentle face, framed by snow-white hair, shows scarcely a wrinkle . . . . Her writing focuses on Creoles, as can be seen in "her first work" [sic], *"A Night in Acadie,"* which was well written and reasonably successful. Afterwards [sic] she published *At Fault* and *Bayou Folk* and then *The Awakening.* "This work is pretentious, and is more nearly what is known as a 'problem novel' than any other St. Louis book. There has been much severe criticism of this book—not so much of the workmanship as of the story; but Mrs. Chopin says she does not mind that." She writes easily and quickly, making almost no changes. "She declares it is either 'easy to write, or utterly impossible,' and therefore she has no fixed plan except a general one of working in the morning.

[1901]

In 1901, Chopin is mentioned briefly in a ten-volume set, titled *The Success Library*, where she is praised as one of several writers whose "studies of local character and environment have made a unique addition and have been brilliantly done" (Marden and Devit 3173–74).

In an editorial on page B1 of the May 19, 1901 edition of the *St. Louis Post-Dispatch*, about why women wore long skirts in the filthy, germ-ridden streets of St. Louis, Chopin herself wrote as follows:

It seems to me the reasons why women wear long skirts are evident. They look best in them. A few women, principally athletic young girls, look well in anything but long skirts.

The women of St. Louis are not at all discreet to wear long skirts in a city which has such dirty streets and sidewalks as we have in St. Louis, but they will do it. They would rather hold a long skirt up[,] tiring the wrist and distressing the wearer in other ways, than wear a short skirt which does not look well upon them. We can scarcely blame some women for refusing to wear anything but long skirts. Stout women, for instance, look bad in anything else. Women are very sensitive about wearing anything that seems lacking in grace, propriety, or dignity, and I suppose that is why they affect the long skirt.

I suppose the long skirt is chiefly condemned in St. Louis because it sweeps up the filth of the streets and sidewalks. We have such a dirty city. If our city were kept clean a woman could get around without soiling her skirt with anything worse than dust. I do not know why St. Louis is so dirty. There seems to be little or no effort to keep it clean. It certainly seems that, with the streets and sidewalks in the condition they are, the women of our city are not discreet to wear the long skirt.

[1902]

In 1902, Chopin is mentioned as one of various "patronesses" for an upcoming lecture by "M. Le Roux" to be given to the "French Benevolent Society Benefit" (*The St. Louis Republic,* April 28, 1902, p. 7. See a similar listing in the same newspaper, April 29, 1902, p. 9).

A particularly interesting article on page three of *The St. Louis Post-Dispatch* for September 9, 1902 contains a portrait of Chopin and is titled "HOW TO SPEND $6000 FOR BOOKS." It is subtitled "Mrs. Kate Chopin, Authoress, Advises Rose Marion." A further heading continues:

"She Would Buy the Best Works from Shakespeare Down and Let Young Readers Select for Themselves." Marion, the author of the article, initially spends part of the piece giving her own opinions but then recounts a visit to see Chopin.

[PARAPHRASE]: Representing the young people of St. Louis, Marion went and asked Mrs. Chopin how she would use the $6000 the school board plans to spend on books. Eventually the article quotes Chopin as saying that she would purchase English and American classics, appropriate to the readers' ages, and let the children choose. "I should select good books, but I should not think of compelling any child to read the books I had chosen." Admittedly, choosing books both good and pleasing would be hard. Some books would not be appropriate. Yet Chopin did not state these opinions so blatantly; rather, they emerged in a light, good-humored conversation with this "dainty little white-haired authoress" whose eyes suggest the depth of her character and insight.

Marion and Chopin discussed books they had read when young. Chopin read much Scott and Fielding, plus other works not considered classics. Neither Marion nor Chopin regretted reading detective stories and fantasies, and Chopin would not want to exclude adventure tales; she even recommended Conan Doyle. Chopin said she loved Dickens but knew that many children do not. She said she admired Dickens' "wonderful imagination and good humor, but not his pathos." Chopin expressed admiration for the stories of Mary Wilkins but thought them unsuitable for children. She admires George W. Cable's early works, such as "Old Creole Days" and the "Bonaventure" tales, but she doesn't know what to make of "The Cavalier," so how would children know?

She likes the style of Robert Louis Stevenson but can't read him at length. She likes Hamlin Garland's "Main Traveled Roads" but finds him generally too serious. "Don't you know I feel sorry for folks that are entirely without a sense of humor? You wonder what is the matter with them and suddenly you discover that they are thoroughly incapable of seeing a joke." William Dean Howells' stories are mostly about love and thus might not appeal to children. Bret Harte's writings are attractive but are emotional. She recommends the works of Sarah Orne Jewett.

"I don't know how they would keep Mark Twain's books out. The children would read them anyhow, whether they were given to them or not. I have a daughter who has read 'Tom Sawyer' and 'Huckleberry Finn' to tatters."

Chopin especially admires *The House with the Green Shutters* but thinks it atypically humorous for an English author. The article ends with the opinion summarized in the third heading: buy the best and let the children decide.

[1903]
Chopin is praised, as a writer about New Orleans, for having "given us, if not the atmosphere of the city, the quality and characteristics

of the life in the surrounding country" (*The Outlook: A Weekly Newspaper* 75 [1903]: 729).

On page five of the February 16, 1903 edition of *The St. Louis Republic*, Chopin is listed as one of a number of St. Louis citizens owning property worth more than $20,000 ($27,880, to be exact). Page eighteen of August 30, 1903 edition of *The Saint Louis Republic* also mentioned that Chopin regularly vacationed at "The Cedars" and was currently chaperoning young people there.

[1904]

In 1904, in a book on the literature of the Louisiana Territory, Alexander Nicolas De Menil discussed Chopin's place of birth, her descent on her mother's side from several of the "old French families of primitive St. Louis" (257), and the wealth of her father. He also mentioned her marriage and her residence in Louisiana. De Menil considered *At Fault* "a good, homely story, not particularly exciting as to the plot, and somewhat crude at times, but still affording pleasant reading," and he said that "in no way did it foreshadow her future work" (257). He praised *Bayou Folk*, however, as being "remarkable" for the "facility and exactness with which Mrs. Chopin handles the Creole dialect, and the fidelity of her descriptions of that strange, remote life in the Louisiana bayous . . . . But she writes of (what she calls) her 'own people,' for by inheritance of birth and by marriage, and I may add — by inclination, she is herself, a Creole" (257).

De Menil wrote that her stories:

> are extremely interesting as studies of life. She has been compared to Mr. Cable, but no two writers could possibly traverse the same ground more at variance with each other. Her touch is far more deft than Mr. Cable's; her insight is more *femininely* subtle (if I may use the word); pain, sorrow, affliction, humbled pride, rude heroism — enter more completely into her sympathies. She feels and suffers with her characters. Nor is this strange: she is herself (as I have said before) to the manor born. Not so Mr. Cable. I do not wish to detract one tittle from the just praise I have given him elsewhere, but the soul of sympathy with which Mrs. Chopin overflows is wanting in his pages;

we may smile with him, we may laugh with him — even grieve with him — but we are forced to realize, nevertheless, that he lacks that touch of humanity that Brunetiere so justly and so eloquently praises in Thackeray and George Eliot. The critics have not as yet fully understood the excellence of Mrs. Chopin' work. (258)

Especially interesting is De Menil's personal reminiscence of Chopin:

I remember Mrs. Chopin, when almost a child, reading one of Sir Walter Scott's novels! Of later years, she is as she was then, an omnivorous reader. She has a strong admiration for the late Guy de Maupassant, whose artistic methods she considers superior to those of any other French author of late days. She is not a "blue-stocking" — she has none of the manners, airs, affectations and eccentricities of the *poseurs bleu.* She has no fads, no serious purposes, no lesson to teach in life. She takes no notes, she has never, she declares, observed or studied people, places, or things, or conditions, or circumstances with a view of using them as literary material. She is simply a bright, unaffected, unpresuming and *womanly* woman. (258)

De Menil ends by noting the existence of *A Night in Acadie* and *The Awakening*, but says nothing about them. He reports, however, that another "work from her pen will appear some time during 1904" (257–59).

Accounts Inspired by Chopin's Death
[1904]
Chopin's death in August 1904 generated much notice and commentary throughout the country. Most of the accounts and obituaries are very similar, but several are worth mentioning specifically (others will be published elsewhere). Thus, the *Kansas City Star* on August 22, 1904 asserted on page six that Chopin's fame rested on her short fiction; it did not mention her two novels. An page three article in the New Orleans *Times-Picayune*, dated August 23, 1904, called Chopin, in its headline, a "Well-Known Writer," and, in its first sentence, a "well-known" authoress," especially known as a

"writer of stories of Creole life." The article stressed Chopin's fame in Louisiana in general and in New Orleans in particular, saying, "She was one of the most popular women in New Orleans society" when she resided there, "and her literary reputation added to her social success." (This last sentence must refer to her social success in St. Louis because Chopin was not yet a published writer when she lived full-time in New Orleans.) The article closes by mentioning all three of Chopin's books, and it says that she was "a social favorite."

A lengthy obituary published on page fourteen of the August 23, 1904 edition of *The St. Louis Republic* reported much factual information, particularly about the circumstances of Chopin's death. It stresses the regard she won by writing short fiction, but says this about *The Awakening*: "while it met approval, seemingly it did not bring forth the true talent of the author" as her published collections of short fiction had done. Even more interesting, however, is this article from part one, page six of the August 27, 1904 edition of *Republic*, which seems worth quoting in full:

Kate Chopin's untimely death, "in the midst of life," deprives St. Louis of its foremost literary personage. Although she had written but little (the whole of her works being hardly a half dozen volumes), no Missourian in late years, and indeed few writers in all the West, created a more distinct literary impression than this portrayer of Creole character. "Bayou Folk" and "A Night in Acadie" occupy distinct places in the complex fabric of American literature. They are as characteristic as the Bret Harte sketches of Western types, as Mary Wilkins's studies of the New Englanders, as any purely sectional portraitures which we have. The ineffable delicacy and sympathy of Mrs. Chopin's delineations, the intuitive touch which imperceptibly invests the subject with a breathing life, place her Creole stories almost beyond compare even in older and more universal fields of literature.

Kate Chopin was a high example of careless genius. She wrote spontaneously and without the pause which heeds second thought or ponders a phrase. Art to her was not second nature—it was first nature. There was no such thing as required technique with her. "Technically," her writings exhibit faults. Frequently there occur passages through which the captious critic or narrowly trained rhetorician might draw a blue pencil, but a sympathy with those self-same faults would find beneath their ingenuousness a peculiar fascinating quality, seemingly of ingenuity, of which the blue pencil would have been a veritable vandal destroyer. To remove such faults would be to steal the perfection of imperfections. Art may be technically perfect, but nature can never be technical and naturalness can never be perfect.

Perhaps a deal of the charm of Kate Chopin's stories lies in the subtle revelation, rarely more than a suggestion, of the writer's personality. It is never an obtrusion, but rather an insinuation which creeps in through the medium of a fine sympathy—the inevitable infusion of self into the work which is done con amore [i.e., "with love"]. Mrs. Chopin's work was purely the work of sincerity. When in the mood for writing she gave herself wholly to it; nor could she be persuaded ever to force the mood or pick up a pen in its absence. She wrote solely for the love of writing. Her utter absence of the so-called "commercial spirit" marked her as almost unique, and she was kept constantly denying flattering overtures and declining attractive invitations from publishers. Such a course would have been called improvident in many another. Happily being removed from such considerations, she wrote, one might say, as a bird sings. "Bayou Folk" and "A Night in Acadie" are not what we might term "great works." They are small and simple expressions of unconscious and unaffected art, which is the very trueness and purity and perfection of writing. They may not "live long," as we apply the phrase to more considerable and pretentious and substantial works. They may not be read by many thousands during many years. But the charm of their delicacy and simple lifelikeness will always endure for the lover of the genuine.

As has already been mentioned, much more information about Chopin's life and works (especially her short fiction) remains to be reported (and reprinted) from newspapers and other periodicals of the time, and some of that "new" information is already in press. For the moment, however, the information reported and reprinted here should suffice to indicate how interesting Chopin seemed to many of her contemporaries—interesting enough that they thought about her, wrote about her, sought her opinions, listened to her read, read her works themselves, and, apparently in some cases, even banned and burned *The Awakening*.

Works Cited

Chopin, Kate. *Complete Works*. Ed. Per Seyersted. 2 vols. Baton Rouge: Louisiana State UP, 1969.

De Menil, Alexander Nicolas. *The Literature of the Louisiana Territory*. St. Louis: St. Louis News Co., 1904.

Marden, Morison Swett and George Raywood Devit, eds. *The Success Library*. 10 vols. New York: The Success Co., 1901.

Seyersted, Per. *Kate Chopin: A Critical Biography*. Baton Rouge: Louisiana State UP, 1969.

Toth, Emily. *Kate Chopin*. New York: Morrow, 1990.

_____. *Unveiling Kate Chopin*. Jackson: UP of Mississippi, 1999.

Wandell, H[enry]. B[razee]. *The Story of a Great City in a Nutshell: 500 Facts About St. Louis*. 1900. 5th rev ed. St. Louis: n. p., 1901.

A Letter to Students as They Read Kate Chopin's
The Awakening

Joyce Dyer

Dear Students,

Until the 1970s, the book you hold in your hands was barely known. Given its current popularity in high schools and colleges, this seems impossible, doesn't it? Now there's a Dover Thrift Edition, a Nook Edition, a Kindle Edition. Until 1969, though, when Per Seyersted published his biography of Kate Chopin, along with her collected novels and stories, American readers and critics were largely unaware of who she was, or of the content of her masterpiece. Looking back, I realize how fortunate I was to be in graduate school with the right teachers at the outset of Chopin's rediscovery. It was simple chance, like so many things in our lives.

My attraction to *The Awakening* was immediate. Was yours, I wonder? I have now published, to my own surprise, over fifty essays about Kate Chopin and her work and a book longer than *The Awakening* itself that's entirely about that novel. I first read Chopin's masterpiece because it was required reading in a literature class I was taking, which may also be true of you. But what about all those times I've read it since?

Although this is difficult to explain, I always resist reading *The Awakening*. You need to understand what I mean by this, because the confession seems to contradict my persistent return. What is it that causes me to hesitate?

As short as *The Awakening* is, and as pleasurable to read, Chopin's book always disturbs me in some profound way and causes me to think about or feel something new that's dangerous. I'm not always sure, I guess, that I have the strength to read the book again. Very good books always take so much out of us. I've never understood what people mean when they say reading is sheer pleasure, or a book is "a good read." Reading books alters us—and instructs the heart—when it's done in a certain way.

That's what I want to talk to you about—reading *The Awakening*. It seems such a simple book. So short, so easy, just translate a few French phrases and pronounce them as best you can and be done with it.

No.

It challenges every assumption I ever had about reading, and about what literature even is. About how art works, and how it works on the reader. What this book has taught me to do, more than any other, is to listen before I draw conclusions.

So what I want to ask you to consider is how to *listen* to this book, and what great rewards might come from that.

I don't mean, of course, that you should read it passively, half asleep in an overstuffed chair. Listening to a book is not a passive act. But what does this kind of reading look like, then?

* * *

FIRST, we readers must stop casting moral judgments so quickly on the books we read. America almost lost *The Awakening* because that old censoring instinct roared up too soon. We need to stop resisting a text five pages into it, and allow a book, instead, time to become irresistible. We often resist a text because of our own beliefs, our own censoring instincts. We approach it with weapons in our hands.

Resistance, oddly, can take the form of liking a character much more or much less than she deserves. If Edna fits our idea of a good or great woman, we, like her, call her a hero and don't notice anything bad; if she disappoints us and fails to show us how to live our lives the way we know we want to, we don't like her, call her a selfish woman, and see nothing good. I would argue that either response, generated by our own desire for a moral center like our own, is problematic in art, and certainly problematic in life.

When I first read *The Awakening*, I saw Edna Pontellier as a role model. I loved the woman. She liked art, she rejected stereotypes

circle will do to us (including our critics and reviewers), and, most of all, what we will think of ourselves if we ever do find the courage to put truth down. Writers are afraid of the truth, just as other people are, and the page is sometimes their battleground. Perhaps you have already discovered this in your own writing.

The Awakening is the closest Chopin ever came to speaking the truth, and it probably had a hand in killing her—at the very least, killing the future of her art. Most scholars feel that the poor critical reception she received caused her to retreat into the world of local color. Some feel that it might have led to the cerebral hemorrhage she suffered at the World's Fair in 1904. Of course, we'll never know.

I cannot always explain, or even rightly guess, why Chopin chose silence in her exploration of certain themes. And I do not even know if it always was a choice. As I describe a few important silences in *The Awakening,* I'll try to consider possible reasons. But my greater hope is that you will think about this matter long after I end this letter, and you hear silences of your own in this great book and in every book you read.

* * *

First, why didn't Chopin do a better job of telling us what's wrong with Edna? I remember that a friend of mine who taught at a nearby school once told me that her class was very upset with Edna Pontellier. "What's wrong with the woman, anyway?" they asked. "She has everything anyone could ever want. What's she complaining about?" Even the narrator, though far more sympathetic than the pupils were, is perplexed about Edna's state and uses language that's indistinct to describe her. We find only vague phrases, at best: "an indescribable oppression, which seemed to generate in some unfamiliar part of her consciousness, filled her whole being with a vague anguish" (Chopin 8); "a certain light was beginning to dawn dimly within her" (Chopin 14); "they were troubled and feverish hours, disturbed with dreams that were intangible, that eluded her, leaving only an impression upon her half-awakened senses of something unattainable" (Chopin

31-32). The narrator occasionally adopts greater clarity, but even then says no more than this: "In short, Mrs. Pontellier was beginning to realize her position in the universe as a human being" (Chopin 14). This is little more than a generality.

It seems a wonderful coincidence, somehow, that *The Awakening* appeared the same year Sigmund Freud published *The Interpretation of Dreams*. Through hints and silences, Chopin seems to be urging a method of analysis (for herself and for her readers) similar to what Freud advised.

We don't know what's wrong with Edna, and that's the way Chopin probably wanted it. Instead of issuing some perilous prescription for womanhood, the narrator watches the protagonist and waits. Silas Weir Mitchell was the most famous nerve specialist in the country during the nineteenth century and prescribed, with great confidence, his famous "rest cure" for Charlotte Perkins Gilman, the author of "The Yellow Wallpaper"—a story that, remarkably, was yet another text that appeared in 1899 and shared the novel's theme of painful domesticity. In her autobiography, *The Living of Charlotte Perkins Gilman*, Gilman tells about the prescription Mitchell sent her home with after treating her for a month in Philadelphia: "Live as domestic a life as possible. Have your child with you all the time . . . Lie down an hour after each meal. Have but two hours' intellectual life a day. And never touch pen, brush or pencil as long as you live" (Gilman 96).

Chopin, stylistically innovative at times, seems to be writing in the omniscient point of view, but often chooses to shift to third person limited—to be less assertive and boisterous in order to let Edna be heard. Chopin will not diagnose Edna with exactitude, nor prescribe a cure. In the last scene, she relinquishes the little authorial control she has assumed and permits an almost first person voice to emerge.

As we psychoanalyze Edna, one silence seems particularly interesting. Edna is motherless, but Chopin treats this matter with such brevity that the first time we read the book we might not even have noticed. But it's an important silence. Although her mother's death has provided Edna with a small inheritance that allows her to begin to explore the dimensions of human freedom, Edna must do a better job of recovering her mother's memory if she is ever to understand how to form loving connections with the rest of the world—certainly with her children, and most certainly with herself. We know only that her mother died when Edna and her sisters were young, but probably not before they witnessed their father's abuse of his wife. The silence about Edna's mother speaks loudly, for it confirms our suspicion that Edna knows her father "coerced his own wife into her grave" (Chopin 68). It is knowledge that is unspeakable.

Let me go one step farther. The general silence about the mother forces us to wonder if she, too, might have chosen suicide. What more convincing reason could there have been than the nineteenth-century shame of suicide to keep the name of the mother off the lips of her own daughter? The people we don't talk about in our lives are often the very people who best explain us, the people who could eventually destroy us if we don't learn how to bring them to the surface and make our peace.

* * *

There is also silence about sex in the book. Oh, we know something's going on, but it's sometimes a little hard to tell what. I don't mean to suggest that Chopin was timid about sex for her time. She was far more bold than most female writers. Although James Lane Allen in *Summer in Arcady* and Thomas Hardy in *Jude the Obscure* had described the breasts of their heroines, women writers did not do that in 1899. As late as 1920, Willa Cather's references to a woman's thigh and breast were omitted from a story published in the *Smart Set: A Magazine of Cleverness*. When Chopin wrote about Adèle's "condition"—her pregnancy, in other words—she was breaking new ground: *The Awakening* is virtually the only American novel of its era to describe a pregnant woman.

But it's also clear that Chopin was strugglingto find a language that allowed her to talk about the female body in a comfortable and honestway. I sometimes wonder if women writers still are engaged in this search. Kate Chopin, like Edna, has difficulty finding "a language which nobody understood" (Chopin 3), the third language the book's trilingual parrot speaks. Think about chapter twenty-seven, when Edna first has sex with Alcée. Its language is full of romantic clichés—not the original language the parrot predicts. Alcée and Edna begin their evening by looking into each other's eyes, and then "he leaned forward and kissed her, she clasped his head, holding his lips to hers" (Chopin 80). Just before the chapter ends, we are given this: "It was a flaming torch that kindled desire" (Chopin 80). And that's what consummation looks like on the page.

Both Edna andChopin are hunting for their own language, and both fall short sometimes. I always feel a little regret about the final image in the book. "There was the hum of bees, and the musky odor of pinks filled the air" (Chopin 109). That was one of the sexiest images in the nineteenth century, but it was also one of the most common. Many other writers used it. Chopin turns it, of course, to her own artistic advantage. In the context of the suicide scene, the images are not light and romantic, but ominous. A deadly sweetness is in those pinks because they come to symbolize nature as Dr. Mandelet understands it—a "decoy to secure Mrs. Kate Chopin, Authoress, Advises Rose Marion for the race" (Chopin 105). It was children—the result of natural desire—that "had driven into her soul like a death wound" (Chopin 106). I'm glad Chopin held a common image of the nineteenth century in a somewhat different light, but I also wonder if, at such moments, she, like Edna, was feeling the constraint of her times.

* * *

And now we come to *race*, one of the most fascinating silences in the book. When I first read Chopin in the 1970s, I remember not being bothered by the question of race in the novel. It didn't cross my mind to ask why black characters seldom had any lines, or why the black race was measured out in tablespoons—octoroon (one-eighth black), quadroon (one-fourth black), mulatto (one-half black), griffe (three-fourths black)—and the white race was not.

But in the 1980s and the 1990s, Chopin began to embarrass me, and I didn't know what to do with her. The evidence seemed pretty clear that she was stereotyping blacks, placing them all in roles of servants and sometimes using epithets to describe them. I feared for a while that she had absorbed the racism of her South—and of her family. Chopin was, after all, raised in a Missouri household of former slaveholders who sympathized with the Confederate cause, and her husband fought in a paramilitary white supremacist group called the Crescent City White League, an association that survived for an entire decade (Thomas 97-109).

Even in 1993, when I wrote a book about *The Awakening*, I was at a loss regarding what to say about race. I knew I had to say something because Chopin's treatment of blacks was becoming a real issue in Chopin scholarship. I knew this was so serious that it could potentially compromise the book's future reputation. So I talked about race in a footnote, my own version of silence, I suppose. I mainly reviewed what other critics had said about race (which was very little), somehow finding the courage to cite Helen Taylor's opinion that the book's "unconsciously racist elements" severely limited Chopin's achievement, even though Chopin had a great deal to say about femininity in the postbellum South (Taylor 156, 202). This argument, by the way, anticipated a major rift between white and black female academics, one that still occasionally flares up. Black female academics believed, understandably, that Edna's liberation was purchased on the backs of black women. For them, her story was not universal because it had nothing to do with them.

For ten years, I didn't teach *The Awakening* or return to it precisely because of this issue of race. And then one day, I discovered a book by Toni Morrison (author of *Beloved*, *Song of Solomon*, *Sula*, *Jazz*, *Paradise,Love*, *Desdemona,Home*), a book that changed my life, and, certainly, my understanding of race in Chopin's 1899 novel. Morrison's book was called *Playing in the Dark: Whiteness and the Literary Imagination*, and I think it's one of the most important books of the twentieth century. I published an essay called "Reading *The Awakening* with Toni Morrison" in 2002, and it finally put to rest my anxiety about race in Chopin's masterpiece.

Morrison, a black intellectual, urged critics to return to texts by white authors, to resist dismissive labeling of them, and, instead, to try to understand how white writers are haunted, for better orworse, by what she calls the Africanist presence. Haunting and silence suddenly looked a great deal alike to me.

It's impossible, she argued, that a white American writer would not be profoundly haunted by race in America. What she believes about every work is that "the subject of the dream is the dreamer" (Morrison 17).And it's what I began to believe about Kate Chopin. *The Awakening* is most importantly Chopin's dream—in other words, the author's dream—and Chopin, we know, has race on her mind. Morrison says, "It would have been an *isolato* indeed who was unaware of the most explosive issue in the nation" (Morrison 50). The 1890s brought Jim Crow laws to the South, legalizing segregation. Between 1890 and 1900, the number of registered black voters in Louisiana fell from 127,923 to 5,320. Are Chopin's black characters really just minor actors whose function is to facilitate Edna's awakening? Are they in the historical background of the novel, or in the narrative foreground of Chopin's dream—which the novel is really a translation of? Could she, a bright Southern woman, have made so little of the hundreds of years there had been a black presence in America?

Now what I see, with Morrison's help, is that the Africanist presence is so loud in *The Awakening* that we would have to clap our hands over our ears not to hear it. Nearly every page of *The Awakening* is a silent, but loud, meditation on the dangerous subject of race. How conscious Chopin was of what she was doing, or of what was being done to her while she wrote, can only be debated—not resolved. How can we understand a dream?

What I began to see in 2002, and what I believe now, is that *The Awakening* is a racially subversive text, every bit as subversive as Melville's *Benito Cereno*.

Why does Chopin rely so heavily on the passive voice when she describes actions performed by blacks? The cake "had been made and frozen" (Chopin 24) by black women Victor Lebrun was supervising; Raoul and Etienne "were being put to bed" (Chopin 48) by the quadroon. Perhaps her frequent choice of the passive voice for the book's servants erupted from the repressed contents of her own mind, with its deep Confederate roots, and guilt. Or from her intelligence, which must have shown her that Edna's freedom from oppression was necessarily connected to her servants' freedom from Edna the oppressor—as active voice is connected to passive. Even in the choice of voice in this book, there is a racial fuse, and it's lit. To use Morrison's image, Chopin was unavoidably, habitually, "playing in the dark." She was asking us to consider the role of race in every decision she made, even if it wasn't deliberate.

Now notice that although the servants seldom speak, they also seldom behave the way that servants are expected to. They are not at all predictable. They are restless, just like Edna. The quadroon nurse who cares for Edna's boys follows them about "with a far-away, meditative air" (Chopin 4). Her mind is clearly not completely on being Edna's servant. The nursemaids who accompany Robert to the beach to find Edna and Adèle look "disagreeable and resigned" (Chopin 19). The quadroon walks behind a wagon Edna's children pull, assuming "a fictitious animation and alacrity for the occasion" (Chopin 51). Chopin also uses the word "fictitious" to describe Edna: "she was becoming herself and daily casting aside that fictitious self which we assume like a garment with which to appear before the world" (Chopin 55).

Sometimes Chopin finds clichés that no one would suspect, and hides her servants behind them. For instance, the quadroon nurse who sits for Edna as she paints is described as "patient as a savage" (Chopin 55). Our initial reaction might be to cringe as we read such language. But then we see. A savage isn't patient. A savage comes right at your neck. The Creole aristocrats better watch out.

Second, think about the terrible whiteness in this book. The white sunshade that hovers over everything. Adèle "dressed in pure white" (Chopin 15). White muslin and white linen collars. Edna's white shawl and white morning gown. Madame Lebrun is dressed in white. Madame Antoine's four-posted bed is "snow-white." Etienne wears a "long white nightgown" (Chopin 38) and the Pontellier house on Esplanade Street in New Orleans is "dazzling white" (Chopin

48). The color white is almost unbearable in Adèle's birthing room. We are nearly blinded by the white of this book.

But often the brightest, whitest chapters alternate with chapters that introduce shadow into the narrative. Edna first realizes her position as a human being in "shadowy anguish" (Chopin 14). How could it be otherwise? An understanding of what it means to be human in America must necessarily take in encounters with people of color. Edna often finds herself not in light, but in "half-darkness" (Chopin 50). When the shadows grow deep, Edna's sorrow, and her knowledge, intensify. Is it any wonder? What's in those shadows we are not told, but one of Morrison's chapters is called "Romancing the Shadow," and she documents this technique throughout the world of nineteenth-century romantics, and feels it is inextricably connected to "meditation on the problems of human freedom" (Morrison 37), and to race.

Third, look closely at the nurse. Do you even remember her? Black nurses in Chopin's stories—including *The Awakening*—often highlight the deficiencies of white women and white marriages. Think about the griffe nurse who helps Adèle during childbirth. The pretty social fictions of the white world cannot survive the leveling experience of childbirth, and the nurse knows this. After Adèle complains about Dr. Mandelet and Alphonse, about being "neglected by every one" (Chopin 104), the nurse cries out, "Neglected, indeed!" (Chopin104) Adèle says nothing in response, but consents to go back to her room, like the spoiled child she is. Chopin then records the nurse's thoughts, and they appear to be very much her own. And ours.

A fourth example shows the way race sometimes damages Chopin's book because she doesn't know how to successfully integrate its force when it arrives. I think Chopin loses her way momentarily in chapter eight, the sewing machine scene, because of race. After we learn that a little black girl is at Madame Lebrun's feet, working the treadle of her sewing machine, we are told, "The Creole woman does not take any chances which may be avoided of imperiling her health" (Chopin 21). In other words, it's okay to have a black child imperil her health, but not okay to imperil the health of a wealthy white woman. From there, the chapter begins to spin out of control. Chopin can't move her eye away from the little child. She cannot keep her on the edge of the scene, on the edge of the white world Chopin seemsto be most interested in writing about, though we can't be sure she's entirely aware of this. She cannot dismiss the child with a single ironic line, nor forget that she is there. The child on the floor is at the very center of the chapter, and Chopin interrupts dialogue between Robert and his mother that seems primary with the repeated refrain of Madame Lebrun's machine—"Clatter, clatter, bang, clatter!" (Chopin 22) Again and again, excessive onomatopoeia intrudes. Chopin would surely have known better. Such a momentary breakdown, if we are to believe what Morrison says, "implies the powerful impact race has on narrative—and on narrative strategy" (Morrison 25). Chopin was at a loss.

Notice, finally, that Edna, before she goes to the pigeon house, dismisses her servants, except for Old Celestine, even though her children ask for them and are going to grow up to desire them as much as their father does. It isn't Celestine they love, of course, but her capacity to serve them. Although Chopin's message is often encoded, nuanced, contradictory, hidden in the shadows, she knew, or at least seemed to sense, that there can be no freedom for Edna without freedom for blacks.

* * *

THIRD, listening implies a relationship with the author. It implies the power and responsibility delegated to an heir. And readers are, to some extent, an author's heirs. The legacy of a writer is passed on through a book's readers. It is one way a book survives.

And what are the responsibilities of an heir?

We must continue to explore the questions that perplex and, finally, destroy Edna Pontellier, so that we won't be destroyed ourselves, as she was. We must find better answers than she was able to. You and I, females and males have inherited from Kate Chopin and Edna Pontellier complicated questions about love, motherhood, art. Those questions are our legacy, which means they now are our questions, too.

* * *

What is love? Can we find an answer more satisfying than the one Edna did? We certainly must try. Will we believe in romantic love and search for that? Edna tried that variety with Robert and found it lacking. The problem with their relationship wasn't that Robert got cold feet and deserted Edna. She would have left him anyway. We hear in the end, as she walks toward the ocean, that "she even realized that the day would come when he, too, and the thought of him would melt out of her existence, leaving her alone" (Chopin108). Robert was a symbol of infatuation and chemistry, *romantic* love—a part of love, yes, but not everything. He was the good-looking guy with boyish charm. But what is love, if not just that? And who could she have loved, loved all her life, not just for a little while? Is that even possible in Chopin's world, or, more importantly, in ours? The domestic love she shared with Léonce was not enough. He hardly thrilled her. Nor did the conventional duties he expected of her. And Arobin was raw *sexual* love, a rogue, a horrible flirt, a temporary pleasure, and she knew it. He would soon be unfaithful to her, if he hadn't been already. So what islove? We must continue to ask.

There's another silence in the text that might help us. There's a character I didn't even notice the first time I read *The Awakening*, but I see him now. His name is Gouvernail, and he appears in only one scene: the dinner party. He is a writer, a journalist at a local paper. In an understated sentence, Chopin tells us that nothing special could be said of him, "except that he was observant and seemed quiet and inoffensive" (Chopin 82). That's all? A perceiver—T. S. Eliot might say a person on whom nothing is lost—and a gentleman and a man, who is neither offensive nor a bully, allows women to have their way. That's all? What more is there? He murmurs only one line in the scene, under his breath. It is a line from Swinburne that suggests he understands exactly what's going on in the dangerous, deadly flirtation he witnesses between Mrs. Highcamp and Victor, as she transforms him into Dionysus. Gouvernail has the lines of the sonnet in his head—memorized. He is a literary man, in other words, with a soul attuned to beauty. He knows this isn't love he sees being acted out before him because heknows what love is. Every time I return to *The Awakening* I take Gouvernail more and more seriously and recognize more fully the sad irony that he is in the same room with Edna, and they never meet. And no matter how many times I read this book, they never will.

But what if they had?

Gouvernail came to life for me largely outside the text because he appears in other stories by Chopin. Maybe another of our obligations as heirs to a writer's estate is to read all the writer wrote. Gouvernail is a recurring character, one of Chopin's many, and I came to know him, and deeply care about him through many meetings, not just one. He's in both "A Respectable Woman" and "Athénaïse," two stories composed before *The Awakening*. Though "in no sense striking" (Seyersted, "Athénaïse" 443), he is desired as a lover by Mrs. Baroda and as a companion by Athénaïse. The saddest thing about love in *The Awakening* is not the collapse of Edna's relationship with Robert. That was a good thing. The saddest thing is that Gouvernail sat at Edna's table, and she never saw him, even though he was her invited guest. Let's hope we don't miss such a person, should he or she one day sit across from us.

* * *

And what are we to do about motherhood, perhaps the most perplexing theme in the book? If I had to say what it was that drove Edna into the sea, what single thing, I would have to say motherhood. Why does the birth scene exist? Why do we need it in the novel? Why does it immediately precede the suicide? Why is the novel written in a nine-month frame?

Edna inherited her century's expectation for motherhood—it was what made women women—and she produced two sons. (Chopin, herself, had five sons and a daughter.) Edna quickly found herself unsuited to be a mother, but how do you reverse a "decision" like that? She could leave Léonce, but the *children*? And that's the last question that remains with her as she walks to her death. "To-day it is Arobin; to-morrow it will be someone else. It makes no difference to me, it doesn't matter about Léonce Pontellier—but Raoul and Etienne!"

Why, we must ask, was she unsuited to be a mother, and how can we be happier in this role, should we choose it? First, of course, let me say the obvious. We must change the world so that women never have to feel that having children is an obligation of their gender—that without children they will necessarily be lonely and unfulfilled. Men and women should not define themselves through their reproductive capability, but only through their humanity. We need to consider very honestly whether we feel pressure to have children, and what the source of that pressure is.

But if we want children, and many women—and men—do, how can we be better, happier mothers and fathers than Edna and Léonce were? First, we must understand, beforewe have children, that we cannot achieve a sense of our selves, of our "position in the universe as a human being" (Chopin 14), entirely through our children. Who we are is not the same as who our childrenare. There is great danger in Adèle's position, in her belief that effacing herself for her children, defining herself solely through their needs, will fulfill her. Edna senses this, but she doesn't know what else to do.

Critics and readers have been offended by Edna for years because they have found her selfish. The implication is that somehow her selfishness is what makes her a horrible mother, and good mothers are not selfish. I cannot refute the critics who point out Edna's selfish acts. They are present in the text. But I can respond by saying something that appears contradictory, but I don't think is: Edna's selfish acts stem from her lack of sufficient self-love.

What can this possibly mean?

There is a difference between "selfishness" and "self-love," and Chopin's novel illustrates it.

Motherhood and "self-love" are not incompatible. Perhaps motherhood and "selfishness" are. The distinction between these words—these two concepts—is what Edna was beginning to explore, and what we all must persist in looking for. The better able Edna is to love herself, the better able she will be to love her children. I'm not talking about narcissistic love, and neither was Edna. I'm talking about true self-love—the ability to know and honor our talent, to understand how deeply we're defined by it, to never grow bored because we have something of great value inside of us, to awaken each day knowing what our true task is. Selfish people are neither content nor generous, but people motivated by self-love are. Selfishness makes you want what other people have because you have not yet awakened to what is distinctly yours. Perhaps Edna's problem is not that she loves herself too much, but too little. She looks for the thing at the center of her soul but fails to find it.

We, her heirs, must look again.

* * *

Finally, what about art? What role will it play in your lives, if any? Although Edna explores painting, Chopin's book invites us to define "art" broadly as we think about its place in our own lives. Art, perhaps, might be best understood as the merger of what we love and of what we know we must do, the idea Robert Frost was getting at in "Two Tramps in Mud Time" when he wrote about a man who loved splitting wood: "Only where love and need are one, / And the work is play for mortal stakes, / Is the deed ever really done / For Heaven and the future's sakes" (Frost 252). Art is the loving work we do for Heaven, however we might understand that, and for the future of the world.

Edna commences her life as a "dabbler," but soon begins to think of painting as her "work." The idea that art was work, both in the sense of difficult labor and of one's true vocation, was not prevalent among nineteenth-century women. Art for most women was genteel accomplishment and pleasant pastime. It was more than that for Edna, but it was still not enough. Art, as we have seen, cannot occur only when the sun is out. And it requires solitude. *A Solitary Soul* was the book's original title. Edna is eager to be alone at times, it's true, but she's afraid of true solitude.

The only real artist in this book is Mademoiselle Reisz, and she's grown poor and ugly, "weazened" and "imperious" (Chopin 79) from her absolute devotion to art. Edna is able to see that Mademoiselle Reisz is "wonderfully sane" (Chopin 79), but Edna isn't able to become her yet. Is Chopin showing us, through the figure of Mademoiselle Reisz, what art inevitably takes from us, or is the author inviting us to consider other ways an artist might pursue her craft?

Will you be the ones to show us what they are?

* * *

You are the heirs to Kate Chopin's masterpiece. Keep looking inside its covers for the wealth it contains. Along with other treasures, there are puzzles there, but don't worry about that:

> questions always last longer than final answers do, and are the heart of any legacy. I hope *The Awakening* remains an important part of your lives, and always informs them, as it has informed my own.

Works Cited

Chopin, Kate. *The Awakening: An Authoritative Text, Biographical and Historical Contexts, Criticism*. 2nd ed. Ed. Margo Culley. New York: W. W. Norton, 1994.

Frost, Robert. "Two Tramps in Mud Time." *Robert Frost: Collected Poems, Prose, & Plays*. Ed. Richard Poirier and Mark Richardson. New York: Library of America, 1995. 251–52.

Gilman, Charlotte Perkins. *The Living of Charlotte Perkins Gilman: An Autobiography*.1935. Intro. Ann J. Lane. Madison: U of Wisconsin P, 1990.

Morrison, Toni. *Playing in the Dark: Whiteness and the Literary Imagination*. New York: Vintage, 1992.

Seyersted, Per. The *Complete Works of Kate Chopin*. Baton Rouge: Louisiana State UP, 1969.

Taylor, Helen. *Gender, Race, and Region in the Writings of Grace King, Ruth McEnery Stuart, and Kate Chopin*. Baton Rouge: Louisiana State UP, 1989.

Thomas, Heather Kirk. "The White League and Racial Status: Historicizing Kate Chopin's Reconstruction Stories." *Louisiana Literature* 14.2 (1997): 97–115.

Defending *The Awakening*: A Response to Hugh J. Dawson

Robert C. Evans

One especially stimulating and provocative essay on Kate Chopin's *The Awakening* seems in fact to have provoked little discussion and response. The essay, published in 1994 by Hugh J. Dawson, offers a vigorous "Dissenting Opinion" about the value of Chopin's novel, both thematically and as a work of art. Dawson comments that, by the early 1990s *The Awakening* was "routinely celebrated as a rediscovered masterwork" (1). In the space of roughly thirty years (he notes), it had gone from being an almost completely neglected text to being included in "lists of the most significant American novels" (1). It had also caused "a flood of critical studies," the convening of symposia devoted to Chopin's fiction," and the "printing of representative works of Chopin in all standard textbook anthologies" (1).

In the two decades since Dawson's essay appeared, this process of "canonizing" Chopin and *The Awakening* has only intensified. The book and its author have been the subjects of hundreds of critical articles as well as numerous books and book chapters. Most important, however, may be the inclusion of complete texts of *The Awakening* in so many standard anthologies of American literature. Few other "classic" American novels have been accorded this kind of prominence. Few American college students manage to graduate without being exposed to one or more works by Chopin, and *The Awakening* is, in fact, one of the relatively few novels they are most likely to read unless they happen to be majoring in literature.

Admittedly, one reason *The Awakening* is so widely reprinted and so often studied is its brevity: it is easier to include Chopin's book in an anthology than it is to reprint *Moby-Dick* or *For Whom the Bell Tolls*. But *The Awakening* is also anthologized for various other reasons besides its relatively compact size. Chopin's novel is clearly written, easy to read, chronologically organized, and rather straightforward in its use of point-of-view. It is not, in other words, an especially "difficult" or experimental book. It is an inviting and accessible text, and it deals with issues that still seem highly relevant, including romantic love and the social roles of men and women. *The Awakening* is now treated not only as a classic work of American literature, but also as perhaps the earliest and, in some ways, one of the most important pieces of American "feminist" fiction.

Dawson, however, is not afraid to challenge this almost worshipful treatment of Chopin's book. Like any good contrarian, he asks us to stop, think, and then think again. Does a novel neglected for so long really merit this kind of sudden elevation? If *The Awakening* were genuinely worth all the praise it has recently received, would it not have received at least some of that praise much earlier and more persistently than it did? Is this book celebrated mainly because its themes are now fashionable and because it now has a natural feminist constituency? Is it acclaimed mostly because its "message" now seems "politically correct"? Is the book really worthy, either intellectually or aesthetically, of all the applause it now generates? These are the kinds of questions Dawson raises, either implicitly or explicitly, in his highly stimulating essay.

And Dawson is not reluctant to answer such questions quite emphatically. *The Awakening* (he asserts) "does not deserve the high place now accorded it" (1). It offers merely "banal gestures toward philosophy and psychology" (2). Its ideas seem confusing and contradictory (2). Often its prose seems meaningless (3), and any "Transcendentalist themes" it employs "do not run deep and lack any sustained development" (9). Chopin's allusions to Emerson merely show her own "intellectual confusion" (9). Edna herself is, in general, a confused, confusing character, and Chopin's presentation of her heroine is often merely muddled. Chopin is "content to play to the pretensions of her era in prose that is unfailingly directed toward the tender-minded" (15). In the final analysis (Dawson believes), "*The Awakening* fails because of Edna," and although "she is often self-pitying, she is never intelligently or truly self-reflective" (16). She is not a "truly compelling" heroine (16), and "*The Awakening* is a frequently affecting but slight novel" (16-17). Chopin "knew enough of contemporary intellectual currents to appropriate, however inconsistently, the clichés of determinism that promised to serve her romantic tale" (17). Ultimately, however, an "attentive, clear-eyed reading of the novel enforces the conclusion that it . . . deserves to be decanonized" (17).

As these quotations show, no one can accuse Dawson of failing to state his opinions clearly. He is, in some ways, the unacknowledged gadfly of Chopin criticism. And, as was the case with that earlier philosophical gadfly, Socrates, Dawson's persistent questioning of received opinion has the great virtue of stimulating real thought, however radical his censure of *The Awakening* may seem. Dawson's questions and skepticism deserve a serious, sustained response— a response I hope to offer here.

I.

Dawson criticizes *The Awakening* for two basic reasons. In the first place, he considers its phrasing and style often embarrassingly inept, right from its very opening words. In the second place, he thinks Edna a highly flawed character and believes that Chopin botched her job of presenting this character in any convincing or compelling way. In attempting to respond to Dawson, I will deal first with his criticisms of Edna and the ways she is presented. Then I will respond to his criticism of Chopin's style. This latter criticism, it seems to me, is the more important and more challenging of the two. If Chopin is a poor, sloppy, sentimental writer (as Dawson thinks she is), then it almost does not matter what her novel "means" or whether its characters and ideas seem worth our attention. *The Awakening*, like any allegedly "great" work of art, must ultimately stand or fall *as* a work of art, not a glorified essay. In responding to Edna, Dawson is one interpreter among many. In offering a severe critique of Chopin's skills as a writer, he is far more unusual and merits a serious, detailed reply.

II.

Dawson's first charge against Edna (as well as against Chopin) concerns Edna's marriage to Léonce Pontellier. Quoting from chapter seven, he notes that it was "'in the midst of her secret great passion'" for an actor that she met and married. She "deceived herself" into thinking that she and Léonce shared similar personalities and thus "gave herself to a marriage 'that was purely an accident, in this respect resembling many marriages which masquerade as the decrees of Fate'" (4-5). This account, Dawson believes, indicates Chopin's own confusion:

> Once again, Chopin's breathless fusing of emotion and philosophy betrays her. Within the same paragraph the reader is told the contrary, that it was this strong-willed individual herself—not blind, irresistible Destiny—that decreed her life's course. Edna's marital partner was not imposed upon her by a despotic parent. Her husband was self-selected, the choice of someone who insisted upon the man and life she wanted, and would have no other. (5)

Edna's marriage to Léonce was probably indeed a mistake, but it is hard to see how Chopin's account of it betrays (as Dawson thinks) any self-contradiction. After all, Dawson himself says that Edna "deceived herself" into marrying Léonce (4), and he quotes the narrator's crucial assertion that Edna's marriage resembled "many other marriages which *masquerade* as the decrees of Fate" (4-5; emphasis mine). Chopin's narrator seems perfectly clear that Edna's marriage was *not* fated or destined to happen—that Edna made a deliberate, willful decision that she now greatly regrets. At the time of their courtship and wedding, she may have regarded herself as fated to marry Léonce, but Chopin goes out of her way to indicate that any confusion between fate and mistake was Edna's, not that of the novel's narrator. The marriage was an "accident" in the sense of being, according to the *Oxford English Dictionary*, "an unfortunate and typically unforeseen event." It was an "accident" in the sense that Edna could not have foretold, months or years in advance, that she would marry someone like Léonce. She merely acted on impulse, motivated by (1) romantic illusions, (2) Léonce's "absolute devotion" (which "flattered her"), (3) her self-deception, and (4) her determination to defy her disapproving father and elder sister, who did not want her to marry a Catholic (Chopin 18). In short, Edna made a mistake, but Dawson does not quote the crucial phrase, in which the narrator makes this undeniably clear: Edna's "fancy" that she and Léonce shared similar personalities and values was "mistaken," and Edna herself now realizes this fact (Chopin 18).

In general, Dawson fails to distinguish clearly among Edna (on the one hand) and Chopin and the novel's narrator (on the other). He seems to assume that Chopin and the narrator consistently endorse Edna's views of things, when, in fact, those views are often merely reported and are sometimes reported with accompanying irony or skepticism. Consider this sentence by Dawson, for example:

> Although she often finds it convenient to represent herself as the innocent victim of forces beyond her control, a plaything of the gods who forge the bonds of emotion . . . and an innocent who 'abandoned herself to Fate, and awaited the consequences with indifference'. . . , Edna's history is that of the self-defining individual. Fate is but a scapegoat. (5)

It is hard to see anything in this sentence with which Chopin or the novel's narrator would disagree. Even the phrase "abandoned herself to Fate" implies deliberate willfulness on Edna's part. She often *chooses* not to choose. Dawson's detailed criticisms of Edna, whom he considers fundamentally self-centered, do not necessarily implicate Chopin or the novel's narrator, both of whom seem quite alert to Edna's shortcomings. The fact that Edna may be confused does not necessarily mean that the same is true of the novel. One can, in fact, largely agree with many of Dawson's often-persuasive censures of Edna without feeling any need to find fault with Chopin, the narrator, or *The Awakening*.

Sometimes, however, even his criticisms of Edna can seem not only severe, but also forced. At one point, for instance, he rejects "the familiar description of Edna as a wife who has been forced into motherhood despite her refusal of that role." Dawson notes that, although:

she recoils from the scene of Madame Ratignolle's pain in childbirth, there is no evidence that she did not wish to have children when she became pregnant with her sons. Surely she must be thought to have known Creole society's expectations of motherhood when—no plaything of Destiny—she rejected the advice of older members of her family and entered upon her marriage to Léonce. Quite simply, Edna's mood has changed, and she wants to be rid of cares she willfully committed herself to but no longer finds congenial. (8)

One can agree that Edna's mood has changed (and perhaps changed irresponsibly) without agreeing that she was "forced into motherhood" or that she "did not wish to have children when she became pregnant." Likewise, when Dawson quotes an admirer of *The Awakening* (Dorothy H. Jacobs) as saying that "Edna is forced to accept maternity," one simply has to appreciate that Dawson and Jacobs seem to mean different things by the word "maternity." Dawson seems to mean "giving birth to children"; Jacobs seems to mean "raising children." Edna would not be the first parent to produce children and then partially (or perhaps even wholly) regret the decision, at least from time to time. In fact, one reason that *The Awakening* probably "speaks to" so many adult readers is that most adults know how it feels to have made any major decision in life and then wonder if they made the right choice. These second-guesses can involve not only children but also spouses, careers, specific jobs, schools, residences, and much else. Edna is surely just one of many women who chose to give birth and then felt conflicted about being mothers. One can sympathize with Edna to some degree without necessarily approving everything she feels, thinks, and does.

Dawson shows little compassion for Edna, and that, of course, is his right. After all, she does commit adultery, does neglect her children, and does, perhaps, commit suicide—acts that trouble Dawson and many other like-minded readers. But Dawson's disdain for Edna extends to disdain for other characters as well. One might expect him to dislike Alcée Arobin, but Arobin is barely mentioned. Instead, Dawson focuses most of his derision on two other characters: Robert Lebrun and Mademoiselle Reisz. He mocks

Robert for displaying devotion to various women, over the years, during summer vacations at Grand Isle. He says that Robert is "quite happy playing the foppish parasite ever-ready to do his woman-of-the-season's bidding" (10). "Small wonder," Dawson continues, "that this simpering pretender later quails rather than declare himself to Edna and ends by seeking to prettify his departure with a gasping protestation of self-sacrifice" (11). For Dawson, Robert is merely "a weakling who has shown himself content to linger as a hanger-on" (11).

Dawson's assessment of Robert, like his assessment of Edna, can seem simplistic and unsubtle. Both characters seem richer and more complicated than Dawson is willing to allow. Robert, for instance, can be seen, at first, as a character with a good sense of humor; neither he nor his various "women-of-the-season" take his devotions seriously. To him, to them, to their husbands, and to their friends, his attentions are simply an amusing game. His devotions are not taken as seriously (one might even say as humorlessly) as they are taken in Dawson's article. Robert can laugh at himself and is willing to be the butt of good-natured teasing by others. The passage in which he spars with Madame Ratignolle (Chopin 11-12) is one of the most amusing in a book full of amusing passages. As for his later behavior, a case can be made that he behaves with much intelligence, sensitivity, and morality. Dawson tends to reduce Robert, as he tends to reduce Edna, to the level of a stick figure in a simple morality play. And, ironically, he does not give Robert much credit for trying to behave morally and selflessly, although he accuses Edna of selfish and immoral conduct.

Dawson's assessment of Mademoiselle Reisz seems equally simplistic. He accuses her of having a "poisonous" view of life (12) and believes that she and Edna enjoy playing "the aberrant roles of tormentor and willing victim" (13). The old lady, he thinks, "delights in meanness" and is "designedly cruel" (13). Dawson suggests that Edna, by continuing to visit Reisz, possibly "seeks unacknowledged punishment" for her attraction to Robert and Arobin (13). Admittedly, some evidence in the book supports these reactions to Reisz; she is by no means an entirely appealing character. But that is just the point: almost *no one* in this novel is entirely appealing—or entirely unappealing, for that matter. Edna is flawed; Robert is flawed; Reisz is flawed; Léonce is flawed; many of the minor characters are flawed. But, after all, almost *all* humans are flawed in one way or another. Almost all people fall short of various expectations, including not only others' expectations but their own. Readers who admire *The Awakening* often admire it precisely because its characters (and the dilemmas they face) seem far more complex than Dawson is willing to allow. Edna has good reasons to love Robert, despite his various shortcomings. She has good reasons to like Mademoiselle Reisz, despite that lady's imperfections. She had what seemed, at the time, good reasons for marrying Léonce, and she has some good reasons, since then, for regretting her marriage and her decision to become a mother.

What seems unfortunately missing from most of Dawson's stimulating article is much sense of the moral and psychological complexity of *The Awakening*. Chopin never seems to have judged any of her characters as harshly or simplistically as Dawson does. Instead, she seems to have tried to present them as complicated human beings—sometimes honest, but sometimes deceptive or self-deceiving; sometimes generous, but often selfish; sometimes simple-minded, but sometimes capable of complex responses to difficult and realistic dilemmas. The many readers who admire the novel presumably do so, in part, because they consider it admirably multifaceted in its presentation of themes, characters, structure, and plot developments. Otherwise, one has to assume that most readers of the book are themselves fairly simple-minded.

And this, apparently, is what Dawson does assume. At one point, he calls some of them "[c]areless readers" (11); at another point, he suggests that *The Awakening* was an effort in the "manipulation of middle-class women" in ways Chopin had learned from "fashion magazines and tawdry fiction" (15); and later, he alleges that Chopin is "content to play to the pretensions of her era in prose that is unfailingly directed to the tender-minded" (15). The novel was once neglected (he says) because of moralistic criticism, but the revival of its fortunes is due to "a more recent moralistic criticism" that endorses Edna's essential selfishness (16). "For some latter-day moralistic critics," Dawson believes, "the rightness of [Edna's] actions is itself sufficient to enshrine the novel as a classic" (16).

Yet, a survey of even the earliest, primarily "feminist" phase of the novel's criticism quickly reveals a surprising number of critics who did not at all entirely endorse Edna's choices or completely admire her personality. Almost from the start of the revival of interest in *The Awakening*, the novel was very often read as a complex book in which Edna was anything but simply an admirable, oppressed heroine.[1] The record of complex reactions to the moral dilemmas posed by *The Awakening* does real credit to its early feminist readers, who were far less unanimously or simplistically sympathetic to Edna than one might have assumed. Ultimately, Dawson believes, "*The Awakening* fails because of Edna," who "is not . . . a truly compelling character" (16). One can argue, however, that he comes to this conclusion not only by simplifying the novel, but also by simplifying the responses the novel has provoked.

III.

More serious than Dawson's charges against Edna are his criticisms of Chopin's prose. After all, one need not admire Edna to admire the novel *if* the novel is well-written. By the same token, if the novel is *not* well-written, then any opinion about Edna is merely an opinion about Edna, not about the aesthetic success or failure of the book. As a work of art, *The Awakening* must stand or fall, in large part, according to how well it is phrased. Once again, Dawson does admirers of the book a big favor by stimulating us to try to explain just why we think *The Awakening* is worth reading *as a novel* rather than simply as a sociological tract.

In critiquing the novel's prose, Dawson begins at the very beginning. He calls the book's opening description of the mockingbird "over-cute" (2) and then continues by claiming that, in general:

> Chopin seems to have made no effort at economy of expression. Again and again, the novella is puffed out with extraneous descriptions. Characters and whole episodes are irrelevant. The narration strains painfully after words equal to the author's pretensions . . . . (2)

Of course, many of these same kinds of criticism have been leveled at other classic American novels (one thinks especially of *Moby-Dick*), and, in some ways, one is tempted simply to reply "to each his own" or merely to say that "there is no disputing about tastes." Dawson finds Chopin's prose embarrassingly inept, whereas many other readers have had precisely the opposite reaction.

One way to try to "defend" Chopin as a stylist is to examine some of the specific passages Dawson censures. Consider, for example, the opening description of the mockingbird, which Dawson believes is "over-cute." A different kind of reader might argue that the description is not meant to be taken completely seriously—that it is, in fact, part of a deliberately comic opening that immediately indicates that humor will be an important part of the book. The descriptions of the parrot and mockingbird seem partly designed to give Chopin an instant opportunity to characterize Léonce Pontellier as somewhat humorless and self-important—someone who, rather than enjoying the birdsong, is instead annoyed by it. And, of course, the opening references to the birds establish an important pattern of symbolism that runs throughout the novel, persisting almost until its very final paragraphs.

As one example, among many, of phrasing that he considers strained and pretentious, Dawson offers two sentences from chapter ten that describe Edna's fear that she may have swum too far out from shore: "A quick vision of death smote her soul, and for a second of time appalled and enfeebled her senses. But by an effort she rallied her staggering faculties and managed to regain the land" (Chopin 28). Again, when one thinks of "great" American writers, who have often been criticized for styles that sometimes seem strained and pretentious, one thinks not only of Melville but of Henry James. Chopin, in fact, seems far less open to charges of stylistic excess than these two authors, and, if they can be and have been defended against such criticism, certainly she seems at least as defensible.

How might one defend the sentences Dawson quotes? For one thing, one might argue that Chopin deliberately wants to emphasize this moment since it so clearly foreshadows the very ending of the book. In other words, she may intentionally have chosen phrasing that may seem a bit overdone precisely because she does not want us to forget this brief episode when we reach the novel's conclusion. The present phrasing is certainly more memorable than if the narrator had simply reported that "Edna feared she might die, and for a moment she felt frightened and weak. Fortunately, she was able to swim back to shore." The sentences as presently phrased seem almost point-for-point ironic when compared and contrasted with the closing description of Edna's final swim: "She remembered the night she swam far out, and recalled the terror that seized her at the fear of being unable to regain the shore" (Chopin 109).

Some of Dawson's objections to Chopin's style could just as easily be (and often have been) leveled at other nineteenth-century American writers, including not only Melville and James, but also Hawthorne and Whitman. Chopin's style is not as crisp, clear, or plain as, for instance, Hemingway's, but she often comes closer to that kind of phrasing than any of the other writers just mentioned.

Consider, for example, this passage about fear of death, which comes from Stephen Crane's *The Red Badge of Courage*:

> Since he had turned his back upon the fight his fears had been wondrously magnified. Death about to thrust him between the shoulder blades was far more dreadful than death about to smite him between the eyes. When he thought of it later, he conceived the impression that it is better to view the appalling than to be merely within hearing. (56)

Crane's language strongly resembles Chopin's, especially in its use of "smite" and "appalling." If she is pretentious, is he pretentious, too? Or consider this passage from "An Occurrence at Owl Creek Bridge," in which Ambrose Bierce describes the senses of a man who thinks he has escaped hanging by plunging into a creek: "Something in the awful disturbance of his organic system had so exalted and refined them that they made record of things never before perceived" (11). If Crane and Bierce, Chopin's contemporaries, can write in these ways and be canonized, is there any reason to exclude *The Awakening* from the canon? Much of her phrasing is simply typical of fiction from her era. In fact, a case can be made that her phrasing often seems far more concise, simple, and "modern" than that of some of the authors already mentioned.

In another example of what Dawson considers "even more desperate prose," he notes that:

> Chopin tells how, several years earlier, Edna had been fascinated by one of her sister's visitors only to find herself chagrined: 'the realization that she herself was nothing, nothing, nothing to the engaged young man was a bitter affliction to her.' (2)

Here, however, it seems fairly obvious that the narrator, using the technique known as "free indirect discourse," is taking us inside Edna's quite immature consciousness and giving us unfiltered access to Edna's childish, exaggerated thoughts. After all, in the first half of the quoted sentence (a section which Dawson himself does *not* quote), the narrator explicitly describes Edna as "a little miss, just merging into her teens" (Chopin 18). Dawson's account of the sentence overlooks what clearly seems to be its intentional irony, and the same can be said of his general response to this often highly ironic novel. Chopin's narrator need not be identified with Chopin, and the narrator is often quite ironic in the way she treats Edna and other characters.

Of course, to argue that *The Awakening* is generally a very effectively-written book is not to argue that its prose is invariably faultless. Consider, for example, this comment by Dawson:

> . . . when the reader is admitted to the scene of Edna's surrender to passion, the florid diction is shamelessly indulgent. In what a century ago no doubt passed for steamy erotic description but has become no less meretricious with time, Chopin relates how Edna illicit lover 'detected the latent sensuality, which unfolded under his delicate sense of her nature's requirements like a torpid, torrid, sensitive blossom' . . . . (2)

What are we to make of prose such as this? Is it as awful as Dawson suggests? Is it worse than some of the sensual prose in other canonical works of American literature? (One thinks of the notorious "rabbit" references in Hemingway's *For Whom the Bell Tolls* and of some of Hemingway's other romantic phrasing in *The Sun Also Rises*.) Most commentators on the passage Dawson quotes have tied it to a pattern of flower imagery that runs throughout the book,[2] so that this sentence makes some sense as part of a larger context and is not to be understood in pure isolation. It is also possible, of course, that the narrator is not taking this moment of romantic passion nearly as seriously as Edna and Arobin seem to take it, especially since the sentence Dawson mocks is immediately followed by one he does not quote—one that seems dry, clear-eyed, and double-edged: "There was no despondency when she fell asleep that night; nor was there hope when she awoke in the morning" (Chopin 99). No sooner, then, does the narrator provide us with prose that might seem "shamelessly indulgent" than she immediately pulls back from it and places the romantic moment in a highly ironic context: sexual contact with Arobin solves none of Edna's problems, as the narrator makes clear and as Edna herself realizes.

Much of the first part of Dawson's article is full of indictments of specific passages from Chopin's novel. In general, he believes that in "her recurrent attempts at verbal artistry, Chopin's purple passages are contrived in ways familiar among aspiring teen-age writers too young to know embarrassment" (2). He is especially unimpressed with Chopin's descriptions of nature, as in the famous, and famously brief, chapter six, which most commentators seem to consider effectively evocative. Dawson instead considers it an example of Chopin stylistic "flatulence" (3), but here, as elsewhere, it is difficult to know what standard of stylistic excellence he has in mind, since he never gives an example of a writer whose style he considers vastly superior to Chopin's. In the final paragraphs of chapter six, the narrator of *The Awakening* repeatedly (and fairly blatantly) echoes Walt Whitman, as numerous scholars have noted.[3] In fact, much of Chopin's phrasing here and throughout the novel— especially in her descriptions of nature—is clearly indebted to Whitman. Is Whitman also guilty of stylistic "flatulence"? Some readers have actually thought so, just as some have found serious fault with the phrasing of Melville, James, Poe, Hemingway, and any number of other "great" American writers. If Chopin's style is less than absolutely perfect, she is in very good and quite canonical company.

Dawson freely admits that his strongly negative opinion of Chopin's prose is definitely a minority position and that even some major critics, whom he himself respects, such as Edmund Wilson, have much admired her writing (3–4). In fact, most recent readers of *The Awakening* seem, implicitly, to admire it. Regrettably, however, less attention often tends to be paid to the novel's structure, style, and phrasing than to its themes and "meanings." The critical fortunes of *The Awakening* began to revive at right around the same time that the influence of critical formalism or "new criticism" (with its emphasis on the "close reading" of works of literature as works of art) began to diminish. Partly for that reason, and partly because renewed interest in *The Awakening* also coincided with the rise of feminism in literary criticism and in the culture in general, Chopin's novel (like the writings of other "minority" authors) has often been read more for what it has to "say" than for how effectively it is written. Even Dawson's article tends to focus more on the "meaning" of the work than on its methods.

Yet Dawson's essay is so valuable precisely because it *does* so vigorously challenge the merits of Chopin's prose and because it does question so unsparingly the novel's value. Like any good gadfly, Dawson forces us to consider matters we are prone to take for granted. He stimulates any real admirer of *The Awakening* to try explain, rationally and in detail, exactly why this novel is really worth admiring *as a novel*, not as an essay or an argument. One hopes that future examinations of *The Awakening* (and of Chopin's other works) will pay more and more attention to them *as* works of art. Formalism is now being revisited and revived; the term "new criticism" is no longer a term of abuse, as it was for so long in the last three decades of the twentieth century. A new "new critical" approach to *The Awakening*—emphasizing what makes the novel a truly splendid *novel*—would be the best way of responding to Hugh Dawson's valuable and thought-provoking essay.

Notes

1. For more on this interpretation, see Rocks (1972), 117; Woolf (1973), 462–65; Berke and Silver (1976), 1170; Justus (1978), 112–22; Fox-Genovese (1979), 273; Candela (1980), 7; Portales (1981), 432–35; and Walker (1983), 89.

2. For more on floral imagery as a recurring symbol and unifying theme in *The Awakening*, see, for example, Dyer 418, Radcliffe-Umstead 132–33, and Showalter 81.

3. For other scholarly references to Chopin's echoing Walt Whitman, see, for example, Barker 77; Bloom 4; Leary 169–70; Mosely 371; and Seyersted 151, to mention just a few.

Works Cited

Barker, Deborah E. "The Awakening of Female Artistry." *Kate Chopin Reconsidered: Beyond the Bayou*. Ed. Lynda S. Boren and Sarah deSaussure Davis. Baton Rouge: Louisiana State UP, 1992. 61–79.

Berke, Jacqueline and Lola Silver. "The 'Awakened' Woman in Literature and Real Life." *Proceedings of the Sixth National Annual Convention of the Popular Culture Association, Chicago, April 22-24, 1976*. Bowling Green, OH: Popular Press, 1976. 1165–79.

Bierce, Ambrose. *"An Occurrence at Owl Creek Bridge" and Other Stories*. Ed. Susan L. Rattiner. New York: Dover, 2008.

Bloom, Harold, ed. *Kate Chopin: Modern Critical Views*. Philadelphia: Chelsea House, 1987.

Candela, Joseph L. Jr. "Domestic Orientation of American Novels, 1893–1913." *American Literary Realism* 13 (1980): 1–18.

Chopin, Kate. *The Awakening*. Ed. Margot Culley. 2nd ed. New York: Norton, 1994.

Crane, Stephen. *The Red Badge of Courage*. Ed. Mary R. Reichardt. San Francisco: Ignatius, 2012.

Dawson, Hugh J. "Kate Chopin's *The Awakening*: A Dissenting Opinion." *American Literary Realism* 26.2 (1994): 1–18.

Dyer, Joyce Coyne. "Lafcadio Hearn's *Chita* and Kate Chopin's *The Awakening*: Two Naturalistic Tales of the Gulf Islands." *Southern Studies* 23.4 (1984): 412–26.

Fox-Genovese, Elizabeth. "Kate Chopin's Awakening." *Southern Studies* 18 (1979): 261–90.

Justus, James H. "The Unawakening of Edna Pontellier." *Southern Literary Journal* 10 (1978): 107–22.

Leary, Lewis. *Southern Excursions: Essays on Mark Twain and Others*. Baton Rouge: Louisiana State UP, 1971.

Mosely, Merritt. "Chopin and Mysticism." *Southern Studies* 25 (1986): 367–74.

Portales, Marco A. "The Characterization of Edna Pontellier and the Conclusion of Kate Chopin's *The Awakening*." *Southern Studies* 20.4 (1981): 427–36.

Rocks, James E. "Kate Chopin's Ironic Vision." *Revue de Louisianne* 1.2 (1972): 110–120.

Seyerstead, Per. *Kate Chopin: A Critical Biography*. Baton Rouge: Louisiana State UP, 1969.

Showalter, Elaine. *Sister's Choice: Tradition and Change in American Women's Writing*. Oxford, UK: Oxford UP, 1991.

Walker, Nancy A. "Women Drifting: Drabble's *The Waterfall* and Chopin's *The Awakening*." *Denver Quarterly* 17.4 (1983): 88–96.

Wolff, Cynthia Griffin. "Thanatos and Eros: Kate Chopin's *The Awakening*." *American Quarterly* 25 (1973): 449–71.

In Defense of Robert Lebrun in Kate Chopin's
*The Awakening*_____

Robert C. Evans

Robert Lebrun is the man Edna Pontellier grows to love in Kate Chopin's *The Awakening*, despite (or perhaps because of) her marriage to Léonce Pontellier and her two small children. Robert is young, good-looking, humorous, sensitive, well-read, and attentive. Léonce, unfortunately, is none of these. Edna's attraction to Robert grows quickly while she, Léonce, and the children are vacationing on Grand Isle, not far from New Orleans. Ultimately, she falls far more intensely in love with Robert than she ever seems to have loved Léonce. Yet, many analysts have often wondered precisely *why* Edna loves Robert, and especially why she apparently kills herself after he leaves her. For many critics, Robert seems unworthy of Edna. He strikes these readers as variously (or in combination) weak, immature, self-absorbed, shallow, and tedious. For some readers, he ultimately seems a conventional sexist male of his era. Some critics have suggested that Robert finally fears Edna's erotic self-assertiveness, and recently, it has been argued that he is probably gay and therefore has little interest in women.[1]

Hugh J. Dawson's negative views of Robert are forcefully and memorably stated. Dawson thinks Robert resembles Edna since both "experience difficulty in achieving a mature relationship with a love-partner" (10). In his relations over the years with various women, Robert has been "quite happy in playing the foppish parasite ever-ready to do his woman-of-the-season's bidding" (Dawson 10). Dawson is, therefore, not surprised when "this simpering pretender later quails rather than declare himself to Edna" (11). Dawson considers Robert "a weakling who has shown himself content to linger as a hanger-on" (11). The charge that Robert is weak is particularly common.

Like Dawson, Pat Shaw also greatly dislikes Robert. According to Shaw, Robert "may deserve Edna's maternal patience, but he does not justify her sexual passion. And he is certainly unworthy of her immolation" (65-66). According to Shaw, Robert excessively reflects "the cloying Genteel Tradition of nineteenth-century American fiction" (66). Modern readers, Shaw says, find it difficult:

> to acquiesce to the relationship between the mature, passionate Edna and the callow Robert. . . . Robert functions metaphorically . . . as a child-lover. . . . Edna's desire for Robert (never consummated) may well have originated in Chopin's own incestuous impulses . . . . (66)

Few readers will want to follow Shaw down this odd Freudian alley, but many readers and critics have agreed that Robert, allegedly immature, does not deserve Edna's devotion.

Can anything be said on Robert's behalf? Does Edna's attraction to Robert make any sense? Is Robert, in any way, a genuinely appealing, sensible, and admirable character—one who may, in fact, be more mature, more thoughtful, and perhaps more worthy of our respect than Edna? Is there any way to argue that Robert is, if not a completely "worthy" figure, at least not entirely "unworthy"? In the essay that follows, I will try to suggest that Robert is far more admirable than some critics have argued.

I.

Reasons for Edna's attraction to Robert are suggested almost immediately. Chapter one already shows how much Robert differs from Léonce—not only physically, but more subtly as well. While Léonce has been reading market reports, Robert has been swimming with Edna. They have shared good times, but, even more important, they share a sense of humor Léonce lacks. Léonce immediately criticizes Edna's foolishness for swimming so late (4). He sees her as a damaged piece of "personal property" (4). Conversely, to Robert, Edna is a friend whose company he genuinely enjoys. Moreover, Edna no sooner returns than Léonce heads off to a billiards game. When he proposes that Robert join him, Robert declines: he "*admitted quite frankly* that he preferred to stay where he was and *talk* to Mrs. Pontellier" (emphasis added; 4).

Robert's frank admission implies his basic honesty. He feels no need to lie, and his candor suggests an absence of ulterior motives. Moreover, his rejection of Léonce's demand ("Come, go along" [4]) shows his willingness to defy an older, wealthier, more influential man—a man who can help his career. The fact that Léonce is not bothered by Robert's response suggests that Léonce himself considers Robert trustworthy (although it may also suggest Léonce's strong self-confidence and even egotism: it never seems to occur to him that Edna might find Robert appealing except as a friend).

After Léonce leaves, the narrator emphasizes the many similarities Edna and Robert share, and she also implies their developing bond. Edna and Robert look alike, share common interests, converse easily, and even have similar foibles, including a tendency to talk too much about themselves. Neither possesses Léonce's social status or financial power, but Robert never criticizes Léonce. In these early chapters, he treats Edna mainly as a friend; his interest in her seems neither romantic nor sexual. He also enjoys the company of "the little Pontellier children, who were very fond of him" (6). Is the narrator here suggesting that Robert is immature? Or is she instead showing us a fundamentally decent person, who genuinely cares about others (including children) from whom he has nothing to gain? Is his fondness for the children a sign of weakness, or does it indicate his basic good nature and the fact that he (unlike Léonce) does not take himself too seriously? If the latter answers seem at all appropriate, then there are at least two more reasons for Edna—and Chopin's readers—to admire Robert.

One reason Robert seems admirable, at least initially, is that he is not Léonce. The narrator makes their contrasts exceptionally clear when she juxtaposes chapters two and three. In chapter two, Robert seems attractive, but he seems even more appealing after we read chapter three, in which Léonce returns from having spent most of the day gambling (and, apparently, also drinking a bit). He awakens Edna from a sound sleep, implies that she has been ignoring the children's health, suggests that she attend to them now that he has awakened them, and then promptly falls asleep himself. Léonce is not intentionally mean or callous; he is not a stage villain. He is simply thoughtless and insensitive in ways Robert never is. In fact, chapter three foreshadows, in ironic ways, chapter thirteen, where Robert lets a tired, ailing Edna sleep until she naturally awakens, when he then gently banters with her, feeds her, and attends to her every need and desire.

Edna's attraction to Robert, then, is not especially mysterious. She has many reasons to find him appealing. Some of these include the following:

- He takes a genuine interest in her work as an aspiring artist and in its results (12).
- He enjoys swimming with her (13).
- He genuinely enjoys children, and they like him (19).
- He is genuinely attentive not only to Edna but also to Adèle (21).
- He likes to read, think, and converse (22).
- He is interested in music as well as the visual arts, and apparently, he is respected by Mademoiselle Reisz, the ascerbic pianist who disdains almost everyone else (25).
- Others respect him and follow his lead (26).
- He goes out of his way to help Edna learn to swim (27).
- By expressing confidence in her, he helps build her self-confi dence (28).
- He is imaginative and whimsical (29).
- He is not easily angered when Edna rebukes him (29).
- He is attentive when he thinks she may need his help (29).
- He enjoys nature (34).
- Attractive women apparently find him attractive (34).
- He shows genuine concern, and provides real assistance, when Edna seems ill (35).
- He is comfortable and friendly with simple folk, who also like him (35-36).
- He is playful and responds with quick wit to the playfulness of others (37).
- He takes good care of Edna after her brief bout of illness (37).
- He sings, and his singing voice is "not pretentious" but is "musical and true" (39).

And so on and so on. This list could easily be extended, but by now, the point is clear: Robert is variously attractive and appealing. He also seems to be a genuinely decent human being. Edna is not the only person in the book who greatly enjoys his company.

In fact, practically everyone in the novel seems to admire, respect, and enjoy Robert—except, perhaps, Alcée Arobin. But Arobin's discomfort with Robert, and the fact that Robert clearly dislikes Arobin (96-97), only enhance our regard for Robert. Arobin is a self-serving cad whose interest in Edna is mostly (and merely) sexual. Robert's contempt for Arobin speaks well of Robert. Indeed, the contrasts between Arobin and Robert typify the ways Chopin uses the novel's other men to highlight Robert's appeal. It is one thing to compare Robert to some imaginary Platonic ideal and find him wanting. It is another thing to compare Robert to almost all the other actual males in the novel. Compared to them—to Léonce, to Arobin, to Victor, to Edna's father—Robert seems quite appealing indeed. The only male who really rivals him as a character and seems decent, thoughtful, sincere, and generously concerned with others is old Dr. Mandelet.

III.

If Edna finds Robert appealing, and if the same is true of Adèle, Léonce, Mademoiselle Reisz, Mariequita, and practically every other character, why, then, do some critics consider him unattractive? As we have seen, the major charges are that he is weak, immature, self-absorbed, shallow, and tedious.

Many of these objections first arise when he appears in chapter five. There we learn that since:

> the age of fifteen, which was eleven years before, Robert each summer
> at Grand Isle had constituted himself the devoted attendant of some
> fair dame or damsel. Sometimes it was a young girl, again a widow;
> but as often as not it was some interesting married woman. (11)

No other character finds this behavior odd or disturbing. All seem to regard it as a game, as does Robert. It is part of a distinctive Creole culture. Creoles, it would seem, just like to have fun, and

Robert is so appealing to other characters (and to some readers) partly because he has a healthy sense of humor. He never takes himself too seriously. Unlike many other of the novel's males, he is not egotistical. He enjoys others' company, feels no need to impose his own values, and is not obviously judgmental (except concerning Arobin, whom he considers dishonest and selfish).

When a woman Robert once playfully courted passed away, he "*posed* [emphasis mine] as an inconsolable, prostrating himself at the feet of Madame Ratignolle for whatever crumbs of sympathy and comfort she might be pleased to vouchsafe" (11). This is simply more playfulness, as the exaggerated language shows. The narrator seems to enjoy Robert's sense of fun as much as the other characters do, partly because the narrator herself is good-humored. Critics who harshly condemn Robert seem to miss his whimsy and the whimsy of the whole novel. They risk taking Robert far more seriously than he takes himself. He begins as a figure of fun but then evolves into a more troubled character. The initial fun emphasizes the later transformation.

Robert is so appealing partly because he is always ready to laugh at his own expense. Rather than targeting others with mocking, satirical barbs, he enjoys jokes on himself and even "sets himself up." This is especially true in his mutually teasing relationship with Adèle:

> "Could any one fathom the cruelty beneath that fair exterior?" murmured Robert. "She knew that I adored her once, and she let me adore her. It was 'Robert, come; go; stand up; sit down; do this; do that; see if the baby sleeps; my thimble, please, that I left God knows where. Come and read Daudet to me while I sew.'"
> "*Par exemple!* ["For goodness sake!"] I never had to ask. You were always there under my feet, like a troublesome cat."
>
> "You mean like an adoring dog. And just as soon as Ratignolle appeared on the scene, then it *was* like a dog. '*Passez! Adieu! Allez vousen!*'" ["Go on! Good-by! Go away!"] (11-12)

This exchange is especially appealing. It demonstrates the easy, relaxed relationship of Robert and Adèle, whose bond seems all the stronger precisely *because* of such teasing and banter. Robert practically *invites* Adèle's comic abuse. This fact suggests not weakness or immaturity but instead a healthy, balanced ego. He doesn't fear public mockery by a woman, even in front of another attractive woman. His openness to teasing implies his openness in general. Would Léonce or Edna's father ever permit, let alone encourage, a woman to mock him? Robert is comfortable in his own skin. Men like Léonce and the Colonel, on the other hand, are never as self-confident as they want to seem. Thus they try to manipulate appearances and dominate others, particularly women.

Robert significantly lacks the insecurity that makes many people take themselves too seriously and try to impose themselves on others. He happily makes himself a figure of fun:

> Meanwhile Robert, addressing Mrs Pontellier, continued to tell of his one time hopeless passion for Madame Ratignolle; of sleepless nights, of consuming flames till the very sea sizzled when he took his daily plunge. While the lady at the needle [that is, Adèle] kept up a little running, contemptuous comment:
>
> "*Blagueur—farceur—gros bête, va!*" ["Joker, comedian, silly! Come off it!"] (12)

How can anyone take this kind of obviously overwrought, self-mocking language seriously? Clearly no one present does, but it is this passage, particularly, that makes Hugh Dawson call Robert a "simpering pretender" (11). No, Robert merely knows his real value, general values, and his own motives well enough to feel unthreatened by such joking. Léonce would never tolerate mockery, let alone invite it. Edna's father would be apoplectic. So would Mademoiselle Reisz. Arobin might tolerate it if he could get profit from it. Once again, when Robert is compared to other actual characters, he seems especially appealing. His behavior here, rather than suggesting weakness and immaturity, may suggest just the opposite.

IV.

Later, Robert twice rests his head against Edna's arm, and twice, she "repulse[s]" him (12). What should we make of this? If Arobin behaved this way, we would instantly know what to think. Robert, however, seems to have no sexual designs at this point—not because he is asexual or homosexual, but simply because he does not yet have sexual feelings for Edna. His physical contact may hint that he *has* begun to develop such feelings. The contact certainly arouses *our* curiosity. Apparently he, however, sees nothing wrong with his conduct ("He offered no apology" [12]), nor, apparently, does Adèle. Robert can rest his head on Edna's arm because, to him, the gesture is insignificant. It is Edna who is bothered enough to "repulse" him. At this point, she is far more strait-laced, conventional, and somber than he. She doesn't know what to make of his behavior, and so she repulses him.

Only later—after a long conversation reveals Edna's youthful romantic fantasies (18–19)—does Adèle become concerned. She doesn't distrust Robert, but she now worries that Edna will misinterpret his attentions. And so, being Adèle (honest, forthright, wise, sensitive, and caring), she doesn't hesitate to speak to him frankly. She assumes he will understand her motives and not be too offended. She candidly tells him that Edna is not a Creole, does not comprehend Creole culture, and may therefore misinterpret his friendship. She therefore asks him to

". . . let Mrs. Pontellier alone."

"*Tiens!*" ["So!"] he exclaimed, with a sudden, boyish laugh. "*Voilà que Madame Ratignolle estjalouse!*" ["Madame Ratignolle is jealous!"]

"Nonsense! I'm in earnest; I mean what I say. Let Mrs. Pontellier alone."

"Why?" he asked; himself growing serious at his companion's solicitation.

"She is not one of us; she is not like us. She might make the unfortunate blunder of taking you seriously." (20)

Robert's ability to shift suddenly from joking to seriousness speaks well of him. He knows Adèle well enough to realize that she is sincere. And for a moment—a long moment—he seems genuinely offended by her final comment:

> His face flushed with annoyance, and taking off his soft hat he began to beat it impatiently against his leg as he walked. "Why shouldn't she take me seriously?" he demanded sharply. "Am I a comedian, a clown, a jackinthebox? Why shouldn't she? You Creoles! I have no patience with you! Am I always to be regarded as a feature of an amusing programme? I hope Mrs. Pontellier does take me seriously. I hope she has discernment enough to find in me something besides the *blagueur* [joker, clown]. If I thought there was any doubt—" (20)

Robert's annoyance is understandable. Adèle has bruised his ego. But he quickly calms down, especially when Adèle reminds him that he is universally considered a "gentleman" (20). Her blunt speech to Robert indicates that she trusts him to react (eventually) in a sensible, mature, generous, and altruistic way. And that is precisely how Robert *does* react. Once he realizes that Adèle sincerely wants to protect Edna, he immediately apologizes for his "rudeness" in responding to her "well-meant caution" (21). He doesn't sulk; he doesn't storm off; he doesn't try to avoid the issue. Instead, he apologizes, and he even says Adèle has helped him not take himself too seriously (21). Are these reactions weak and immature? Arguably they suggest just the opposite. Robert can discipline his emotions and admit his errors. Instead of remaining angry, he shows real concern for Adèle as the episode ends (21).

V.

The common charge that Robert is a milquetoast is hard to sustain. In chapter eight, for instance, he emits a "shrill, piercing whistle which might have been heard back at the wharf" to summon his distant brother Victor, who is in many ways Robert's opposite

(Chopin 22). It is Victor, not Robert, who seems immature: he talks non-stop, pokes his nose into others' business, craves attention, and is generally such a nuisance that even his mother often grows exasperated. Thus, when Victor ignores both Robert's whistle and his own mother, Robert generously tells Mrs. Lebrun, "Whenever you say the word I'm ready to thrash any amount of reason into him that he's able to hold" (22). Later, Mademoiselle Reisz tells Edna that "It's a wonder Robert hasn't beaten [Victor] to death long ago" (47). In fact, Reisz reveals that:

> he thrashed him well enough a year or two ago . . . . It was about a Spanish girl, whom Victor considered that he had some sort of claim upon. He met Robert one day talking to the girl, or walking with her, or bathing with her, or carrying her basketI don't remember what;and he became so insulting and abusive that Robert gave him a thrashing . . . ." (47)

Robert, then, is not a weakling. Physically, at least, he seems able to hold his own. And notice his typical treatment of women. Although the Spanish girl is far from wealthy or socially prominent, Robert apparently treats her with much the same kindness he seems to show to all women. As Adèle said earlier, he is indeed a "gentleman" (20).

It is, in fact, precisely *because* he is a gentleman that he suddenly decides to leave for Mexico when he realizes that Edna's feelings for him, and his own for her, have become too emotional, romantic, and intense. Clearly they are falling in love, and this time Robert distrusts his ability to discipline his emotions. His abrupt decision to depart catches everyone by surprise, including the novel's readers. Edna, in particular, is "bewildered" (40), and she is also clearly hurt and angry or annoyed (43). Why does Robert leave? Apparently, he fears giving in to his emotions and possibly committing adultery. Apparently, he worries that he will be unable to remain simply Edna's close friend (43). The narrator doesn't make very clear precisely why Robert leaves. Instead, readers are left almost as mystified as Edna.

But what do Robert's critics expect him to do? Commit adultery with Edna (and thus not only violate his conscience, but also take advantage of her present confusion), thereby betraying Léonce and possibly bringing Edna, her husband, their children, his own family, and Robert himself into disgrace? Adultery was considered seriously immoral in Chopin's time. But instead of behaving like Alcée Arobin and exploiting his opportunity, Robert does indeed act like a "gentleman."

Why does he not explain himself more fully? Perhaps to save himself—and Edna—from embarrassment and/or avoid an argument. Surely he does not want to hurt her more than his departure already will. Therefore, he chooses to leave quickly, with little fanfare. He *does* bravely and maturely go to see Edna before departing (43). Rather than merely disappearing, he is sufficiently strong and grown-up to risk her wrath and/or tearful grief. Certainly his own feelings here seem stronger and more mature than hers:

> For the first time she recognized the symptoms of infatuation which she had felt incipiently as a child, as a girl in her earliest teens, and later as a young woman. . . . The present alone was significant; was hers, to torture her as it was doing then with the biting conviction that she had lost that which she had held, that she had been denied that which her impassioned, newly awakened being demanded. (44)

Such phrasing is worrying: Edna may be in the grip of yet another adolescent obsession, as Adèle had feared. Robert is partly to blame, of course: he *did* pay intimate attention to her even after Adèle had advised him not to, and perhaps he feels guilty for not following Adèle's advice. Neither he nor the narrator explains precisely *why* he leaves, thus encouraging speculation. Apparently when Robert realizes his intensifying feelings for Edna, he decides to withdraw. We may disagree with *how* he withdraws, but it is hard to think him mistaken in deciding *not* to commit adultery with the mother of two small children. The children—as even Edna later admits (108)—are the truly complicating factors. Robert seems to realize this, and he seems to respect the complex reality of Edna's situation. Here and elsewhere, he thinks more clearly and rationally than she. Little wonder, then, that in the next chapter, his mother alludes to his general wisdom while Edna's strong emotionalism is stressed (45).

VI.

Except for scattered references, Robert now disappears until chapter twenty-one, when Edna and Reisz discuss him at length (60–62). Robert has written Reisz a letter full of inquiries about Edna, and when Edna reads it while Reisz plays the piano, Edna passionately weeps (61–62). Clearly, Robert has not lost his interest in her, and clearly, her own passion has intensified *because* of his absence. A similar discussion about Robert occurs in chapter twenty-six. By that point, Edna has read a number of his letters to Reisz and often the letters mention Edna. He never writes to Edna herself for reasons Reisz intuits: "It is because he loves you, poor fool, and is trying to forget you, since you are not free to listen to him or to belong to him." From one of these letters, Edna learns of his planned return to New Orleans (77). Reisz tells Edna that if *she* were young and in love, the man she would love "would have to be some *grand esprit*; a man with lofty aims and ability to reach them; one who stood high enough to attract the notice of his fellowmen. . . . I should never deem a man of ordinary caliber worthy of my devotion" (77).

If Reisz is implying that Robert is *not* such a man, then she is faulting him precisely as some critics have done. But clearly Reisz admires Robert, so it is not at all clear that she is implying he is unworthy. Besides, the ideal man she describes is exactly the kind of man Edna has romantically—and foolishly—fantasized about in the past. Fortunately, Edna here rejects Reisz's superficial criteria. She loves Robert even though he is *not* lofty, prominent, wealthy, or distinguished (78). Yet, her reasons for loving him all seem superficial. They involve his physical appearance, not his character, values, or personality (78). Reisz's reasons for loving seem quite unrealistic; Edna's seem relatively trivial. Surely Edna loves Robert for reasons other than the color and part of his hair, the angle of his nose, and the shapes of his chin and little finger (78), but these are the only reasons she explicitly mentions. Neither Reisz nor Edna mentions all the qualities of character than make Robert an appealing—and genuinely lovable—human being.

When Robert finally does reappear—in chapter thirty-three—he meets Edna accidentally. Both are surprised. Clearly, they still love each other, but just as clearly, Edna is at the center of her own universe. Although Robert has been back for only two days—one spent working—Edna is frustrated that he did not come earlier to see her (92–93). She has long fantasized about their reunion (93), but reality disappoints her (as it often does). Yet, although she speaks angrily—or at least bluntly—to Robert (93), he still tries to be courteous (94). Before long, tensions dissolve, although they briefly flare up again when Robert realizes Edna's connection with Alcée Arobin (93).

VII.

Later, when Edna and Robert once more accidentally meet, Edna again criticizes Robert for having kept his distance. With unintentional irony, she says, "You are the embodiment of selfishness . . . . in sparing yourself you never consider for a moment what I think, or how I feel" (100). It doesn't seem to occur to Edna how selfish her own words and conduct may seem—words and conduct that even the gentlemanly Robert calls "cruel" (100). She insists that he address topics he would rather avoid because he sees no point in discussing them (100). Nevertheless, he accompanies her back home, and it is there that Edna literally takes matters into her own hands by kissing him while he is leaning his head back, his eyes apparently closed. Robert probably would not have kissed her first—not because he is asexual, homosexual, weak, or immature, but simply because she is a married mother of young children. But when Edna kisses him, he instinctively responds and passionately returns her kisses. He also confesses his love, admitting that it was *because* of this love that he went to Mexico (101).

Reactions to the ensuing scene will reveal as much about particular readers as about the scene itself. Robert fully confesses his love and passion for Edna and says he even dreamed that Léonce might free her from their marriage. To this, Edna responds in one of the book's most intriguing statements:

"You have been a very, very foolish boy, wasting your time dreaming of impossible things when you speak of Mr. Pontellier setting me

It seems just as possible to argue, however, that Robert here has simply come to his senses. He realizes that a satisfying relationship with Edna is no more possible now than it was earlier, and perhaps he is shocked by Edna's own narcissism. Her smug comment that she can now "give" herself where she chooses may make him realize that she has already "given" herself to Alcée Arobin (as, indeed, she has) and that she has already, therefore, been as unfaithful to him as to Léonce. Perhaps he thinks that Edna is too capricious—and too irrational and obsessed with fantasies—ever to make anyone a reliable partner. Perhaps, too, he thinks her betrayal of himself and Léonce with Arobin is above all a betrayal of her children—a failure to consider them and their long-term best interests.

One need not agree with all of Robert's probable reasons, in _____ to think that they are hardly unreasonable. Robert, far from _____ in deciding to end his relationship with _____ stronger and *more* mature than

free! I am no longer one of Mr. Pontellier's possessions to dis[pose of]
or not. I give myself where I choose. If he were to say, 'Here, [I]
take her and be happy; she is yours,' I should laugh at you[
(102)

Robert seems shocked ("His face grew a little white. 'What do [you]
mean,' he asked" [102]). Ironically, however, Edna's condemnat[ion]
of Robert's foolishness recalls Léonce's condemnation of Edna[']
foolishness in chapter one. In both cases, the tone seems patronizin[g]
and condescending. Most readers will probably sympathize with
Edna's claims that she is no longer Léonce's possession, but her
apparent assumption that her status as a wife (and mother) is
unimportant and that she can give herself where she chooses is
simplistic, to say the least, and perhaps it is even highly foolish.
Edna accuses Robert of being immature, but one might just as [easily]
reverse the accusation. Some readers will find it [difficult to]
complete seriously when she

meiodramatically proclaims, "Oh! I have suffered, suffered! Now you are here we shall love each other, my Robert. We shall be everything to each other. Nothing else in the world is of any consequence." Similarly, one can argue that if Robert ever actually appears weak and immature, it is when he begs Edna not to honor her prior commitment to visit Adèle when the latter is giving birth: "Don't go; don't go! Oh! Edna, stay with me . . . . Why should you go? Stay with me, stay with me" (103). For one brief moment, Robert begins to sound like Edna—passionate, irrational, melodramatically "romantic," unrealistic, and fundamentally self-centered.

It should not surprise us that this mood does not last. Throughout the book, Robert has been more sensible, thoughtful, and responsible than this immature language would suggest. As Edna returns from assisting Adèle, she again melodramatically fantasizes about Robert (106), but then, stunned, she finds his farewell note: "'I love you. Goodby—because I love you'" (106). For some readers, this note epitomizes Robert's shallow worthlessness. Dawson, for instance, thinks Robert seeks to "prettify his departure with a gasping protestation of self-sacrifice" (11).

---

order to . . .

seeming weak or immature . . .

Edna, can instead be seen as much s... ...g... ...

she. The Robert who is arguably weak and immature is the Robert who exclaims, "Don't go; don't go! Oh! Edna, stay with me . . . . Why should you go? Stay with me, stay with me." The Robert who writes "I love you. Goodby—because I love you" is arguably the Robert who shows real strength, real maturity, and a real sense of the often difficult complexities of life and love.

Note

1. For a small sampling of these various views see, for instance, Fox-Genovese (277), Jones (180), Lant (173), Thornton (56), St. Andrews (53–54), Wolff (460), and Toth (117).

Works Cited

Chopin, Kate. *The Awakening*. Ed. Margot Culley. 2 nd ed. New York: Norton, 1994.

Dawson, Hugh J. "Kate Chopin's *The Awakening*: A Dissenting Opinion." *American Literary Realism* 26.2 (1994): 1–18.

Fox-Genovese, Elizabeth. "Kate Chopin's Awakening." *Southern Studies* 18 (1979): 261–90.

Jones, Anne Goodwyn. *Tomorrow Is Another Day: The Woman Writer in the South, 1859–1936*. Baton Rouge: Louisiana State UP, 1981.

Lant, Kathleen Margaret. "The Siren of Grand Isle: Adèle's Role in *The Awakening*." *Southern Studies* 23.2 (1984): 167–75.

Shaw, Pat. "Putting Audience in Its Place: Psychosexuality and Perspective Shifts in *The Awakening*." *American Literary Realism* 23.1 (1990): 61–69.

St. Andrews, Bonnie. *Forbidden Fruit: On the Relationship between Women and Knowledge in Doris Lessing, Selma Lagerlof, Kate Chopin, Margaret Atwood*. Troy, NY: Whitson, 1986.

Thornton, Lawrence. "*The Awakening*: A Political Romance." *American Literature* 52.1 (1980): 50–66.

Toth, Emily. "Kate Chopin's Unvarnished Life Story." *Southern Studies* 8.1-2 (1997): 111-19.

Wolff, Cynthia G. "Thanatos and Eros: Kate Chopin's *The Awakening*." *American Quarterly* 25 (1973): 449–71.

Tourism and Landscape in *The Awakening*

Jeffrey Melton

Readers cannot complete Kate Chopin's *The Awakening* without being affected. The ending is particularly challenging, and critics over the generations have struggled with its ambiguity and provocative imagery. Most readers agree that Edna unsuccessfully negotiates the conflict between social respectability and her own subversive tendencies. Her struggle drives the action of the novel and plays out in her inward battle between romantic and realistic sensibilities.

For Edna, a realistic worldview is an adult one, an attitude that she takes directly from mainstream, middle-class culture in the late nineteenth century. She marries Léonce in an expression of her willingness to accept adult (realistic) responsibilities and expectations. However, as readers quickly discover, Edna retains a strong romantic sensibility as well, and it manifests itself most obviously in her relationship with Robert Lebrun, which provides the core romantic plot device. Readers who disapprove of her actions, especially at the end of the novel, rest their case on her inability to close "the portals forever behind her upon the realm of romance and dreams" (19).[1] Although it earns the most attention from readers, her love for Robert represents only part of her romantic life.

Readers often come down on one side or the other regarding their opinion of Edna's final act. On one hand, some see her choice as a strike against patriarchal oppression in a triumphant, though tragic, political act of selfhood; on the other, some see her choice as adolescent cowardice, an impulsive act of selfishness. Both views are supportable, which attests to the artistry of Chopin's writing. Critics nonetheless tend to simplify the idea of romanticism on both sides of the debate. For Edna's detractors, her romanticism is simply melodrama, defined only by sentimentalism. For Edna's supporters, romanticism is the catalyst leading her to recognize and to escape her domestic trap. However, Edna's developing romantic eye for nature offers a much stronger and nuanced way to measure her intellectual and physical experiences. She embarks upon a quest for full understanding of her environment and her place in the world. That journey is best illustrated by her evolving relationship with nature. It is true that Edna's romance with Robert is mired in childish fantasies, but her romance with the natural landscape is much more positive and aspirational.

Resort Life and Social Change

Although American resort life in the late nineteenth century evolved in support of pervasive values and cultural stability, in effect, it served as a subversive force. The popular adage and marketing slogan for modern Las Vegas, "What happens in Vegas stays in Vegas," derives in no small part from the culture wars initiated by the development of resort vacations in the era. The implications of the phrase are that vacationers in Las Vegas are tempted to participate in behaviors that would not be suitable back home. Americans on vacation often not only depart from their workaday lives, but also free themselves from restrictive value systems. This behavior is in no way restricted to Las Vegas—"Sin City"—nor is it new. Americans on vacation have always flirted with trouble.

Even the term "vacation" itself has had a complex existence. From the beginning, the idea of taking time off from work to indulge in pleasure carried significant challenges to a national value system defined by a strong work ethic. Cindy Aron writes, "vacationing generated fear and anxiety among the nineteenth-century middle class, because vacationers were people at leisure and leisure remained problematic. Work, discipline, and industry were the virtues that allegedly counted for the success and well-being not only of individuals, but of the nation itself" (5). In short, a vacationer was not working and thus not contributing to the common good. In addition, the pleasures of vacations could lead to self-indulgence and self-degrading behavior that could undermine the moral integrity of the nation. Vacations were nonetheless established as respectable activities for elite classes and upper-middle classes as long as the leisure time was also legitimized by self-development. If Americans were fortunate enough to be able to take vacations, they needed to justify them by taking the opportunity to improve their minds, bodies, and spirits. The term "recreation" became more in vogue in that it asserted leisure as "re-creation" or rejuvenation. By the 1890s, it became a widely held belief that vacations could improve the work life of the nation as a whole and thereby be justified as productive behavior. The social debates on the validity of vacations were legitimate arguments. Aron writes, "resorts themselves became sites of change—creating environments in which vacationers not only could enjoy new sorts of pleasures but could also experiment with new, often less restricted, rules of conduct and behavior" (3). The tides of change initiated by vacationing in the late nineteenth century were especially transformative for women, who traditionally had faced a moral code of behavior much more restrictive than men and who had little opportunity to venture out of the domestic sphere.

The ideals of work as indicative of American moral and industrial power held the work of men as the standard. The work of women, in turn, although vital to mainstream values, resided wholly in the domestic sphere and, as such, held no economic power. Women gained status from being married to male providers who could relieve them of the necessity of working for wages and even of working in the household beyond overseeing domestic servants. Leisure for women "was not a condition fraught with either moral or political risks but rather a culturally sanctioned requirement" (Aron 8–9). In other words, the standard of middle class women at the turn of the century was to demonstrate status by being as inactive as possible. On vacation, women were, like the men, obligated to improve themselves in some degree to justify the time at a resort, but the irony of the contrasts between home life and resort life in practice encouraged and even supported women in efforts to become more active in all facets of a worldly life. Edna Pontellier is just such a woman.

Women of leisure embraced respectable resort activities that, in the end, introduced the pleasures of substantive physical and intellectual development, which many found invigorating. Edna's struggles, while tied to her personal issues, also represent those of a generation of Progressive Era women, who, for the first time, gained the opportunity to join men in physical activity (Edna learns to swim) and to explore their talents (Edna develops her artistic skills). Such aggressive self-development went well beyond the normal Victorian expectations that women use their talents to adorn and elevate the middle-class home. Middle class women were primed to gain and lose the most from resort culture because their dependent status left them vulnerable to the shifting sands.

Upon returning to New Orleans after her summer of expansion, Edna cannot readjustto normalcy—inactivity on all levels, includingmind, body and spirit. Once she returns to the more rigorous social structures of the city, she no longer fits within its boundaries. Her example is emblematic of how resort life began to push against the norms of mainstream society as many women sought to continue their vacationactivities year round. Once they experienced the opportunities to challenge themselves physically and intellectually in vacationing contexts, many found the return to inactivity unacceptable. Edna's small subversions of normalcy upon her return home have immediate disruptive effects on the peace of the household. The best example is her choice not to observe her traditional Tuesday visitation days. This is an especially apt symbol for Edna's disenchantment with the return of mannerly passivity. Her task on Tuesdays is simply to stay at home and wait to entertain visitors. She chooses instead to go out, symbolically to be active by moving rather than remaining still. According to Tara Parmiter, her experiences at Grand Isle resort "inspire the re-evaluationof self and home" (12). Upon returning to the traditional restrictions of patriarchal society, Edna "can no longer tolerate the petty constrictions of her social set" (12). She is no longer compatible with leisure as simply performance of status. She prefers to use leisure for an active pursuit of happiness through self-definition.

The dramatic changes that would not come to symbolic fruition until a generation later, with women gaining the right to vote in 1920, were due in no small part to the experiences of women on vacation. As Aron observes, "women both discovered and helped create a resort culture that freed them from some traditional middle-class constraints and allowed them to exercise new forms of personal autonomy" (70). With exposure to the joys of such privileges, many women sought to remain active upon their return home. What one does in Las Vegas or, in this case, Grand Isle never remains there.[2]

Nature and Landscape[3]

Chopin makes substantive use of framing devices and compositional techniques aligned with late nineteenth-century art. Readers encounter a rich use of color and imagery that evokes a deep appreciation of the visual romanticism of nature and the environment. Michael Gilmore connects Chopin's style in creating imagery with that of the Impressionists, arguing that the similarities apply "both to subject matter and technique" (64). The connections are especially evident in how Chopin uses light and color to create an environmental mood that matches the emotional state of Edna in particular. Gilmore continues, "More telling than these surface affinities is the deeper kinship between Edna's evolving state of mind and the objectives of Impressionist art. Rather than aspiring to an unmediated vision of reality, Impressionism is concerned with a given scene's effect on the individual consciousness" (64). It is a symbiotic relationship: natural surroundings influence human experience; humans influence natural surroundings by defining them (painting them, describing them) in personal terms. Although Chopin clearly incorporates Impressionistic ways of seeing into the narrative, the American art tradition that she evokes is much broader and is tied to the romantic landscape art that permeated American consciousness throughout the nineteenth century. The first significant contribution to high art in the United States was made by the Hudson River School.[4]

Romantic landscape art by painters such as Thomas Cole, Asher B. Durand, and Albert Bierstadt obtained a wide popularity, while also earning critical acclaim. Although—like American romantic writers—artists had European models, they formed an indigenous artistic expression that celebrated the American landscape in both personal and national terms. If the Impressionists emphasized the individual's remaking of the environment in personal terms, the Hudson River painters did much the same thing, but also created a national narrative that aligned the personal pursuit of happiness with Manifest Destiny. Key to that narrative is a sense of belonging within the American landscape that offered the backdrop for personal and national expansion. The two were intertwined. Leo Marx, in his seminal 1964 book *The Machine in the Garden*, notes that the American continent, from the European perspective, always carried an "immense burden of hope" and formed in the public's eye a devotion to a pastoral ideal, the confidence in the natural landscape to provide the backdrop for a "truly successful 'pursuit of happiness'" (74).

Although by the 1890s, when the Hudson River School had fallen out of favor among art critics, the popular imagination that saw the American landscape as symbol of potential and hope had not waned. Widely regarded as the Father of the Hudson River School, Thomas Cole asserts, in his 1836 "Essay on American Scenery," the personal connection that an American shares with the natural landscape. He writes, "it is his own land; its beauty, its magnificence, its sublimity—all are his; and how undeserving of such a birthright, if he can turn towards it an unobserving eye, an unaffected heart!" (Par. 2, line 2). This idea of ownership is vital, and it implies dominion not only of the view itself, but also of the poetic and cultural implications of the American landscape as a whole. Although the historical reality of the nineteenth century limited this ownership to landholding males of European ancestry, the concept nonetheless resonates among the population at large. If political progress was slow to offer similar opportunities for pursuing happiness, the imagined symbolic landscape was still available to all. Cole notes that the value of embracing the beauty of the landscape is that it allows anyone with a "loving eye" to "obtain a free horizon." The land remained at the turn of the century (and still remains) tied to the American Dream in popular consciousness, and this legacy is crucial to recognizing the depth of Edna's own artistic imagination and her efforts to reach her own horizon.

The novel's first landscape image is also readers' first glimpse of Edna. Léonce, looking up from his newspaper, watches Edna, escorted by Robert, walk up the beach toward the vacation cottage: "He fixed his gaze upon a white sunshade that was advancing at snail's pace from the beach. He could see it plainly between the gaunt trunks of the water-oaks and across the stretch of the yellow camomile. The gulf looked far away, melting hazily into the blue of the horizon" (4). It is crucial to note that Léonce focuses on the sunshade (umbrella) rather than Edna or Robert. This characterizing of his wife as "it" matches Chopin's later comment that he sees her as "a valuable piece of personal property" (4). However, it is the following line that places Edna in the center of a compelling landscape image worthy of a Hudson River School painter. In effect, the small figures (Edna and Robert) are centered within a vast panoramic image of the natural surroundings. They are framed by large trees in the foreground and granted color by the expanse of yellow flowers (camomile, or chamomile) that surround them. The image is given depth by the vastness of the gulf waters behind them, becoming hazy in the distance and commingling with the blue of the sky at the horizon. It is a beautiful image, carefully composed to parallel the closing of the novel. Here, Edna is object, a woman in a garden, defined not by her individuality, but by a sunshade, a focal point of virginal white. Her back, not coincidentally, is to the horizon.

Chopin sets up Edna's relationship to her surroundings from the beginning, the object of Léonce's gaze as adornment to the landscape that he has inherited as a Euro-American male. Her relationship to landscape when considered in the company of men is consistently placed in the context of domestic beauty rather than the panorama itself. Léonce is but the primary symbol of male power. The two other young male figures, Alcée and Robert, likewise assert a landscape imagery that encloses Edna rather than providing her access to the broad stroke of landscape imagery. In traditional gender codes, men belonged to the outside, women to the inside. The expansive out-of-doors was defined as a masculine realm. However, women were increasingly encouraged to embrace nature, but in a domestic context. Therefore, home gardening became an allowable pastime for women and encouraged an intimacy with nature that also matched their assumed natural inclinations as nurturers. Plants and flowers, then, were symbolic of children. In the first image above, the yellow flowers not only frame the white sunshade but also imply the natural beauty of Edna as matron.[5]

Alcée sees Edna not as an object of personal property as does Léonce; rather, he sees her as a sexual object. His view of her nonetheless repeats the use of flowers as an assertion of her connection to nature. Having moved from Léonce's house into her own "pigeon house," Edna still remains enclosed by male notions of feminine nature. Alcée has arranged to fill her new home with flowers placed around the interior. This is a romantic gesture related to his sexual intentions, but it also reflects the cultural limitations women faced in regard to establishing an open relationship with nature itself. The associations with nature from the male point of view are represented by cut flowers in vases, which, although pleasing to the senses, are a synecdoche for nature and women under masculine control—cut from nature and placed in restrictive containers for domestic consumption. Edna, like the flowers in the vases, is subject for a still-life painting, not a panoramic landscape.

Edna demonstrates a capacity to intuit the freedom implied by landscape imagery. The first time readers witness Edna responding to a broad natural scene, she is seated alongside Adèle. Alone, they are free of the male gaze and are thus able to talk with some intimacy. Chopin writes, "Edna Pontellier, casting her eyes about, had finally kept them at rest upon the sea. The day was clear and carried the gaze out as far as the blue sky went; there were a few white clouds suspended idly over the horizon" (16). Somewhat restless, Edna takes some time to match her mood to the scene in front of her. When her eyes come to "rest," what follows could easily be a painting, with the same capacity to draw the attention into the middle distance of the horizon and the same expression of contentment with the details of the sky. The scene is peaceful and inviting.

Edna immediately begins to let her imagination engage the scene. Although the tone emphasizes the lack of movement—clouds "suspended idly"—she responds with active thought, so active that Adèle notices her "expression which seemed to have seized and fixed every feature into a statuesque repose" (16). When asked what she was thinking of, Edna chooses to explore her thought process in some depth. She shares a vital connection that illustrates her innate capacity to embrace nature with anintensity that goesbeyond traditional assumptions. She says, "'the sight of the water stretching so far away, those motionless sails against the blue sky, made a delicious picture that I just wanted to sit and look at'" (16). Her response is intimate, as indicated by her rapt attention to its detail and her desire to maintain a connection with the "delicious picture."

Chopin's word choice is not incidental; it reveals the commonplace tendency of Victorian era Americans to see landscapes in terms of framed images created by popular artists. This scene, in addition, sets up Edna's artistic sensibility, introducing her capacity to see into a scene and invoke meaning. She then makes a connection not only to a childhood memory of intimacy with her natural surroundings but also, by implication, to standard pastoral imagery associated with agrarian society and westward expansion. Her sensory experience harkens back to "'a summer day in Kentucky, of a meadow that seemed as big as the ocean to the very little girl walking through the grass, which was higher than her waist. She threw out her arms as if swimming when she walked, beating the tall grass as one strikes out in the water. Oh, I see the connection now!'" (17). The connection is between the grass and the water and how both offer enfolding encounters with nature. Edna is yet to experience the joy of swimming at Grand Isle, so she speaks of herself as a child in third person because her current "realistic" self is so distanced by time and sensibility from that ecstasy initiated by the child's exploration through the grass. Edna's comment that she may have been running away from church and Adèle's joking response encourage a further distancing from her younger self, whom she calls an "unthinking child." This phrase is unfortunate in that it focuses on the oppressive fundamentalism that she was fleeing without fully considering the romantic pantheism that she was running toward. She has already begun to seek that grassy meadow again and the sense of belonging that it provided long ago.

She finds that feeling in the waters of Grand Isle. Being given the opportunity and encouragement to learn to swim was typical of beach resort vacations, and that context provides the catalyst.

After struggling for most of the summer, when Edna finally feels the power of her body within the embrace of the water, she is exultant and swims away from the shore alone. Here Chopin provides Edna's second landscape image at Grand Isle: "She turned her face seaward to gather in an impression of space and solitude, which the vast expanse of water, meeting and melting with the moonlit sky, conveyed to her excited fancy" (28). The passage emphasizes romantic patterns of describing (or painting) landscapes. She seeks to gain "space and solitude," and the framing of the scene again uses the horizon, the "unlimited" space of expansion. She panics upon turning to shore when she realizes how far toward that horizon she has moved. Although this moment emphasizes that she is only beginning to regain a sense of competency with her body and confidence in the landscape, the fact remains that she composes herself and swims ashore. The success of that swim is unequivocal.

The freedoms of resort life renew within Edna her desires to negotiate her own life with her own sense of place and self. But summer vacations end, and families return to cities defined not only by a more rigid social structure but also a denuded natural environment. The Pontellier home itself provides a crucial glimpse into the workaday world. It is filled with Léonce's many stylistic possessions, the outside is painted "dazzling white," and its yard is "kept scrupulously neat" with "flowers and plants of every description" (48). All facets of this beautiful scene are the subject of Léonce's control and oversight. The features, including the flowers in the yard, are meticulous presentations of social status. With this domestic ideal, Edna's intimacy with landscape is greatly restricted. For Victorian culture, nature had become increasingly ornamental, resulting from nostalgic reverie for a pastoral past in contrast to a rapidly urbanizing and industrializing present. Parks with elaborate ornamental landscaping burgeoned in response, creating highly stylized presentations of nature in urban settings. This translated into family life as well for middle and upper classes; the grounds of homes became gardens. The social structures built around gender were likewise applied to urban interaction with nature, and women became the keepers of nature within the domestic sphere. Women often worked in home gardens and most often were encouraged to focus on ornamental plants as opposed to food gardening, which would be left to servants. More often, however, the female interaction with nature simply took the form of cut flowers as decoration inside the home.

With this context in mind, Edna's urban life in reference to flowers becomes indicative of her overall connection to nature. Soon after returning to the city and after she and Léonce have an argument, Edna goes to her room highly agitated. As her first act, she goes to an open window and gazes into "the deep tangle of the garden below" (50). The garden is the only landscape available to her, and she seeks it for solace. She does not find any, however, and Chopin's description of it reflects Edna's impressionistic response to it. She sees a "deep tangle," as opposed to a well-maintained space. She feels the "witchery of the night" and is put off by the "torturous outlines of flowers and foliage" (50). Her reaction to this semi-natural scene is telling. The problem is context; this overly-controlled pseudo-natural space can provide no solace for her after her awakening to panoramic nature on Grand Isle. She becomes more frustrated and takes off her wedding ring, throws it to the floor, and stomps on it. This is one of the most quoted moments of the novel as it demonstrates her growing anger at her entrapment in domesticity. However, it is the second violent action here that is more instructive: She then grabs a "glass vase" from the hearth and slams it to the floor (51). That vase is supposed to contain cut flowers to add a feminine touch to the home and to represent nature as adornment. However, it is empty. In this scene, she finds that she cannot destroy the ring, but she can destroy a container designed to control the natural world. Edna's outburst equates the two types of confinement.

The following scene at Adèle Ratignolle's home provides the applicable contrast. Adèle, the clear embodiment of domestic grace and beauty, creates a much different response to flowers in the home. Upon entering the scene of domestic harmony, Edna is taken by Adèle into the front "salon, where it was cool and sweet with the odor of great roses that stood upon the hearth in jars" (53). This image captures the blend of home and garden that typifies allowable female-nature interaction. Edna's now vase-lesshearth, in contrast, is a symbolic rejection of middle-class values and the use of flowers as commodification. Her natural imagination has expanded well beyond such small, restricted displays of approbation. For Adèle, cut flowers in vases bring a bit of the beauty of nature into the home to typify familial bliss. For Edna, a cut flower is simply a dying flower.

Edna is never able to reestablish herself with any sense of balance in New Orleans, and she steadily loses control. She extends the freedoms that she experienced on Grand Isle outside of the resort life context, thus proving the fears that many Victorians felt regarding the pernicious effects of resort life on mainstream culture. She expands her artistic eye and develops into a professional who gains some level of legitimacy, earning money and respect from her customers. Moreover, she pursues her sexuality with Alcée Arobin and continues her love for Robert. In the end, she casts off the perpetual limitations that those relationships will provide for her and returns to the only promise of self-affirmation that she has encountered, the romantic natural landscape of Grand Isle.

In the end, Edna returns to the source of the inspiration for self-affirmation that she discovered in the natural and free setting of Grand Isle. Naked at the edge of the water and looking into the distance, Edna begins swimming, following the initial impulse she had the previous summer upon discovering her physical strength in the water—to swim out into the romantic imagery where the sea meets the sky. Chopin writes, "She did not look back now, but went on and on, thinking of the blue-grass meadow that she had traversed when a little child, believing that it had no beginning and no end" (109). Although she remembers the fear she had upon her first swim, the key here is that she "does not look back" for any sense of security from the shore. Any fear is inconsequential at this point. Her intentions are clear. She claims a landscape of her own that is tied both to her life experiences with nature and to the pursuit of happiness imbued in American nature imagery.

The final paragraph begins with "She looked into the distance" (109). Although a momentary terror flares, it quickly subsides without causing her any hesitation. While looking into the distance, Edna has a series of impressions from her youth, but the last line confirms her awakening: "There was the hum of bees, and the musky odor of pinks filled the air" (109). Her willingness to embrace the natural landscape and its Emersonian power to affirm life free of restrictions has made possible Edna's final assertion of her will. The last image refers to the beauty of nature free of Victorian restrictions on the intimacy women could seek in the natural landscape. The smell of flowers (pinks) envelops her, just as the sea itself does. The imagined flowers are not contained by the Victorian rage for domestic order. Edna, like those flowers, is free to fill the air.

Notes

1. Chopin, Kate. *The Awakening: An Authoritative Text, Contexts, Criticism.* Ed. Margaret Culley. New York: Norton, 1976. All references to the text are from this edition.

2. For an excellent discussion of tourism on Grand Isle, see Steilow.

3. Throughout the essay, I will use the term "landscape" to also include "seascape." This is for convenience and also to apply the word, in its broadest sense, to a symbolic representation of a panoramic view of the natural environment.

4. For a strong introduction to the history and paintings of the Hudson River School of art, see *American Paradise*.

5. For an overview of women, gardens, and domesticity, see Norwood.

Works Cited

Aron, Cindy Sondik. *Working at Play: A History of Vacations in the United States.* New York: Oxford UP, 1999.

Avery, Kevin J., Oswaldo Rodriguez Roque, John K. Howat, et al. *American Paradise: The World of the Hudson River School.* New York: Metropolitan Museum of Art, 1987.

Chopin, Kate. *The Awakening: An Authoritative Text, Contexts, Criticism.* Ed. Margaret Culley. New York: Norton, 1976.

Cole, Thomas. "Essay on American Scenery." *The American Monthly Magazine.* Jan. 1836 University of Minnesota. Web. 27 Nov. 2013. <http://www.tc.umn.edu/~danp/rhet8520/winter99/cole.html>.

Marx, Leo. *The Machine in the Garden.* 1964. New York: Oxford UP, 2000.

Norwood, Vera. *Made from This Earth: American Women and Nature.* Chapel Hill: U of North Carolina P, 1993.

Parmiter, Tara. "Taking the Waters: The Summer Place and Women's Health in Kate Chopin's *The Awakening.*" *American Literary Realism* 39.1 (2006): 1-19.

Steilow, Frederick. "Grand Isle, Louisiana, and the 'New' Leisure, 1866-1893," *Louisiana History* 23.3 (1982): 239-57.

Kate Chopin's *The Awakening* and Her Louisiana Fiction as Travel Literature_____

Thomas Bonner, Jr.

Kate Chopin's connections with Louisiana began when she was Kate O'Flaherty, listening to her maternal great grandmother in St. Louis spin tales of life along the Mississippi River. In these early years, she began to be a traveler in spirit and in fact. Madame Victoire Charleville and her family had owned a boat line that plied the river from St. Louis to New Orleans. There were visits down river by the St. Louis family to those in the region of Natchitoches, Louisiana and upriver from the family who lived along the Cane River. These stories and journeys in her youthful years serve as clues to how her literary imagination developed and how literal and remembered travel to Louisiana fitted into it.

"The literature of travel" marks much writing in eighteenth and nineteenth century British and American literature. An easily accessed volume addressing this subject is the *The Cambridge History of English and American Literature*, where the writers indicate that authors of this kind of literature are known more as authors than travelers (for example, Laurence Sterne is known for his 1768 novel *A Sentimental Journey Through France and Italy* and Robert Louis Stevenson for his 1878 travelogue *An Inland Voyage*). Two points about the writer of travel literature emerge: that the writer must possess something of the traits of "a born traveler" and that the writing must "possess the spirit and the passion of travel which possesses the writer" (Ward et al. 7.1).

On this basis alone, one can categorically argue that Chopin is both a traveler and a writer of travel literature. Her response to her pre-wedding visit to New Orleans in 1869 reveals that she has an innate sense of the place she is visiting becoming part of herself and a passion for what she is seeing, which seemsalmost a dream come true—dreams often being an element of much writing about travel.

She describes New Orleans as the pristine image of a pastoral city, implying a contrast to her native city of St. Louis. She is describing a neighborhood along Esplanade Avenue, running from the Mississippi River to Bayou St. John, or between St. Charles Avenue and Magazine Street in what has become known as the Garden District. There is something new in the architecture she describes, and it is pastorally complementing the climate and environment of a spring that has yet to arrive in St. Louis. Her observation in her Commonplace Book (see Chopin, *Private* 85) suggests that she is merely an adolescent using prose in lieu of outbursts of enthusiasm.

The diary of Chopin's grand tour of Europe, following her wedding, has seeds of these earlier descriptions, as well as the beginnings of more mature ones, emphasizing an increased element of realism and risk-taking. She does things for which a young Victorian woman in the American Midwest would have been criticized: she drinks beer in a German *Ratskeller*; she smokes cigarettes in public; and most importantly, she walks *alone* along streets in European cities. Furthermore, she shows an awareness of world-changing events and the people who bring them about. For example, she describes her meeting with the Prussian General Von Moltke in a Stuttgart hotel before his conquest of France in the Franco-Prussian War (*Private* 110). She also describes the revolt by the French during that period when the Napoleonic eagles, still on the city's light standards, were being brought to earth. Her taking a European wedding trip during this war was itself an act of risk-taking, but war prior to the world wars was for Europe more to do with political change and less to do with the subjugation of people and the destruction of cities.

Within a more contemporary theory of travel literature, both Larzer Ziff in *Return Passages: Great American Travel Writing, 1780–1910* and Alison Russell in *Crossing Boundaries: Postmodern Travel Literature* raise, as Julie Prebel observes, the question: "How does American travel literature function as an index of cultural self-awareness and individual self-definition?" (406). Such questions expand the perspective for judging travel literature from that frequently found in the two characteristics of: (1)the traveler being one with the travel and (2)the writing reflecting that. For it is evident that many of the nineteenth-century writers of travel were not only what Ziff calls "eyes to the world" (140), but were also eyes reflecting their own world, their own varied establishments, often Colonial ones. Critical values about travel writing then and now emphasize the recognition of the Otherness found in the travel; it is an awareness involving not only the views of the writer's own culture, but alsowhat the writer can perceive from the perspective of the "Other."

Many people claim that a person not born in Louisiana cannot be a true Louisianian.People who hold such a position rarely change their closed perspectives. Kate Chopin was born in St. Louis in 1850 and came to New Orleans twenty years later as a bride. Her father-in-law welcomed her as a visitor but rejected her French heritage because it was marred by her father's Irish origins. Furthermore, she arrived during Reconstruction, a time when local people were suspicious of the many visitors who had come from the North to take advantage of the economic rebuilding (a climate not terribly different from that in New Orleans following the flood from Hurricane Katrina). It was during this period that the distinctions between the French Quarter and the American Quarter—the lower Garden District and the Garden District itself—became more acute, even as the French were moving out to more spacious grounds along Esplanade Avenue.

When Kate and Oscar arrived in New Orleans in 1870, they lived at 443 Magazine Street, likely a so-called "shotgun double" structure. They later moved to the corner of Constantinople and Pitt Streets. In 1876, they moved again to a larger double at 209 Louisiana, now numbered 1413. It is at the upper edge of the Garden District. Emily Toth describes the house in her initialbiography: the "downstairs area included front and back parlors with elaborate acanthus-leaves ceiling medallions and two fireplaces, one of blackened stone and the other of reddish brick. Behind the parlors were a dining room or kitchen, and stairs leading to three or four large bedrooms" (130). The house "was surrounded by a lush profusion of shrubs, trees, and flowers" (Toth 130).

Chopin writes about Louisiana with passion and feels its extraordinary sense of place, but she also writes with concerns about cultural self-awareness and individual self-definition. For a late nineteenth-century writer, she reveals an unusual sensitivity to what recent writers and critics would term "the Other." The general chronology of Chopin's experiences in Louisiana begins inNew Orleans, moves toGrand Isle, and then moves toCentral Northwestern Louisiana. Chopin responds in her writings to the people, places, and cultures she encountered in each of these places and found a role for her*self* in this process.

Most readers of American writing know Chopin's second novel, *The Awakening*, which isset in New Orleans and Grand Isle, most likely in the 1870s. Her images of the French Quarter in that bookreflect a closely and highly structured architecture, a kind of purposeful urban environment aimed at producing high income and the leisure that goes with it. The best image of such architectureis the Ratignolle structure with the business locatedon the first floor and the home on the second—business and family arranged cheek by jowl in the European urban tradition. The Ratignolles represent an older society comfortable with this close placement of fiscal and familial properties. Both husband and wife exhibit behaviors indicating comfort in their financial and social roles. The location of the structure, deep in the French Quarter, further exhibits a sense of the family's having been there long enough for them to be considered part of the socialestablishment.

Although the narrator of *The Awakening* seems to develop a nearly objective point of view, Edna Pontellier, the central character, stands clearly as an outsider to this society. Enough evidence exists in the narrative to suggest that Chopin to some degree identifies with Edna. In a later published comment addressing Edna's scandalous ideas and behavior,Chopin playfully suggests some ownership of Edna while admitting that characters can get away from their authors (Chopin, *Private* 296). If we look at Chopin's late adolescent description of the city and the one that develops through this novel, it is clear that the comfort she found in the first response has not lasted.

The location of the Pontellier house on Esplanade represents the movement of the younger French families away from the French Quarter to a more pastoral, less intensely urban environment. Two old homes at the corner of Esplanade and Galvez Street reflect the architecture and gardens of the Pontellier home.Psychologically, Edna likewisetries to be free of confined spaces and limited light. She often leaves her home to walk alone in search of something missing in her life. Edna speaks of the importance of what one learns or discovers in the walking, especially for women, who (she suggests) live in a form of cloister. When she walks and climbs the steps to Mademoiselle Reisz's apartment, a small dark space with a view of the "crescent of the [Mississippi] River"(59), she is moving deep inside herself as she walks from the outskirts of the Quarter to a site deep within it. When she avoids the regularTuesday callers, wives of her husband's clients, she is avoiding the trap of a social architecture that cages her within custom. When she walks out Esplanade toward Bayou St. John to Catiche's al fresco café, she is finding a light and a freedom that she had discovered in her summer on Grand Isle. Curiously, when she leaves the family home for the small cottage, described as a pigeonnière, she retreats into herself like the birds that are kept in such a place to be captured and slaughtered for someone's dinner. Here, she uses architecture as a way of distinguishing what is happening within her. And when "the lamp sputtered and went out," she searches for what light she has come to know, even a winter light (106).

Chopin does not describe the winter journey from New Orleans to Grand Isle, a journey which wasno small task in those days, as it had to be accomplished by land route (train and coach) and water way. She describes Edna on her arrival as "looking tired and a little travel-stained" (107). There the images of her earlier visit at the opening of the novel flash up: the open air, the expansive Gulf, and the light. The water is not warm as it was in summer. The light does not have the same glow. The easy ambience of summer visitors is missing, as Victor Lebrun is "patching a corner of one of the galleries" (106) and his mother and the cottages' servants are away. Edna is a visitor, a traveler who has come here at a time when she is not part of the social center. How often Chopin came here as a summer visitor is not known, but clearly she was less than half French Creole and certainly not an Acadian, and, as a result, would have felt her position on the margin of the society that habitually made its way to the shore of the Gulf each summer.

Grand Isle in the summer, from Chopin's perspective, was a lush tropical paradise, heavy with humidity when the sea breezes waned. Its water oaks, lemon trees, and orange trees complement "the yellow chamomile" (4). One could speculate that the fecund landscape at the edge of the Gulf reflects the fertile body of the novel's protagonist and that the changes in Edna are mirrored in the manner in which the landscape is portrayed. What is so rich in summer declines in winter, paralleling the acquisition of *self* in that first summer on the island and its potential and actual loss during winter. Her uses of the beach, specifically, work in this manner. During summer, the beaches are social with processions of walkers and the presence of bathers—teeming with life, but night scenes on it are empty of society and foreshadow the winter vacuity, emphasizing the title Chopin almost used for the novel, "A Solitary Soul" (see plate, Chopin, *Awakening* [2]).

Critics and scholars since the 1960s have written much about the Gulf of Mexico in *The Awakening*, attending to its symbolic functions of growth, freedom, and even, ironically, beginnings in endings, all amplified by the transcendent effect of sea birds. Chopin's descriptive style moves closer to the romantic than the real when she is using the island as a setting for her characters. Her various echoes of Walt Whitman's lines about the seductiveness of the sea and her composition of vistas across the water to the horizon offer impressionistic images that nearly rival those ofLafcadio Hearn in his novel Chita: A Memory of Last Island (1886). Except when describing the night scenes, she bathes the islands—both Grand Isle and the nearby island of Chênière Caminada—in extraordinary light. It is the same kind of light that the British romantic poets sought in Italy and the Mediterranean, a light that almost transforms the natural and gritty world of sea meeting land into an idyllic vision. In truth Chopin used the light on the sea and its beaches almost as a magic agent, similar in some respects to the magic one finds in medieval romances, for it is in this setting that Edna experiences her epiphany, and yet it is also here where she realizes that she cannot reach the horizon before her and sinks into the depths of the Gulf.

John R. May in his essay "Local Color in *The Awakening*" reminds readers, after the explosion of psychological and early feminist examinations of the novel, that the literal setting in local color writing was central to symbolic and wider realist readings. He compares Chopin's use of color to Stephen Crane's, but he finds the "strokes of her brush less jarring," pointing out the similarity between the meadow of Edna's youth and the sea of her adult circumstance, and linking the architecture of the Pontellier house on Esplanade Street to the social "restraints of the Creole city" (1031-40). The term *local color* was still a widely used one in 1970 when May wrote his essay. It had been used somewhat derisively to describe writing that was limited to extolling the features of a region at the expense of characters' psychological development as the controlling force in a story's composition. And yet it had its defenders who would cite Flaubert's dictum that all realism begins in the local. While Chopin's short fiction defined her status as a local color writer for many years, her use of setting actually serves as a beginning of a larger vision.

In 1879, after nearly a decade of living in New Orleans, Kate Chopin and her family moved to Cloutierville, Louisiana, where they resided until 1884, two years after her husband's death. Kate Chopin's mother-in-law, Julia Benoist Chopin, was actually born in Cloutierville, and sometime after her marriage, she moved to the nearby McAlpin Plantation. We know that her husband treated his son's wife as an outsider, but there is little or no evidence of his wife's attitudes towards her daughter-in-law. If Chopin was on the margins of society in New Orleans, she was definitely an outsider here in this village near the Cane River. Toth addresses this aspect of Chopin's life at some length, commenting on her urban fashions and manner (141). As New Orleans had provided a base for travel in South Louisiana for Chopin, Cloutierville provided her with a similar opportunity in Central Northwestern Louisiana.

The Chopin, Kate house—later known as the Bayou Folk Museum—burned to the ground in October 2008. The chimney now overlooks the ruins around it. The house stood on Louisiana Hwy 495 in Cloutierville. The size of the town, closer to that of a village, has changed little since the early 1880s when Chopin lived there with her family. Horses and wagons once traveled the then dirt street with wooden sidewalks. From the front gallery of the house, Chopin could look across the slowly meandering Cane River to the cultivated fields beyond. The house itself, built on brick piers, would have survived any high water from an overflow of the river. The main rooms were six to seven feet above a ground-level basement. The house was more charming and gracious than elegant, for in the Mississippi Valley, it was rare to have an elegant home far from the Mississippi River, the route which artisans in the fine building trades traveled.

As she had doneearlier in New Orleans, Chopin collected characters and experiences for her fiction in and around the settlement on the Cane River. In her writing, she used "the village" (as she often referred to Cloutierville) in a many stories, at least once describing it as "two long rows of very old frame houses" (*Works* 105). She set her first novel in the country near this village, where the modern world had begun to arrive in the form of the railroad and the lumber mills. In *At Fault*, Chopin re-creates the landscape of Central-Northwestern Louisiana, including its plateaus, its bayous and swamps, and its near mountain-like hills. Her literary treatment of these areas follows mostly in the realist tradition, and she frequently contrasts characters rooted in the landscape to Northern visitorsto develop her fiction as social criticism. The arrival of the railroad as part of this post-Civil War change affected the Chopin family and agricultural business as the railroad divided the Chopin plantation, which was being managed by Oscar Chopin's brother Lamy. While *At Fault*, Chopin's firstnovel, is not closely autobiographical, it does draw on her experiences and observations from her nearly five years of residence.

At Fault, like her later novel *The Awakening*, focuses on change, here on characters and their society, whose pastoral culture is in the process of being altered by the latest iterations of the Industrial Revolution. Chopin names the plantation "Place-du-Bois"—"Place of the Woods or Forest"—and emphasizes the disturbance of industry by Thérèse LaFirme, the protagonist, having to move the plantation home because of the arrival of the railroad. In the South, the "highways" about which towns developed in pre-Civil War years were the navigable rivers and streams; in the post Civil War period, the railroads provided the catalysts for that kind of development.

The close association of landscape and mind set—even body consciousness—in *The Awakening* has at least one prelude in *At Fault*. When Thérèse's nephew takes the St. Louis visitor Melicent into the cypress swamp, the setting reflects the psychological uncertainty of their early stage of romance. The descriptions of the swamp have some of the uncertainty and beauty that she used in handling the places where water and land meet in *The Awakening*. The swamp here lies near *Lac du Bois*, which the couple enters by pirogue after traversing the swamp. Chopin's descriptions have a less urgent and more relaxed quality than in the other chapters of the novel and in the early short stories: for instance, she describes"the dense canopy of an overarching tree . . . whose extreme branches dipped quite into the slow moving water," and she also depicts "the bayou, that was now so entirely sheltered from the open light of the sky by the meeting branches above, as to seem a dim leafy tunnel." Chopin also engages more than visual images by emphasizing the aural: "The dull plash of some object falling into the water, or the wild call of a lonely bird were the only sounds that broke upon the stillness, beside the monotonous dipping of the oars and the occasional low undertones of their own voices." Chopin gives us threatening images as well, including "the doleful hum of a gray swarm of mosquitoes" and "the black upturned nozzle" of a water moccasin. When the couple moves into the openness of the lake, "with the broad canopy of the open sky above them" (*Works* 749), Chopin paints a narrative of this watery landscape from its peril to its beauty, offering us a nearly allegorical look at the nature of romantic relationships.

While *At Fault* has a structure and general technique that remind readers more of popular romances than literary novels, embedded in its development are elements that we would associate with travel literature. The use of the summer visitor is a convention in much popular fiction, but Chopin makes the presence of Hosmer, who represents the sawmill industry, more a matter of an invading force, not unlike the federal forces that decimated so many plantations and towns in this area just thirty or so years before, but the romances between Thérèse and Hosmer and that between Melicent, Hosmer's sister, and Grêgoire blunt the blade of what is happening to the terrain and its constituent society.

Chopin traveled regularly in this country for social and family occasions at the homes spread out along the Cane River and beyond. Although she had six children, it is obvious that she had assistance to allow her the freedom to travel about nearby Natchitoches and the region. When her husband died in 1882, she took over the management of the plantation. Chopin set all or parts of well over twenty stories in or around Natchitoches.

While many of these stories have mainlyincidental settings, some have settings that have psychological implications. The most anthologized of her stories, "Désirée's Baby" is set along the Texas Road between Cloutierville and Natchitoches. As in *At Fault*, a swamp scene is critical to the narrative: Désirée with her child "disappeared among the reeds and willows that grew thick along the banks of the deep, sluggish bayou; and she did not come back again" (*Works* 244). In *The Awakening*, published seven years later, Edna merelyacquiesces to her fate in the Gulf, butDésirée purposefully chooses death in water rather than having a death-in-life experience. Chopin uses bodies of water as catalysts for change, but she also uses them as barriers, as in "Beyond the Bayou," in which a black woman has a shock early in her life and the bayou becomes an agent of her separation from a full and sound life for many years. In that story, the old woman finally conquers the power of an incident long in memory and crosses the bayou to a full life. Chopin offers the prose effect of a painted scene: "When she had made her way through the brush and scrub cottonwood-trees that lined the opposite bank, she found herself on the border of a field, where the white, bursting cotton, with the dew upon it, gleamed for acres and acres like frosted silver in the early dawn" (*Works* 179).

The town of Alexandria, just south of Cloutierville, has minor roles in Chopin's stories, but in "Vagabonds," the narrator encounters a man down on his luck walking to Alexandria to look for a job. Two details make this story significant: (1)the crossing of the river by ferry, suggesting a near mythical encounter with the boatman Charon and (2)the emphasis on walking by the female first person narrator—the lattera motif that alsodominates *The Awakening* four years later. In her fiction, Chopin always cites Alexandria as a comparatively urbane and economically progressive destination.

Chopin's fiction takes readers from the vacation spot of Grand Isle to the trade and agricultural center of Shreveport, from the train depot in Gretna to war-devastated Grand Coteau, and from river plantations in Iberville Parish to the rude frontier life of Sabine Parish. In several stories, Chopin shows that keen awareness of "the Other" in society, but she showsthe Other having a specific identity tied to race and ethnicity. In a sense, she identifies with the people she describes, looking through others' eyes and abandoning her own uniqueness as an individual. In "A Gentleman of Bayou Têche," she creates a situation in which a visitor to the Hallet Plantation asks an Acadian to pose as subject for his sketching. For the visitor, the Acadian is clearly an exotic. At first, the man agrees to pose for him and then changes his mind. Later, after rescuing the visitor's son from drowning, the Acadian agrees to sit for him, so long as his dignity is observed. Gesturing with his finger as if he were writing, he demands, however, that beneath the illustration in the magazine would appear this caption "Dis is one picture of Mista Evariste Anatole Bonamour, a gent'man of de Bayou Têche" (*Works* 324). At the close, even though this man is illiterate, Chopin gives him a dignity, a sense of worth. This story is a comment by Chopin on the range, if not the abuses, of some of the writing that became known as local color. The artist here is associated with a magazine, and magazines like *Harper's* advanced this type of literature to audiences in the Northeast who were fascinated with anecdotes brought back by veterans of the Civil War.

The reference to the Têche evokes the legend of Longfellow's poem "Evangeline" as the story "At Chênière Caminada" reaches into the romantic world of the Baratarians.

Chopin creates a situation of a dream coming true for a young Acadian fisherman who falls in love during a summer at the island with a daughter of a famous Creole lawyer in New Orleans. During the winter, she dies, and his grief turns into feelings of liberation like those of Louise Mallard in "The Story of an Hour," published the following year.

"At Chênière Caminada,"published six years before *The Awakening*,foreshadows the novel's geographical settings and the role of the Other in society. Unlike "A Gentleman of Bayou Têche," in which Chopin turns a humorous anecdote into a societal lesson, "At Chênière Caminada" hints at the dissolution of Tonie's dream; it refers to deaths in the islands amid a storm on Barataria Bay, all the while maintaining a detached point of view, so important in *The Awakening*.

If passion and enthusiasm are requisites for a writer of travel literature, Chopin demonstrates those traits, especially in her presentation of the culinary culture of French Louisiana. Both novels and stories contain descriptions of various dishes, including gumbo and court-boullion. Dinners in her writings reflect the social occasions of this culture, but she also uses them as narrative devices, sometimes signaling shifts of thematic direction, as in *The Awakening* when Edna, "bewildered" at news of Robert's leaving for Mexico, embarrassingly reveals her affection for him (40). Of course, the farewell dinner at the Pontellier home with Edna's friends offers a captivating description of fine dining in New Orleans, but it is also a ritual shift toward an intensified interior life in her subsequent move to a smaller residence and its "shallow *parterre* that had been somewhat neglected" (87).

Accordingly, Chopin presents a full picture of culinary customs in this region, as in *The Awakening* at the Creole dinner on Edna's birthday: "Oh, it will be very fine; all my best of everything—crystal, silver, and gold, Sèvres, flowers, music, and champagne to swim in. . . . . wax candles in massive brass candelabra, burning softly under yellow silk shades; full fragrant roses, yellow and red." Chopin also describes "the garnet lights" of a cocktail—a relatively new term then—invented by Edna's father to celebrate her birthday (81, 83). The elegant images of cuisine here have similar effects of wonder as those in contemporary slick magazines. The description of a breakfast setting with "a small golden-brown crusty loaf of French bread at each plate" in "Athènaïse" has a simple and *appealing* elegance (*Works* 443). In contrast, Chopin offers several robust descriptions of Acadian gumbos. In "A Night in Acadie," Chopin describes the process of cooking a gumbo: ". . . into the pot went the chickens and the pans full of minced ham, and the fists-full of onion and sage and piment rouge and piment vert" (*Works* 489). It is in the descriptions of cuisine and culinary experiences that Chopin nearly breaks from her disciplined narrative detachment.

As a writer of travel literature, Chopin translates the experience of travel, the value, as Robert Louis Stevenson noted, beingin the journey and not the arrival. Furthermore, the real traveler is changed in some way by the people, places, and situations she encounters. Chopin, indeed, bears the marks of change throughout her life. Because Chopin was born in the gateway to the West, it was not unusual for her to be conscious of women and their families as they passed through St. Louis moving west. In fact, seven years before her birth, The Great Migration initiated the most populous patterns of westward migrations. The regular river traffic of Chopin's great grandmother's steamship line between St. Louis and New Orleans alsobroadened Chopin's perspectives about place and boundaries. When a friend suggested that she write a memoir, a witty discussion ensued, at the conclusion of which her friend said, "I guess you'd better stick to inventions." She said, "I guess I had" (*Works* 717). Indeed, it has been Chopin's fiction that has carried us through her various journeys. By the time she was writing what was to become *The Awakening,* her use of place had largely changed to that of a symbolist, a writer with distance on her material, a traveler geographically and psychologically.

Works Cited

Chopin, Kate. *The Awakening.* Ed. Margo Culley. 2nd ed. New York: Norton, 1994. 1976.

_____. *The Complete Works of Kate Chopin.* Ed. Per Seyersted.Baton Rouge: Louisiana State UP, 1997. 1969.

_____. *Kate Chopin's Private Papers.* Ed. Emily Toth and Per Seyersted. Bloomington: Indiana UP, 1998.

May, John, R. "Local Color in *The Awakening.*" *Southern Review* 6 (1970): 1031–40.

Preble, Julie. Review of *Return Passages: Great American Travel Writing* by Larzer Ziff and *Crossing Boundaries: Post Modern Travel Literature* by Alison Russell. *American Literature* 74.2 (2002): 406–408.

Toth, Emily. *Kate Chopin.* New York: Morrow, 1990.

Ward, Adolphus and William Trent, et al. *The Cambridge History of English and American Literature.* Vol. 14, Part 2. New York: G.P. Putnam's Sons, 1907–21. *Bartleby.com.* 2000. Web. 22 Oct. 2013. <www.bartleby.com/cambridge/>.

Ziff, Larzer. *Return Passages: Great American Travel Writing.* New Haven: Yale UP, 2000.

Catching Up with Kate Chopin: Reading Chopin Reading_____

Mary E. Papke

Martha Graham, echoing Edgard Varese among others, declared that "No artist is ahead of his time. He is his time; it is just that others are behind the times." We have certainly been a very long while catching up to Kate Chopin's "time," and in many ways, the dimensions of her time still elude us in our understanding of *The Awakening*. Virtually forgotten for half a century, recuperated by male Southern specialists and non-American Americanists, then by second-wave feminist scholars, Chopin's major work continues to call forth a steady stream of criticism that seeks to unveil and explain the mystery of her novel's appeal. Categorized during her life first as a local color/regionalist Southern writer, then more broadly as a realist, and most recently as a naturalist, Chopin neatly fit the parameters of these related literary movements in most of her works.

Yet, *The Awakening*, seems different. While many of her early and mid-career writings openly address issues of gender, class, race, and sexual preference that mark her work as social fiction, *The Awakening* also reaches for what Raymond Williams called a "new structure of feeling," a desire for a new way of being in the world that is as yet nascent, under construction, not yet fully conscious (131–132). Chopin's novel famously refuses closure precisely because she worked so hard to introduce and develop this new structure of feeling that she hoped would speak powerfully to her readers and move them to translate private feeling into social action.

I would like to focus attention on four novels from Chopin's "time," all of which are rarely discussed at length in Chopin scholarship, though their affinity with The Awakening is striking. Two are American works, and two are not, for, as several critics have reminded us time and time again, Chopin was of at least two distinct cultures—American and French—and read widely in several

hiding in another city with a religious family. Here the novel takes an important turn, refocusing on Petra's innate ability to become an artist of the stage and also onthe unique ability of art, unlike life, to speak truth. As one character posits:

> "But supposing you read a fictitious story which resembled your own experience in such a manner that it made you understand yourself; would you not say of that story which gave you the key to your life, and which gave you the comfort and courage gained by knowledge, that you found more truth in it than in your own life?" (Björnson 227–228)

At the end of the novel, we see the promise of Petra's coming into her own, performing for the first time for an audience that includes her ex-lovers, her second family, and her mother. The last line is "Then the curtain rose!" (274).

The novel's effect depends on the exceptionalism of the two main female characters and on the factthat each must learn that "no person becomes perfectly true in all his relations before he has found his right calling" (266). We see in the novel the negative effects of an authoritarianism, whether this be channeled through parent, priest, or lover, that deems it appropriate to bend others to one's will. We also witness the man instinct of possession in two of Petra's suitors, an instinct that effectively denies a woman's desire for self-possession. Such will to power leads repeatedly to the repression of sensuality and pleasure. Standing apart from, but always present in this scenario of thwarted desires, is the sublimity of the inhuman landscape. In particular, the sea is a constant presence for the fisher-maidens and a means of escape from untenable romantic attachments. While the novel ends happily—everyone (even Petra's father) finds his or her true relation to others—it also ends with a beginning, literally Petra's opening enactment of self in all her mutual contradictions. In light of all this, it should not surprise us that Chopin wrote "Emancipation. A Life Fable" shortly after reading Björnson's novel. In her fable, her reimagining of Plato's myth of the cave, an animal happens to find its cage door open one day. Taking a chance on finding its true relation to a real world, it forgoes the security of the cage/cave for "seeking, finding, joying and suffering" (38). Perhaps Chopin did not copy extracts from Björnson's novel into her Commonplace book, but instead translated his heroine's quest for self-authenticity and life into her own "time" and language. "Emancipation" nevertheless also went under erasure, kept in her private papers and made available to readers only in 1969 with Seyersted's edition of her complete works. Key elements of her fable and Björnson's novel will reemerge in new forms later in *The Awakening*.

A much more direct and traceable influence on Chopin was her intense study of Guy de Maupassant's fiction. As she recalled in "Confidences," a private document written in 1896:

> Here was life, not fiction....Here was a man who had escaped from tradition and authority, who had entered into himself and looked out upon life through his own being and with his own eyes; and who, in a direct and simple way, told us what he saw. When a man does this, he gives us the best that he can; something valuable for it is genuine and spontaneous...Someway I like to cherish the delusion that he has spoken to no one else so directly, so intimately as he does to me. (700-01)

Chopin translated several of his stories in the years immediately preceding and overlapping with her work on *The Awakening*. Almost all the stories she chose depict passion taken to the extreme, madness, intense alienation, and moral vacuity. No publisher would touch the volume once she was done. Despite this rejection (perhaps a warning), Chopin would address similar issues of divorce, sensuous awakening, obsession and suicide in her last novel. Perhaps the rejection of her Maupassant volume did affect one longstanding mystery in her novel—the withholding of the name of the novel Edna reads at Grand Isle and finds so shocking, although the other women do not and discuss it openly at meals. We know that two other volumes are being circulated and read, something by Daudet and a book referred to as the Goncourt (novels, then, of classic French naturalism). The mystery novel could be Honoré de Balzac's *La Femme de trent ans* of 1834, and Dieter Schulz draws cursory parallels between Edna and Balzac's Marquis d'Aiglemont, but Balzac's novel hardly fits the seeming propensity for naturalist works among the readers at the resort. Gustave Flaubert's *Madame Bovary* of 1851 naturally comes to mind, with its tale of adultery and grotesque suicide, so much so that Willa Cather immediately labeled Chopin's work "a Creole Bovary" in her review (170). The book might even conceivably be Emile Zola's *Thérèse Raquin* of 1867 or his *Nana* of 1880, although we know that Chopin was not altogether sure of Zola's artistic agenda and questioned the truth of his vision (see, for example, her review of *Lourdes*). Another serious possibility would be Maupassant's *Une Vie* (*A Life*), published in 1883, its title resonating with Chopin's original "A Solitary Soul." In both works, a woman of high social class is led to believe in the sacredness of marriage, the rite conceived of, at first, as the natural extension of idealized romance and, then, after that delusion is put to rest by the realities of quotidian co-existence and the wife's expected full submission to the husband's will, as nothing more than a plot to reproduce the same social hegemony endlessly and at the cost of a woman's individual desires. Maupassant's Jeanne is raised by a free-thinking father and a virtually absent mother, trapped as she is in a grossly obese body and suffering a weak heart. Jeanne is later sequestered in a convent until she comes of age. She then makes the terrible mistake of misrecognizing the man who courts her as the ideal lover and husband. Instead, he proves to be a miser, an inveterate philanderer (he forces himself on Jeanne's maid as soon as he and Jeanne return from their honeymoon and then takes up with her best friend), a poor father, jealous of any attention given to his child—in short, a cad of the first order. I'm not so sure that any of the above would necessarily shock Edna since she has already given up any illusions about why she married and what many men are like. What would have shocked and shamed her into reading the book in private is the explicit physicality of certain scenes, particularly that of the violence of the wedding night and, somewhat later, the highly eroticized depiction of Jeanne's sexual awakening. Erotics give way quickly to two graphic birth scenes: the first highly disturbing, since Jeanne's maid suddenly gives birth before her to her husband's illegitimate child, the second dramatically overwrought, as Jeanne gives birth prematurely to her own son. Two other birth scenes come much later in the text, Jeanne's delivery of a much-desired, but stillborn, daughter, after her husband and his lover are killed by her husband. Then, there is the whelping of a litter, made grotesquely tragic when the local priest, infuriated at any such reminder of sex and its consequences, beats the helpless bitch and then tramples her to death. His gruesome act saves Jeanne from an increasing religious fanaticism, though it also marks the loss of any sort of recompense or comfort through the Church. Jeanne in her life loses, not unexpectedly, her parents, but she also suffers the unexpected loss of her husband's affection, then her husband himself, and the woman she considered her best friend, the daughter she craved, her son, who proves too like his father and is seduced by big cities, big money, and an easy woman, and then her faith. Later, she loses her chateau and most of her property, and, for a time, her mind. Perhaps the most subjective loss is her connection and communion with the sea that she views daily from her bedroom window before she is made to move. When she had returned to the chateau after years at the convent, the narration tells us that "She developed a passion for bathing. She would swim off into the distance, strong and bold, oblivious to the danger. It felt good to be in this cold, clear, blue water that lifted her up and rocked her to and fro. When she was far from the shore, she would lie on her back, her arms folded across her chest, and gaze into the deep blue of the sky broken only by the sudden flight of a swallow or the white silhouette of a seabird" (19). After she loses the chateau, she slowly comes to realize what the sea signified for her alone:

> it was the sea that she had been missing so much, her great neighbor for twenty-five years, the sea with its salty air, its angry moods, its scolding voice, its powerful gales, the sea which she could glimpse every morning from her window at Les Peuples, whose air she breathed day and night, of whose presence nearby she was always conscious, and which she had come to love like a living person without realizing that she did. (217)

The sea, then, is her idealized lover who will never betray her.

Ironically, Jeanne is rescued from utter despair by the maid who slept with her husband. Rosalie comes back to nurse Jeanne back to health, takes over the run of her properties, and helps her reconnect with her son, albeit in a very strange fashion. Paul writes Jeanne that he has married his lover just before she died giving birth to a daughter whom he entrusts to Jeanne's care. Whether this child brings joy or sorrow remains to be seen. However, the ending is another beginning of sorts, an odd conclusion to an otherwise grim naturalist account of a woman's life.

Edna might also have been shocked not only by the intensity of Jeanne's sexual awakening but by her consequent decision to reject sex and sensuality completely, to repress the deeply-felt pleasure she discovers and to invest herself instead in becoming a mother-woman, only then to be later abandoned and yet repeatedly manipulated by her son. Another novel Chopin admired greatly documents, in even more detail for a whole social milieu, the effects of the repression of desire and the refusal to feel empathy for others.

We know from Chopin's "Impressions. 1894," published in 1976 in *A Kate Chopin Miscellany*, how much she admired Mary E. Wilkins (later Freeman). On May 12, 1894, she wrote, "I know of no one better than Miss Jewett to study for technique and nicety of construction. I don't mention Mary E. Wilkins for she is a great genius and genius is not to be studied" (90), a curious sort of putting a whole body of work under erasure, as in some ways unapproachable except through adoration. On June 7, 1894, in an entry bemoaning the critical vacuity of the press notices for *Bayou Folk*, she abruptly turns attention to Wilkins' *Pembroke*, calling it "the most profound, the most powerful piece of fiction of its kind that has ever come from the American press," noting as well the "senseless" newspaper reviews it received (96). Wilkins' reviewers, as will eerily occur later in the case of Chopin's novel, show "no feeling for the spirit of the work, the subtle genius which created it" (96). No doubt written to make Chopin feel better about her own reviews, the entry also directs us to yet another examination of the consequences of exacting will that Chopin may have recalled when laboring over her own great novel.

Pembroke is still today considered a minor regionalist work, part of the so-called New England twilight literature. It focuses on the dying off of the Puritan legacy of communal iron will and little mercy for those who transgress the will of the patriarchs. Wilkins herself introduces the novel as such, which description does not, however, preclude our reading the work as demonstrating the inheritance of most white Americans. Again, it is a story of thwarted love but multiplied in a community so inbred and authoritarian in the extreme that it is hard to distinguish one character from another. We see a patriarch working in collusion with a mother, who has taken over the power of a father, a patriarchy signified openly in the names of the two major adult figures—Cephas, Peter's Aramaic name in the Gospels, and Deborah, recalling the prophetess and judge of Israel. Ironically, even though Cephas is the instigator of the terrible communal tragedy in the novel, he will be allowed redemption by the end, whereas Deborah is not, suggesting that the community must give up the harsh ways demanded by the Old Testament for the more forgiving and inclusive Christianity of the New Testament. In short, the characters must learn and then embrace a new structure of feeling.

The story is simple, yet complicated by continual duplication of betrayal and self-alienation. Deborah's son Barnabas loves Charlotte Barnard, but because of a ridiculous argument with her father, Cephas, over politics, he simultaneously abandons her, is banished from her house, and exiles himself from his family home to the half-finished structure he was building for Charlotte. Trapped by this argument in Cephas's house by her sister Sarah, Charlotte's mother, Sylvia misses her standing visit from her long-time suitor, who then abandons her because he feels betrayed. Hannah, Sarah and Sylvia's other sister, will later be witness to another disastrous effect of the argument, as her son becomes secretly involved with Deborah's daughter, whom Deborah then casts out of the family home when she discovers Rebecca's pregnancy. The novel goes on to detail the long suffering of the majority of characters, who nevertheless prove intransigent in their willful harsh judgment of others. And so years pass—miserably.

Two events bring the novel's perverse scenario to an ending that is, like those in the previously discussed novels, a sort of beginning. Deborah prides herself on her righteous authoritarianism, particularly in the case of her extremely fragile son Ephraim, her denying him the simplest of pleasures and the common experiences of rustic boyhood supposedly for the good not of his health but of his soul. After he commits a minor transgression, she begins to beat him, and he dies at the first stroke. While Deborah believes she was acting from "a high purpose," the narration gestures instead to "the part which her own human will" had in her choice of actions, her will to power over all others (194). She later learns that her son had secretly gone sledding the night before his death and eaten a large slice of mince pie, his forbidden fruit. Deborah grasps at this knowledge as exonerating her of causing his death. She then immediately suffers a stroke and dies shortly thereafter. She does call for her two other children before dying, including the daughter she cast out, but we cannot be sure whether she meant to express love, something she has not done anywhere in the story, or to assure herself that she has done right by them, no matter the consequences. That is, she remembers the children, but whether it is because she is a good mother-woman or powerfully self-centered, we cannot be sure.

The second incident involves Sylvia, long abandoned by her lover and, as we intuit as the story progresses, by her kinfolk and community as well. Her family, we learn, "were interested in not knowing" (214) how close to abject poverty Sylvia comes after years of selling off property. Her own sisters claim they "knew nothing whatever," a sort of willful ignorance that absolves them from having to act on behalf of someone else's well-being. In fact, just before Sylvia is forced into exiling herself to the poorhouse, they shame her into giving up the last two items of value to her as a wedding gift for Hannah's daughter—her family's silver spoons and the sofa she bought for her lover's courting of her. Her lover, not her family, rescues her at the last moment.

If Sylvia's suffering is pathetic, that of Barnabas is incomprehensible except as illustrative of the consequences of intransigent will. He is repeatedly given chances to forgive and forget the actions that have isolated him not only from his lover but from his community, but he cannot do so, admitting that his own self-centeredness has hurt his soul. And, by the end of the novel, he is physically manifesting his soul's sickness in a crippling deformity of the spine that some witness and others do not. At the same time, he experiences an intense man-instinct for possession of Charlotte, whom he believes will marry another, but, like Sylvia before her rescue, can only cry piteously and bemoan fate. He, in turn, must be rescued by the lover he abandoned who cares for him during a near-fatal illness, despite her father's threat of permanent banishment. Humbled by her love for him, Barnabas sends her home and then makes a penitential trek to her house, literally standing up straight by the end for himself and his lover. Cephas welcomes him in, and the novel closes with this beginning: "And Barney entered the house with his old sweetheart and his old self" (254).

Why did Chopin consider this the greatest of all American novels of its kind? Perhaps, as I have suggested, it illustrates the legacy of many Americans, a legacy of the drive to individual self-satisfaction coupled with a will to power that is purposefully oblivious to the suffering of others. Perhaps, if we look forward to Chopin's critique of regionalism's limitations evident in her critical essays, this novel eschews "provincialism" for "human existence in its subtle, complex, true meaning, stripped of the veil with which ethical and conventional standards have draped it" ("Western Association" 691). The novel most certainly strips bare the pretensions, obsessions, and self-delusions of its various characters but leaves open any final judgment on those left standing at the novel's end. Is Barney's "old self" worthy of resurrection? Will Charlotte's decision to live according to a new structure of feeling change community ways of being? Again, as with any open ending, much remains to be seen.

Lafcadio Hearn's *Chita*, the last novel to be considered, has the most obvious affinities with Chopin's work, though I cannot verify that Chopin ever read it. Christopher Benfey, the editor of the Library of America edition of Hearn's works, agrees, writing of *Chita*, "it's such an exquisite balance of natural forces, tragic characters, and the bewitching landscape of the Gulf islands….I'm convinced that *Chita* had a major influence on writers like Kate Chopin, who covered some of the same terrain in her classic novel *The Awakening*" (Kelley 4). Set in the Gulf and in New Orleans, *Chita* recalls the 1856 destruction of Last Island by hurricane and the aftermath for a child who survived, who is, in essence, born out of the sea and given a new life. Beyond this, the intricacies of plot need not concern us, but the back history and impressionistic rendering of the setting should. Arlin Turner claims, in his introduction to the novel:

> It stands all but unique in our literature. Its special qualities result from the refraction of an exotic scene and extravagant action through the mind of an author who was a thorough-going romantic by temperament and conviction and who was, nevertheless, a disciple of Herbert Spencer and an exponent of evolutionary theory. (ix)

We will, of course, see the same heady mixture of romanticism, naturalism, and impressionistic evocation in Chopin's novel.

Part one of *Chita* offers us provocative insight into the setting of part one of *The Awakening*. Here Hearn describes the Grand Isle resorts as "plantation-residences…converted into rustic hotels, and the negro-quarters remodeled into villages of cozy cottages for the reception of guests…." (11). Here, then, slave history is reinscribed after it has been whitewashed, erased. Part one goes on to record the legend of Last Island, includinghow four hundred Creoles danced in the grand hotel while French-speaking servants waited upon them even as the hurricane approached. The Southerners' willful obliviousness to impending disaster results in the death of virtually all present, a foreshadowing of the losses that will be suffered in the coming Civil War. The girl rescued and renamed Chita is saved both through the agency of her mother and by chance, signified by the billiard table on which Chita is found, bound to her mother's corpse.

Chita will later be haunted by her mother's spirit, but she is also, early on, haunted by the very element in which she is discovered. As Hearn writes, "the Voice of the Sea is never one voice, but a tumult of many voices—voices of drowned men, —the muttering of multitudinous dead, —the moaning of innumerable ghosts, all rising, to rage against the living" (19). Later, the narrative voice insists that one may desire to swim out alone, but one will do this only once: "Then the fear of the Abyss, the vast and voiceless Nightmare of the Sea, will come upon you" (26). Only in a crowd of bathers can one feel safe: "numbers give courage, —one can abandon one's self, with fear of the invisible, to the long, quivering electric caresses of the sea...." (27, ellipsis in original). Chita, however, does not have the luxury of such a leisurely group swim; as her foster father makes clear, "'The world is like the sea: those who do not know how to swim in it are drowned; —and the sea is like the world,' he added.... 'Chita must learn to swim!'" (157, ellipsis in original). Once she does so, she becomes one with the ocean, and she is thereafter never alone: "But always, —always, dreaming or awake, she heard the huge blind Sea chanting that mystic and eternal hymn, which none may hear without awe, which no musician can learn;—" (152). Because Chita affiliates herself so strongly with Nature, she enters the permanent dream state of Gulf life: "Then slowly, caressingly, irresistibly, the witchery of the Infinite grows upon you: out of Time and Space you begin to dream with open eyes,—to drift into delicious oblivion to facts,—to forget the past, the present, the substantial,—to comprehend nothing but the existence of that infinite Blue Ghost as something into which you would wish to melt utterly away forever...." (21, ellipsis in original). Hearn's work thus suggests to readers of our time that despite the despair that Chopin's heroine experiences in her last days, her naked reunion with the sea can also be read as a new beginning, in which she is at last freed to enjoy the ceaseless sensual caresses of the sea while surrounded by "the hum of bees and the musky odor of pinks" (109).

In all five of the novels discussed here, the central female character must lose virtually everything she values before imagining a new structure of feeling that would enable self-presentation and community revitalization. Petra is allowed to embrace her mutual contradictions and so changes the hearts of the people who cared for her; perhaps her art will speak truth to a larger community.

Jeanne literally embraces a new structure of feeling about class and privilege when she takes in her illegitimate granddaughter and allows her one-time maid the authority she once exercised over her. Charlotte quietly lives according to a new structure of feeling and so saves Barney's heart and soul; whether she can teach her larger community the importance of compassion and empathy for others remains in question. Edna desperately wishes to embrace a new structure of feeling once she is awakened to it, but she remains, throughout her experience, a solitary soul. For her, there will be no rescue; for her, it is too late or, perhaps, too early, simply not her time, but Chopin refuses to end the novel in despair or death. Through her, nevertheless, we are granted insight into the invidious ideological proscriptions that deny any possibility of anyone's true relation to self, calling, and community. This is why *The Awakening* still matters, why we continue to be moved by the story of one woman, one life. As Chopin intimates in the last lines, we must choose either simply to close the book on poor Edna, erasing her from our thoughts, or to take up the challenge of following in Edna's wake until we reach Chopin's dream of a new way of being in this world.

Works Cited

Björnson, Björnstjerne. *The Fisher Maiden*. Trans. Rasmus B. Anderson. NY: Doubleday, Page & Co., 1882.

Cather, Willa [Sibert]. "A *Creole* Bovary". *The Awakening*. Ed. Margo Culley. 2nd ed. NY: W.W. Norton & Company, 1994. 170–172.

Chopin, Kate. *The Awakening*. Ed. Margo Culley. 2nd ed. NY: W.W. Norton & Company, 1994.

_____. "Common Place Book. 1867-1870." *A Kate Chopin Miscellany*. Eds. Per Seyersted and Emily Toth. Natchitoches: Northwestern State UP, 1979. 47–88.

_____. *The Complete Works of Kate Chopin*. Ed. Per Seyersted. Baton Rouge: Louisiana State UP, 1997.

_____. "Confidences." *The Complete Works of Kate Chopin*. Ed. Per Seyersted. Baton Rouge: Louisiana State UP, 1997. 700–702.

_____. "Emancipation. A Life Fable." *The Complete Works of Kate Chopin*. Ed. Per Seyersted. Baton Rouge: Louisiana State UP, 1997. 37–38.

_____. "Emile Zola's 'Lourdes.'" *The Complete Works of Kate Chopin*. Ed. Per Seyersted. Baton Rouge: Louisiana State UP, 1997. 697–699.

_____. "Impressions. 1894." *A Kate Chopin Miscellany*. Eds. Per Seyersted and Emily Toth. Natchitoches: Northwestern State UP, 1979. 89–99.

_____. *A Kate Chopin Miscellany*. Eds. Per Seyersted and Emily Toth. Natchitoches: Northwestern State UP, 1979.

_____. "The Western Association of Writers." *The Complete Works of Kate Chopin*. Ed. Per Seyersted. Baton Rouge: Louisiana State UP, 1997. 691–692.

Freeman, Mary E. Wilkins. *Pembroke*. New Haven: College & UP, 1971.

Hearn, Lafcadio. *Chita: A Memory of Last Island*. Chapel Hill: U of North Carolina P, 1969.

Kelley, Rich. "The Library of America Interviews Christopher Benfey About Lafcadio Hearn." *The Library of America e-Newsletter*. Web. 20 August 2013.

Maupassant, Guy de. *A Life: The Humble Truth*. Trans. Roger Pearson. Oxford: Oxford UP, 1999.

Schulz, Dieter. "Notes toward a Fin-de-siècle Reading of Kate Chopin's *The Awakening*." *American Literary Realism, 1870-1910* 25.3 (Spring 1993): 69–76.

Seyersted, Per. *Kate Chopin: A Critical Biography*. Baton Rouge: Louisiana State UP, 1980.

Toth, Emily. *Kate Chopin*. NY: William Morrow and Co., Inc., 1990.

Turner, Arlin. "Introduction." *Chita: A Memory of Last Island*. Chapel Hill: U of North Carolina P, 1969. ix-xxxxiv.

Williams, Raymond. *Marxism and Literature*. Oxford: Oxford UP, 1977.

In Praise of Folly: Gendered Discourse in *The Awakening*

Robert D. Arner

On three separate occasions (and on one linked occasion) in Kate Chopin's *The Awakening*, Léonce Pontellier accuses his wife of "folly," which is a gendered term historicallyapplied principally to women. (The first-person speaker of Erasmus's *In Praise of Folly* [1509], for example, certainly—except for certain chapters in Proverbs, the best-known literary work in which the character of Folly appears—is a woman.) Léonce's first use of the term occurs early in the book, specifically in chapter one, as Edna and Robert Lebrun make their way back from the beach, and Léonce criticizes Edna for swimming so late in the day: "'What folly to bathe at such an hour in such heat'" (4). Despite her use of the sunshade, he claims she has been "'burnt beyond recognition'" by the sun and looks disapprovingly "at his wife as one looks at a valuable piece of personal property which has suffered some damage" (4).

Léonce's idea that his wife is already beyond his recognition is truer than he knows; something has begun to happen to Edna in her proximity to the ocean, her exposure to the ocean's sensory stimuli that the novel attempts to articulate in its famous refrain. Hers is clearly an awakening of the sensual and sexual self:

> The voice of the sea is seductive, never ceasing, whispering, clamoring, murmuring, inviting the soul to wander for a spell in the abysses of solitude; to lose itself in mazes of inward contemplation.

> The voice of the sea speaks to the soul. The touch of the sea is sensuous, enfolding the body in its soft, close embrace. (14)

Among the things left out of the novel (Léonce's age as contrasted with Edna's twenty-eight years, for example) is how often the Pontelliers have been guests at Madame Lebrun's *pension* on Grand Isle. Is this contact with nature Edna's first, since her childhood days amid the bluegrass of Kentucky? In chapter seven, the book seems to suggest it is, as though she'd been confined in and by the urban spaces of New Orleans or elsewhere since her youth; later, in the city, she has lost most of the tan, the emblem of her awakened sexuality, which she had acquired at the seashore (50).

The "damage" that Edna has sustained as Léonce's property arises chiefly from never having allowed her skin to become darkened, something that proper ladies of the late Victorian and early Edwardian period ought never do, as such darkening calls into question their breeding and social status and, in the case of this novel, links them to such other characters as the nameless quadroon nursemaid and, especially, Mariequita, the "Spanish girl" (32), whose loose sexual morality is never in question; the basket she carries that is full of shrimp (33), considered an aphrodisiac in sexual folklore, connects her sexuality to the sea. Darkened skin would also associate Edna with foreign races, including those in Cuba and the Philippines, which the American nation was in the process of "subduing" (or had only recently subdued) when the novel was published. It also associates Edna with the ethnically undesirable and frequently "swarthy skinned" immigrants who were then flooding the United States. Léonce's anxiety about his wife's darkened skin may, therefore, reflect his anxiety as a Creole about his own status in the broader American commercial and consumer-oriented society that was expanding in the nation and in which he seeks to participate as an equal or even major player. His will to dominate not only in domestic, but also in entrepreneurial matters becomes clear in his declaration to Dr. Mandelet that he is leaving for New York "'on business very soon. I have a big scheme on hand, and want to be on the field proper to pull the ropes and handle the ribbons'" (64). Of course, pulling the ropes and ribbons is also what he has been repeatedly trying to do with regard to his wife and her wishes, so far with little success, and it is as well an excellent description of the American capitalist's attitude toward the acquisition of new "possessions."

Léonce's second accusation of Edna's "folly," more complex than the first, takes place in chapter eleven, following Edna's exhilarating and liberating swim in the Gulf of Mexico, after she and Robert have walked back to the *pension,* and Robert has spun his fable about the Gulf Spirit's taking possession of her soul. She sits on the porch, awaiting, but also dreading, the arrival of her husband, who immediately demands that she come inside: "'What are you doing out here, Edna? I thought I should find you in bed'" (30). He bends down to look at her closely but still fails to see her true nature any more than in chapter one. "'You will take cold out there,'" he says irritably. "'What folly is this? Why don't you come in?'" "'It isn't cold,'" replies Edna. "'I have my shawl'" (30). Here she, and not he, is given the rational response, but he fails to understand this. "'The mosquitos will devour you,'" retorts Léonce. "'There are no mosquitoes,'" Edna responds (30), apparently forgetting the "little stinging, buzzing imps" (8) that disrupted her earlier nighttime reverie in chapter three. When Edna still does not comply with Léonce's entreaties, he repeats the charge of folly, verbally upping the ante: "'This is more than folly . . . I can't permit you to stay out there all night. You must come in the house instantly'" (31).

By chapter eleven, however, Edna Pontellier's self-recognition has moved well beyond "a mood" or being "moody," if either of those simplistic terms ever applied to her. Léonce's earliercurt command for Edna to "'come in the house instantly'" (31) provides the catalyst for a new, if only temporary (at this point), state of self-awareness, one that deepens as the novel progresses and extends as well to a heightened understanding of exactly how completely and, as matters will prove, irretrievably she is trapped within her physicality and within her marriage socially, which constitute "the conditions which crowded her in" (31).

> She wondered if her husband had ever spoken to her like that before, and if she had submitted to his command. Of course she had; she remembered that she had. But she could not realize why or how she should have yielded, feeling as she then did . . . . [But] the physical need for sleep began to overtake her; the exuberance which had

sustained and exalted her spirit left her helpless and yielding to the conditions which crowded her in. (31)

The need for sleep, that is, engenders an oppression of spirit that leaves her once again vulnerable to Léonce's bullying and to her situation as a married woman, leading to the reversal of roles by husband and wife at the end of the chapter discussed a few paragraphs above.

The perceptive reader of Léonce's first two accusations of Edna's so-called folly will have noticed that folly is anything the male character says it is, specifically any female behavior, of which the man doesn't approve at the moment. In this case, it is two contradictory things: a woman's exposing herself to heat and sun and then later exposing herself to the cool night air. So a woman in the late nineteenth-century world of this novel (and in the world beyond the novel also, which seems to be Kate Chopin's larger point) is compelled to inhabit a social milieu, in which rules she has had no hand in making are constantly changing, although her status does not change regardless of whatever "rule" is in force at any given moment. She is, by reason of her gender, condemned to be seen as an emblem and representative of folly.

In each case, the concern that Léonce expresses is apparently motivated by his worries about his wife's health, itself a male preoccupation in the late nineteenth and early twentieth centuries. However, it is actually a verbalization of the male's will to dominate the behavior of the woman to whom he is married and whom he believes he owns, thinking himself responsible for and, therefore, implicated in her conduct in all matters. His reputation is at stake because of his wife's behavior, as Léonce demonstrates, when he publishes the story that Edna has moved out of the house on Esplanade Street because of renovations. Doubtless, in his mind, it is another act of folly, which he must cover up for his own sake, although Léonce doesn't say as much, as shown in chapter thirty-two. Above all else, a wife's behavior should not call into question her husband's intelligence and discretion in choice of a wife, as Léonce admits it has done when he speaks to Doctor Mandelet:

"I have a quick temper, but I don't want to quarrel or be rude to a woman, especially my wife; yet I'm driven to it, and feel like ten thousand devils after I've made a fool of myself. She's making it devilishly uncomfortable for me." (63)

Here Léonce displays a chivalric attitude. But the repetition of the concept of devil—"ten thousand devils," "devilish"—betrays Léonce's actual thoughts about his wife and, as he says, women in general. Even though he ascribes feeling like "ten thousand devils" to himself, it is apparent, in context, that he blames his wife's behavior, not his own, for making him feel that way. The problem for Léonce is not his wife's struggles with her own identity or with gendered social and cultural issues in the United States, but his own male ego in being made to feel like a "fool," that is, in becoming himself, if only momentarily by his account, an accomplice in and victim of his wife's folly.

The third occasion, on which Edna Pontellier's husband accuses her of folly (by now we might say he has all but come to identify her with the goddess Folly) occurs in reference to her painting—that is, to her artistic striving, another occupation that, from Léonce's point of view, is feminine rather than masculine, as in his profession as a cotton broker and avid reader of market reports. As a man who applies himself to "the task of reading the newspaper" and who is "already acquainted with the market reports," thus having no recourse from boredom but to glance restlessly "over the editorials and bits of news he had not had time to read before quitting New Orleans"(3), he stands revealed, even as the book opens as a person to whom the general flow of opinion and events—unless related to monetary matters and especially any idea related to the world of art—is an affront and an anathema. And by affront and anathema, it is meant: a feminine pursuit that produces no profit, except when professionally engaged in, perhaps, but never when indulged in by a mere housewife.

Léonce's impatience with the mockingbird "whistling his fluty notes out upon the breeze with maddening persistence" and with the Farival twins, practicing their duet from Zampa (3) establishes his antipathy to art in the opening pages of the novel. It is a point upon which the novel insists (even though bird song might not generally be regarded as art, and the Farival twins' playing does not appear to be among the best) by foregrounding the symbolism of birds and music throughout the rest of the book. These are languages with which Léonce has no sympathy and which he does not understand. Thus it is no surprise when, in a moment of further impatience at what he takes to be Edna's "absolute disregard for her duties as a wife" (55), he angrily declares: "'It seems to me the utmost folly for a woman at the head of a household, and the mother of children, to spend in an atelier days which would be better employed contriving for the comfort of her family'" (55). Despite his apparent dislike of music, he praises Madame Ratignolle for keeping up her household as well as her music, forgetting, perhaps, that her household is mainly maintained by black servants: "'[S]he's more of a musician than you are a painter,'" he tells his wife, imagining that he knows enough about either art to be a judge of quality. Edna sets him straight: "'She isn't a musician, and I'm not a painter'" (55). The key word in this heated exchange, besides "folly," is, of course "employed," as if the only world that matters (to Léonce, it *is* the only world that matters) is the world of work, including, as he makes clear, the world constructed of Edna's traditional domestic duties. To his accusation, at any rate, Edna mildly but infuriatingly replies, "'I feel like painting . . . Perhaps I shan't always feel like it'" (55). Such a response, emphasizing feeling or "whim" over purpose, could only have confirmed to Léonce his conviction of his wife's essential folly.

Léonce has no way of knowing that Edna has already internalized some of his accusations of folly. After the episode of the smashed vase and stamped-upon wedding ring in chapter seventeen, for example, she "could not help but think that it was very foolish, very childish, to have stamped upon her wedding ring and smashed the crystal vase upon the floor" (54). These are the very words that Léonce might have used had he known of her actions, and the thoughts occur to her, it should be noted, just before her confrontation with her husband about the time she invests in her painting. However, those words are followed immediately by the narrator's description of how Edna "began to do as she liked and feel as she liked" (54).

There is an even greater rebelliousness against the confining regulations of male morality for women's conduct than has so far been recognized in criticism, and that is saying a great deal, since so much has thus far been written on the subject. As her comments to Léonce (above) indicate, she does not even paint with a purpose; although the money she earns from her art enables her to establish the Pigeon House as a separate residence, the novel presents that pecuniary advantage almost as an afterthought. Without attempting to seem psychiatric, one might suggest that such vacillation of feelings or moods has all the marks of bipolar disorder, and the novel might usefully be read to illuminate that disease insofar as the demands of society engender it—and in Edna's case (and among disempowered people in general), that seems to be to a very large degree indeed. There are many frightening psychological moments in the novel, only one of which I present below (every reader will offer her or his own):

Edna looked straight before her with a self-absorbed expression on her face. She felt no interest in anything about her. The street, the children, the fruit vendor, the flowers growing there under her eyes, were all part and parcel of an alien world which had suddenly become antagonistic. (51)

As if Léonce's repeated characterizations of Edna's various behaviors as folly weren't enough to label her as an alien, by reason of her gender, another character in the novel associates Edna Pontellier with folly. This time, it is not her husband, but Robert Lebrun. The use of the word thus establishes a verbal link between Robert and Léonce, foreshadowing Robert's unimaginative and conventionally masculine response to Edna's remark that she is "'no longer one of Mr. Pontellier's possessions to dispose of or not'" (102). After their trip to the church in chapter twelve and its aftermath in chapter thirteen, Robert remarks that "'it was folly to have thought of going in the first place, let alone staying. Come over to Madame Antoine's; you can rest there'" (35). Robert's apparent solicitude for

Edna's fatigue, though apparently well-intentioned, combined with the word "folly" and his insistence that she "'rest,'" seems to rule out, from Robert's point of view at least, any other than a physical reason for Edna's discomfort with the religious service. He seems to assume frailty and liability to weakness and disease, although within the context of the novel, her behavior may well have arisen as a result of the content of the sermon or merely the confinement of the church itself. At this moment in the novel, Robert might at first appear to be taking some responsibility for un-masculine folly, since he agreed to accompany Edna to church, but the attentive reader will recall that it was Edna's notion to go (32). The "folly" of going to the Chênière, therefore, falls entirely upon Edna Pontellier's head.

In thus casting aspersions upon Edna's character as a woman of folly, the two men in the novel who are most important to her, although in different ways, link her through implied scriptural allusion with promiscuity and adultery. As such, the accusation of "folly" suggests perhaps an unconscious understanding on the part of both men that, within the Judeo-Christian tradition, Edna's folly—her resistance to automatic deference to masculine commands and instructions and her dalliance with younger unmarried men—will lead her morally into adultery, first with Alcée Arobin and then, if she is lucky (or unlucky), with Robert Lebrun. Most biblical exegetes understand the first nine chapters of Proverbs as mainly intending to contrast, as wisdom literature, the female figures of Wisdom, a virgin or chaste wife, and Folly, an adulterous woman. Proverbs 2:16-18, for example, counsels young men against keeping company with the "strange woman, even from the stranger which flattereth with her words. 17 Which forsaketh the guide of her youth, and forgetteth the covenant of her God. 18 For her house inclineth unto death, and her paths unto the dead" ("Proverbs").

Likewise, Proverbs 6:29 cautions that "he that goeth to his neighbor's wife; whoever toucheth her shall not be innocent" (King James Version) and warns about the danger of encountering a jealous husband in 6:33-34: "33 A wound and dishonor shall he [the adulterous young man] get; and his reproach shall not be wiped away. 34 For jealousy is the rage of a man; therefore he [the wronged husband] will not spare in the day of vengeance" ("Proverbs"). And much of Proverbs 7 consists of racy descriptions of the wiles and behavior of the adulterous woman, especially 16-19: "16 I have decked my bed with coverings of tapestry, with carved works, with fine linen of Egypt. 17 I have perfumed my bed with myrrh, aloes, and cinnamon. 18 Come, let us take our fill of love until the morning: let us solace ourselves with loves. 19 For the goodman is not at home, he has gone a long journey [to New York, presumably]" ("Proverbs").

Finally, in Proverbs 9:13-18, there are even intimations of the lavish dinner parties that structure *The Awakening*, especially the one given at the Pigeon House, although in other chapters of Proverbs such dinners are ascribed as much to Wisdom as to Folly:

13. A foolish woman is clamorous [like the voice of the sea?], she is simple, and knoweth nothing.
14. For she sitteth at the door of her house, on a seat in the high places of the city,
15. To call passengers who go right on their ways:
16. Whoso is simple, let him turn in hither: and as for him that wanteth understanding, she saith to him,
17. Stolen waters are sweet, and bread eaten in secret is pleasant.
18. But he knoweth not that the dead are there; and that her guests are in the depths of hell. (King James Version)

Attitudes toward female sexuality, such as those expressed in the above scriptural passages certainly number among the conditions, which crowd Edna in. Edna has only recently become aware of exactly how restrictive is the world she has inhabited all her life, including the world of religion, when it comes to female behavior. The verses from Proverbs also narrowly define a woman's sexual behavior exclusively from a male perspective—the early chapters of Proverbs especially represent advice narrated by an older man (allegedly Solomon), a mentor, to a younger one, much of it (as above) concerned with how to avoid predatory females, and there is, of course, nowhere within the book anything pronounced from a female perspective. But such one-sided moral judgments derived from scripture, as Kate Chopin certainly realized, cannot begin to capture the complexity of gender relationships, sexual desire, and human psychology as the world of the late nineteenth century knew and experienced these things. *The Awakening* is filled with descriptions and accounts of vacillating, contradictory feelings on Edna's part, with attempts to use experiences from the past— Edna's childhood experiences in the deep grass of Kentucky, her infatuations with a tragedian and an unnamed cavalry officer, her fantasies about pirate gold and her relationship with her father (he of the military rank and padded shoulders, other signifiers of male imposture), Léonce's money, and so on—to understand her present confusions and their relation to gender inequalities.

Kate Chopin's interest or disinterest in the prescriptions of scripture and religion in general have not been well documented, in my opinion, but there are at least some intimations of her attitudes in *The Awakening*. One might be found in Edna's belief, when she encounters Robert in Catiche's garden and restaurant in the suburbs, that "a designing Providence had led him into her path" (100). Providence, of course, especially as conceived and positioned within the verses from Proverbs we have just been considering, would not assist an already adulterous woman to the location of her next "prey," and so Kate Chopin's larger point in Edna's reflection seems to be rather with the way in which Providential guidance and scriptural verses can be and have been construed by individuals in ways that best suit their own designs and desires—unless, of course, one imagines that Providence has led Edna to Robert as a way of furthering and, indeed, insuring her own punishment, death, and damnation for having already committed adultery, but I believe that such a reading would be pushing the book where the text does not authorize our going. In any case, Edna's idea demonstrates her continuing susceptibility to conventional explanations of why and how things happen in the world, pointing toward her inability to be totally sexually iconoclastic and, therefore, to her eventual suicide in keeping with the mores prescribed by males.[1] Robert's being led by Providence into her path would make Edna the predator rather than, as the book seems to demonstrate in various ways almost from start to finish, the traditional prey of any available male and would make Providence complicit in both her and Robert's downfall, or, alternatively, would make Providence intent upon testing Robert's moral resilience, transforming him into a version of the tempted and resistant male of Proverbs.

More important in the context of the implied references to Proverbs that activate and underline the repeated charges of Edna's folly, I believe, is the fact that on her visit to the Ratignolles (54) Edna explicitly calls into mind Proverbs 15:17— "Better is a dinner of herbs where love is, than a stalled ox and hatred therewith"—a text that, in Edna's mind at least (and in this reader's, too), seems invoked in order to offer a countervailing justification for the behavior of the "strange woman" identified with folly from the first page of the novel and the second chapter of Proverbs. Where there is no love or understanding in a house, as there assuredly is not in the house on Esplanade Street, a woman might be considered justified in seeking other venues or avenues for her emotional attachments and sexual activities. As it turns out, the meal served up to Edna is not "dinner of herbs" but "a delicious repast, simple, choice, and in every way satisfying"(54), but this description of the meal also invites the reader to recall Léonce' s annoyed impatience with his food in chapter seventeen, which is, in fact, a displacement of his irritation with his wife for not keeping her visitors' Tuesdays, and his subsequent angry decision to take his "dinner at the club" (50). Madame Ratignolle's keen interest in everything her husband says during the dinner becomes a touchstone of the great degree of marital discord between Edna and Léonce. Small wonder, then, that when Edna leaves this dinner party, she is "more depressed . . . than soothed" by the couple's performance (54). Marital harmony, dependent upon "blind contentment," is not for Edna, and neither, as matters turn out, is "life's delirium" (54).

In offering this account of but one aspect of *The Awakening*, its verbal patterning and implied allusions (in one case, a direct allusion), this essay, of course, has neglected other and, many would say, more important elements of the novel. Nor has this essay attempted to frame the discussion theoretically or politically, although it might be argued that some political implications lurk in the use of the word "folly" to describe the behavior of a woman, and in Dr. Mandelet's categorization of women as peculiar organisms, characterized by whimsical and moody behavior (64). This essay has also refused to be concerned with whether unified authors really exist or, indeed, whether there is such an author or any author in this book. The approach taken perhaps manifests a bit of whimsy and peculiarity on its own, a sort of throwback to what used to be called New Criticism, which had numerous problems with its underlying assumptions about what constituted literature—Kate Chopin was not in the canon in those days, for example—but which still seems occasionally useful in providing a methodology for reading literary texts. This essay seeks to illuminate at least one small part of Kate Chopin's novel and her craft of fiction, which is too often overlooked.

Note

1. For a discussion of this unsatisfactory (to some readers) aspect of the ending of *The Awakening*, see George Spangler, "Kate Chopin's The Awakening: A Partial Dissent," *Novel: A Forum on Fiction* 3 (Spring 1970): 249-55.

Works Cited

Chopin, Kate. *The Awakening*. Ed. Margot Culley. 2nd ed. New York: Norton, 1994.

"Proverbs." *The Official King James Bible*. KingJamesBibleOnline.org. November 2007. Web. 9 Dec. 2013. <http://www.kingjamesbibleonline.org/Proverbs-Chapter-1/>

Spangler, George. "Kate Chopin's *The Awakening*: A Partial Dissent," *Novel: A Forum on Fiction* 3 (Spring 1970): 249-55.

Humor in Chopin's *The Awakening*

Robert C. Evans

The Awakening focuses on such issues as an unhappy marriage, thwarted love, psychological depression, eventual adultery, and possible suicide. Yet, it is often a humorous and sometimes even very funny book. Its frequent humor, however, has not been the subject of much discussion. Partly, Chopin uses humor to highlight, by contrast, the book's darker tones and themes. Partly, she uses it to suggest how much the novel's first half differs from its second. Partly, she uses humor to characterize different personalities, as well as her characters' complex interactions. And she especially uses humor to imply the values and perspectives of the novel's narrator. Humor is used so frequently and variously throughout *The Awakening* that this book deserves to be called one of the more amusingly serious novels among the "classics" of American literature. It is not, of course, anywhere as nearly or consistently funny as *Adventures of Huckleberry Finn* by Mark Twain or even *Moby-Dick* by Herman Melville, but it is certainly far more regularly amusing than other classic novels by such writers as Hawthorne, James, Crane, Hemingway, or Fitzgerald. Chopin herself had a fine sense of humor, and she clearly reveals it in this book.

The very opening sentences of the novel are already amusing. A caged parrot exclaims, "*Allez vous-en! Allez vous-en! Sapristi!* [Go away! Go away! For God's sake!]" (Chopin 3). And no sooner does the parrot so exclaim than Léonce Pontellier—a central character—obeys the bird's advice. Disgusted by the racket the parrot and another bird are making, Léonce gets up and moves to an entirely different location so he can read his newspaper in peace. Already, then, Chopin uses this comic conflict between Léonce and the birds to characterize Léonce as a somewhat humorless person. He is accustomed to having his own way and unwilling to tolerate a disturbance that others might find funny or ridiculous. Part of the function of humor in *The Awakening*, in fact, is to present Léonce as one of the least humorous characters. Unlike his wife, Edna, or his eventual rival, Robert, or even the man with whom his wife eventually has sex (Alcée Arobin), Léonce finds little in life that strikes him as funny. He tends to take himself, and anything that concerns him, a bit too seriously. It is partly his lack of humor that helps make him increasingly unappealing to Edna, while it is precisely Robert's ability to see the humor in life that helps cause Edna to find him increasingly attractive.

Chopin already implies this basic contrast between Léonce and Robert in the novel's opening chapter. After Edna and Robert return from her beginner's efforts to swim in the Gulf of Mexico, the very first words Léonce speaks to her are "What folly!" (Chopin 4). Clearly, he is not amused, and his lack of humor here and elsewhere is a keynote of his character. And then, when Robert and Edna, facing each other, begin to laugh together, neither can successfully explain to Léonce why they find a particular incident so funny: "It did not seem half so amusing when told" (Chopin 4). Part of the problem, of course, is that they are trying to explain the incident to *Léonce*, of all people, who is not the sort of person to find anything very humorous. If Léonce and Edna shared more of a sense of humor, their marriage might be in better shape. It isn't simply that Léonce is not especially funny and cannot particularly appreciate humor in others. It is partly that his essential seriousness makes him somewhat boring. Thus the narrator engages in humorous irony of her own when she has Léonce tell Edna, regarding Robert, that she should "send him [that is, Robert] about his business when he bores you" (5). The joke, of course, is on Léonce: it is Léonce, not Robert, whom Edna will dispose of when he bores her. Most students, when this passage is read to them, instantly laugh out loud. They can already see where this novel is heading. They already sense that Léonce is the butt of the narrator's irony. Right from its very first chapter, then, *The Awakening* is an often funny book.

I.

Interestingly enough, the moment when Edna and Léonce seem closest also comes at the end of chapter one, when Edna automatically intuits that Léonce may not return immediately from gambling at a nearby hotel. She instinctively understands that the time of his return will depend on "the size of 'the game.' He did not say this, but she understood it, and laughed, nodding good-by to him" (Chopin 5). This is a rare moment when Chopin hints that Edna and Léonce may share a sense of humor, and even here it is *Edna* who laughs, not Léonce. For the most part, Edna seems the more vital, more vibrant of the two because it is she who is often capable of finding life funny—a trait she shares with Robert. Thus, in chapter two, she and Robert once again chat about "their amusing adventure out in the water," which "had again assumed its entertaining aspect"—now (that is) that Léonce is gone (Chopin 5). In general, Edna shows, throughout the book, a real capacity for good humor, although she also shows a real capacity for great depression and melancholy. Her frequent sadness makes her possible suicide at the end of the novel seem less than completely surprising, while her gift for humor and joy make her death seem all the more tragic and sad. Partly because she *is* often funny and *can* appreciate humor, Edna is an appealing character. One function of humor in the novel, then, is to help make us like Edna, so that her final fate seems all the more regrettable. If Edna were as humorless and self-important as Léonce, we would care much less for her or about her.

Yet, it is not only Edna who is often characterized as good-humored. The same is true of various other characters, especially Robert, and also Adèle Ratignolle. Most important, however, is the sense of humor revealed by the narrator. By implying the narrator's humor—which is sometimes ironic, sometimes gentle, sometimes sharp, sometimes generous, sometimes whimsical, etc.—Chopin implies a person who is, perhaps, *the* most complex personality in the book. The narrator is able to see the humor in many of the characters and situations she describes, and she therefore often appears wise, insightful, good-natured, and trustworthy. Unlike Léonce, the narrator is not hyper-serious, nor is she especially judgmental. She sees the foibles of the people she describes, but she rarely if ever condemns them. The narrator, by implication, is not only the teller of this story, but also a good role-model for the story's readers. Her traits help illuminate, by comparison and contrast, the narrower, more limited personalities of most of the novel's characters.

Consider, for instance, these sentences: "Robert talked a good deal about himself. He was very young, and did not know any better. Mrs. Pontellier talked a little about herself for the same reason. Each was interested in what the other said" (Chopin 5-6). Here the narrator gently mocks both Robert and Edna, but *only* gently. It is as if the narrator finds their self-centeredness amusing, while also recognizing that it is a common human trait—one we all share, especially at particular ages in our lives. Implicitly, the narrator herself once behaved this way when she was young, and so the joke is partly on Robert and Edna, partly on us, and partly on herself as well. And then, as if to make it clear that she is not judging Edna and Robert harshly, she hastens to add that "Each was interested in what the other said" (Chopin 6). The narrator of this book, unlike Léonce, has a healthy sense of humor, but rarely, if ever, is her humor mean or harsh. We sense that she is intelligent, sensible, genial, and tolerant. She seems willing to forgive nearly all her characters their inevitable foibles. Her attitude toward most people in *The Awakening* seems affectionate rather than censorious. In that sense, she is a fine role model for the novel's readers, and she would be a fine role model for most of its characters, if they could only get to know her.

At one point, for instance, she says that Robert's mother, Madame Lebrun, enjoyed "an easy and comfortable existence which appeared to be her birthright" (Chopin 6). A different, more judgmental narrator might have made that final comment seem more of a dig. Chopin's narrator, however, seems merely to smile at Madame Lebrun's sense of entitlement. Whatever the narrator says about the characters almost always makes the narrator seem appealing because she herself seems good-humored. Thus, when she tells us that Robert "amused himself with the little Pontellier children, who were very fond of him" (Chopin 6), her comment reflects well on Robert as well as on the narrator. Each seems fond of children, especially the actual or potential humor of children, and thus each seems appealing in his or her own right.

When Léonce returns from the hotel from his night of gambling and (presumably) drinking, the narrator tells us that he "was in an excellent humor" (Chopin 6)—a subtly funny way of implying, perhaps, that he is tipsy. Here again, it is in the early sections of the book that Léonce seems most appealing, partly because he seems most humorous because he is most human. Very quickly, however, he seems less attractive when he suggests that Edna has been neglecting a sick child, who does not seem sick at all. And the more critical Léonce becomes of Edna, the more critical the narrator seems of Léonce. Chapter three is a particularly humorous chapter of *The Awakening*, even though it is also a particularly serious chapter as well, since it is the first chapter, in which we sense real trouble in the Pontellier marriage. Most of the humor in chapter three is fairly pointed, and it is almost entirely pointed at Léonce. Thus, we cannot help noticing the multiple ironies of Léonce's belief that Edna is "the sole object of his existence" (Chopin 7); that she fails to pay him sufficient attention (Chopin 7); that he is somehow an expert on childhood illnesses (Chopin 7); and that, even though he supposedly values her more than anything, he instantly falls asleep after he thoughtlessly awakens and upsets her (Chopin 7).

The narrator doesn't overtly judge Léonce; she doesn't need to. She describes his behavior and lets us draw our own conclusions. She manages to keep her own good humor even while depicting Léonce as slightly obnoxious. And, before the chapter ends, she not only makes Léonce seem somewhat appealing once more (by making him seem not only financially generous but also the object of his young boys' obvious affection); she even lets him laugh for one of the few times in the novel (Chopin 8). Then, in another moment that often draws laughter from students, the narrator concludes chapter three by reporting that all the wives on Grand Isle "declared that Mr. Pontellier was the best husband in the world. Mrs. Pontellier was forced to admit that she knew of none better" (9).

Why are these sentences funny? There seem to be several reasons, and the fact that there *are* several (and that they combine with and reinforce one another) implies the frequent complexity of Chopin's skills and achievements as a humorist. First, the sentences are amusing because they imply that the wives on Grand Isle have fairly superficial standards for judging excellence in husbands. (Léonce, after all, has merely sent Edna a box of edible goodies.) Second, the sentences suggest that these wives may be less than fully happy with their own husbands. Third, Edna's admission that she knows of no husband better than hers may be less than enthusiastic if not actually somewhat extorted. Finally, her admission may imply that most husbands *are* no better than Léonce (who does not exactly set the highest standard). A chapter full of tension thus ends of a light, wry note—a note that simultaneously and subtly characterizes Léonce, other husbands, Edna, other wives, and, especially, the shrewd, clever narrator.

II.

The narrator's ability to mock characters gently, without making them seem utterly ridiculous, is especially on display when she describes Adèle Ratignolle. Before we meet Adèle, we are introduced to various women whom she resembles in certain ways:

> The mother-women seemed to prevail that summer at Grand Isle. It was easy to know them, fluttering about with extended, protecting wings when any harm, real or imaginary, threatened their precious brood. They were women who idolized their children, worshiped their husbands, and esteemed it a holy privilege to efface themselves as individuals and grow wings as ministering angels. (Chopin 9)

Here, the sarcasm, although still lighter than it could be, seems obvious (perhaps *too* obvious), especially in the ever-lengthening extended metaphor, in the adjective "precious," and in the verbs "idolized" and "worshiped." One senses, in this passage, that the narrator does not much respect these women because they seem to have so little respect for themselves. They seem exaggeratedly subservient, and so the narrator's prose itself seems a bit exaggerated in its ridicule.

When the narrator turns to describing Adèle Ratignolle, however, the tone relaxes. It is still humorous, but the humor no longer seems especially sharp. In fact, the whole long passage comparing Adèle to a "bygone heroine of romance and the fair lady of our dreams" (Chopin 9)—a passage too long to quote in full— seems all the more light-hearted because it is preceded by perhaps the first genuinely "laugh out loud" line of the novel: "If her husband did not adore her, he was a brute, deserving of death by slow torture" (Chopin 9). As we will see later, Chopin is often especially funny when she imagines implausibly extreme violence. Sentences like the one just quoted are particularly humorous because they violate so completely the subtle, sophisticated tone of the rest of the novel. Like much of the rest of the novel's humor, such sentences are effective because they surprise us by contrasting so completely with most of the phrasing that precedes them. Such sentences imply that the narrator has her tongue firmly in her cheek: she does not take herself, such sentiments, or the people who may actually embrace them completely seriously. She is indulging in some good, silly fun.

The narrator's general presentation of Adèle is both amusing and affectionate. This is especially obvious, for instance, when we are told how Adèle dresses a baby like an Eskimo to protect it from "treacherous drafts" that "came down chimneys" and from "insidious currents of deadly cold" that "found their way through keyholes" (Chopin 10). Yes, the narrator is having some fun here at Adèle's expense, but it is good-natured fun, not biting satire. This humorous description of Adèle helps highlight, by contrast, Edna's far more relaxed attitude toward her children, even as it suggests just how devoted Adèle genuinely is to her ever-growing brood. As the novel develops, Adèle comes across as an increasingly attractive character—one who is truly concerned for and about Edna and one who has real insight into the dangers Edna faces from her environment and from her own personality and values.

One of the most obviously and appealingly humorous sections of the novel occurs in chapter five, in the memorable back-and-forth between Adèle and Robert about his former devotion to her. Robert, speaking in Edna's presence, begins the comic banter:

> "Could any one fathom the cruelty beneath that fair exterior?" murmured Robert. "She knew that I adored her once, and she let me

adore her. It was 'Robert, come; go; stand up; sit down; do this; do that; see if the baby sleeps; my thimble, please, that I left God knows where. Come and read Daudet to me while I sew.'"

"*Par exemple!* [For goodness sake!] I never had to ask. You were always there under my feet, like a troublesome cat."

"You mean like an adoring dog. And just as soon as Ratignolle appeared on the scene, then it *was* like a dog. '*Passez! Adieu! Allez vousen*! [Go on! Good-by! Go away!]'" (Chopin 11-12)

Moments such as this—and there are a number of them in *The Awakening*—serve various functions. This one not only helps highlight, through contrast, the loneliness and tragedy that develop later in the novel, but it also helps emphasize the attractive sense of community that exists among the Creoles—a sense of community from which Edna becomes increasingly distanced. The playful teasing between Adèle and Robert here foreshadows the similar playful teasing between Robert and Edna that appears later in the book, when they visit the *Chênière Caminada* and are alone together there for much of the day. In the meantime, the ability of Adèle and Robert to tease one another as they do here suggests how comfortable they are together, how much they understand one another, but also how different their relationship is from the one that will soon develop between Robert and Edna.

Perhaps most important of all, however, is the way these humorous passages characterize Robert. Adèle obviously likes him, and it is easy to see why: he does not take himself too seriously; he is willing to make himself the butt of other people's jokes; he enjoys life and laughter; and he seems admired and trusted not only by Adèle, but also by her husband and by the entire community of Creoles, who have known him for years and who seem to like and respect him. It is easy to see why Edna herself finds Robert appealing. His sense of humor, his lack of self-importance, his ease around women, his ability to *understand* women, and his open joy in his relations with others make him very much the opposite of Léonce Pontellier. Robert and Edna seem to share, at least at first, the same sense of fun, and a sense of fun is apparently one crucial trait most lacking in her marriage with Léonce. Critics who have wondered what Edna finds appealing in Robert have often neglected his sense of humor. Compared to Léonce—and also compared to Edna, for that matter—Robert seems far more humble and good-humored and far less pompous. Léonce and Edna, who otherwise seem so different, both tend to take themselves too seriously. Robert's sense of humor helps make him, in some ways, the most appealing character in the book. Nearly everyone likes him (Arobin is one possible exception) and enjoys being in his company, and his sense of humor is one key to his popularity.

Another especially appealing part of the book involves the comic banter between Edna and Robert in chapter thirteen. Their dialogue here reminds us of the earlier comic exchanges between Robert and Adèle (quoted above), but here the tone is far more intimate. Part of the function of humor in the book, in fact, is to imply in subtle ways any changes in tone and any development in relations between the characters. Thus, the following exchange is both funny and revealingly serious. Edna has just awoken from a deep sleep in the home of Madame Antoine at *Chênière Caminada*; Robert has been spending the time reading. They are alone together for one of the few times in the book:

> "How many years have I slept?" she inquired. "The whole island seems changed. A new race of beings must have sprung up, leaving only you and me as past relics. How many ages ago did Madame Antoine and Tonie die? and when did our people from Grand Isle disappear from the earth?"

> He familiarly adjusted a ruffle upon her shoulder.

> "You have slept precisely one hundred years. I was left here to guard your slumbers; and for one hundred years I have been out under the shed reading a book. The only evil I couldn't prevent was to keep a broiled fowl from drying up." (Chopin 37)

Once again, Robert seems immensely appealing because of his sense of humor. So, for that matter, does the often-too-serious Edna. It is Edna who initiates the playful exchange (the kind of conversation she never initiates or responds to with Léonce). This detail already suggests how comfortable she feels in his presence. Meanwhile, Robert immediately plays along, and this whole episode, in fact, recalls the easy familiarity they seemed to enjoy when we first met them together in chapter one (Chopin 4). Now, however, Léonce is not present to spoil the fun. Although Edna and Robert joke about an entirely new phase of existence, such a phase is precisely what seems to be inaugurated here. Moments of humor are especially useful to Chopin in implying how close her characters feel to one another. This is true not only of Edna's relationships with Robert but also of her relationships with most of the other characters, especially Mademoiselle Reisz. Reisz is never more appealing than when she is teasing Edna.

III.

Chopin uses humor, however, in many more ways than simply to imply intimacy between her characters. Frequently, for instance, she uses it to mock excessive romanticism and naïve desires. This function of humor is especially important because Edna is often the target of the narrator's satire, which is sometimes implied and sometimes overt. Anyone who assumes that Edna is the unblemished heroine of the book, with whom the narrator completely sympathizes, is missing much of the novel's fun.

Much of the humor at Edna's expense appears in chapter seven, when the narrator indirectly report's Edna's account of her early life to Adèle Ratignolle. Indeed, the fact that Edna herself offers this account suggests the possibility that she may even be making fun of herself. If that is the case, then Edna is a more mature, more self-aware character than she sometimes seems to be. However, the point of view in chapter seven is not obviously clear, and so it is possible that it is the narrator, rather than Edna herself, who refuses to take the youthful Edna completely seriously. In either case, the young Edna described in chapter seven seems silly in some of the ways most of us are silly when we are young. And that is an important point: Edna is not being mocked for being unusually foolish; she is merely being teased for the typical follies of youth.

At one point, for instance, Edna is described as "a little miss, just merging into her teens," who has become smitten with her older sister's beau. But when the beau pays *Edna* no attention, "the realization that she herself was nothing, nothing, nothing to the engaged young man was a bitter affliction to her" (Chopin 18). Surely this language—especially the "nothing, nothing, nothing"—is not meant to be taken seriously, although it has, in fact, been condemned by some as evidence of Chopin's stylistic immaturity (Dawson 2). More subtly humorous is the description of young Edna's next obsession, this time with the appearance of a renowned actor: "The persistence of the infatuation lent it an aspect of genuineness. The hopelessness of it colored it with the lofty tones of a great passion" (Chopin 18). Here, Chopin is at her understated best when implying that this "infatuation" is not to be taken seriously. However, a few sentences later, the mockery is far more obvious when we learn how young Edna often treated a framed portrait of the actor: "When alone she sometimes picked it up and kissed the cold glass passionately" (Chopin 18). *Passionately*? Surely, Chopin is having fun here at the expense of her heroine's former self. But she may also be suggesting that Edna has still not entirely outgrown her adolescence.

In any case, throughout the book, sentimentality is often mocked—sometimes overtly, sometimes more subtly. The "two lovers" who appear again and again are sometimes the focus of such amusement. In chapter eight, for instance, the narrator describes how they walk together: "There was not a particle of earth beneath their feet. Their heads might have been turned upside-down, so absolutely did they tread upon blue ether" (Chopin 21). It is easy to imagine Chopin smiling as she wrote those sentences and many other, similar sentences, including the one in chapter twelve, in which the narrator says of the lovers, "They saw nothing, they heard nothing." Their concentration on each other is so complete that Mariequita even asks Robert whether the lovers, who are now leaning on each other, are married. Robert instantly replies, "Of course not!" and laughs

(Chopin 21). The lovers, then, are sometimes the targets of gentle ridicule, but at other times, they are used to suggest that conventional marriage can drain a relationship of passion and devotion. Chopin jokes frequently throughout *The Awakening*, but her jokes, as here, almost always have some significant implication for the book's larger themes and meanings. Her treatment of the lovers suggests that the ideal relationship between a husband and wife would be one that is less blinkered than theirs, but one that nevertheless preserves some of the lovers' real mutual devotion.

IV.

The ways Chopin uses humor in *The Awakening* are so numerous and diverse that a brief essay cannot begin to do justice to them all. Often, they imply or illustrate the foibles of human personalities and conduct. Collectively, they imply the narrator's shrewd perceptions of the characters and of human nature in general. The humor in *The Awakening* helps complicate the book in all kinds of enriching ways, and it makes a novel that might easily have become a grim social tract seem, instead, to reflect real wisdom and compassion. Ultimately, the humor helps make both the novel and the narrator seem far more attractive than they would have been if the humor had been absent.

Consider, for example, this passage describing preparations for the trip to *Chênière Caminada* in Beaudelet's boat:

> Beaudelet grumbled because Mariequita was there, taking up so much room. In reality he was annoyed at having old Monsieur Farival, who considered himself the better sailor of the two. But he would not quarrel with so old a man as Monsieur Farival, so he quarreled with Mariequita. (Chopin 33)

These sentences are not essential; they do nothing to help characterize the book's main personalities. They are not obviously relevant to the novel's main themes. But they do imply the wit, wisdom, and whimsy of the narrator. They imply the comic egotism of Beaudelet and Farival, and they thereby enhance our sense that *most* of the characters in the novel are egotistical to one degree or another, often in ways that have far more unfortunate consequences than the ones suggested here. Egotism or pride (in the negative sense of the word) is a major motif of *The Awakening*, and most of book's humorous passages help reinforce that theme.

Thus, Farival later laughs at Beaudelet's abilities as a sailor, and Beaudelet swears at Farival under his breath (Chopin 33). Mariequita is humorously frustrated (twice) because Robert pays more attention to Edna than to her (Chopin 34). Later still, Victor Lebrun behaves so egotistically that the frustration of other characters is described in especially comic ways, as when the narrator comments that "Farival thought that Victor should have been taken out in mid-ocean in his earliest youth and drowned," while Victor wishes the same fate for "obnoxious" old people, such as Farival (40). Later, however, Farival is laughing hysterically at one of Victor's stories (41), so the bitterness between them is balanced by soothing good humor. By using humor so often when depicting her "minor" characters, the novel's narrator gives us the sense that we are being admitted into a rich and complex social world—one in which even the least obviously important characters have "real" personalities.

Further examples of this kind of humorous and therefore enriching characterization involve Mademoiselle Reisz's opinion that "hanging would be too good" for Victor (Chopin 47); her comment that "It's a wonder that Robert hasn't beaten [Victor] to death long ago" (Chopin 47); and her comment that the summer would have been "rather pleasant, if it hadn't been for the mosquitoes and the Farival twins" (Chopin 47)—annoying little girls who are the subject of much of the book's humor. Yet Mademoiselle Reisz herself is the target of much humor, as when a shopkeeper tells Edna that he "knew Mademoiselle Reisz a good deal better than he wanted to know her" and when he later says that "He thanked heaven she had left the neighborhood, and was equally thankful that he did not know where she had gone" (56). Thus, Mademoiselle Reisz is annoyed by the self-centeredness of Victor and the Farival twins, but her own self-centeredness annoys others (the shopkeeper is just one of many). The same thing is true of Edna's father and of various other characters. Chopin's humor, then, often reinforces two pervasive themes: that we are all more egotistical in the eyes of others than we seem from our own perspectives, and that self-centeredness is ultimately the source, in this book, of much laughter but also of much suffering and even tragedy.

Ironically, one of the comic highlights of the novel occurs in the final chapter, just before Edna dies. Victor has been trying to make Mariequita jealous by implying that he is in love with Edna:

> She got it into her head that Victor was in love with Mrs. Pontellier, and he gave her evasive answers, framed so as to confirm her belief. She grew sullen and cried a little, threatening to go off and leave him to his fine ladies. There were a dozen men crazy about her at the *Chênière*; and since it was the fashion to be in love with married people, why, she could run away any time she liked to New Orleans with Célina's husband.

> Célina's husband was a fool, a coward, and a pig, and to prove it to her, Victor intended to hammer his head into a jelly the next time he encountered him. This assurance was very consoling to Mariequita. She dried her eyes, and grew cheerful at the prospect. (Chopin 107)

This splendidly funny passage, like many funny passages in *The Awakening*, serves several functions at once. It contributes to the characterization of Victor and Mariequita. It enhances the pervasive theme of self-centeredness. It reminds us that romantic passions can sometimes seem silly and even laughable. It, therefore, may imply that Edna's own passions are themselves somewhat silly, or perhaps it makes them seem, by contrast, serious and profound, or perhaps some mixture of the two. The quoted passage, by making us laugh out loud, only highlights the sadness of the book's rapidly approaching conclusion, and perhaps the passage also reminds us that there is life outside of Edna's narrow perspective—that although she will soon die, life will go on in its normal, often funny ways for most of the rest of the book's characters. Ironically, the characters who may be least likely to experience much laughter in their later lives, after Edna dies, will be Léonce (who is fairly humorless to begin with) and Robert (whose native sense of humor may be crushed by guilt). And then, of course, there are also Edna's young sons, two of the most comical and good-humored characters in the novel, whose lives will be changed forever by their mother's death.

Works Cited

Chopin, Kate. *The Awakening*. Ed. Margot Culley. 2nd ed. New York: Norton, 1994.

Dawson, Hugh J. "Kate Chopin's *The Awakening*: A Dissenting Opinion." *American Literary Realism* 26.2 (1994): 1-18.

"Casting aside that fictitious self": *The Awakening* as a Cautionary Tale

Peter J. Ramos

Going back to the late 1970s, at least, the most prominent critical readings of the ending of Kate Chopin's *The Awakening* havemaintained that Edna Pontellier demonstrates eitherthe heroic victory of a female protagonist over patriarchy through suicide, or the inevitable, fatal defeat of any strong-willed and independent woman seeking to escape the patriarchal structure. Both readingsimply a society dominated by an institutionalized sexism that is insurmountable for any woman who challenges it in the name of equal rights or autonomy.[1]

The majority of my own students believe that Edna frees herself from patriarchy by committing suicide. Without exception, my students argue that Edna is forced to commit suicide by the patriarchal society in which she wishes to live a more autonomous life. Yet, this view may be too simple (see Ramos). Another way to read Edna's behavior is to see it in the service of a cautionary tale, against stripping yourself of identity. Identity is, in some ways, a kind of arbitrary and inhabitable fiction: at what point does one have the right to call oneself an artist? Does having a child (or raising someone else's) automatically make one (or preclude one from being) a mother? And yet, in order to actually inhabit an identity, one must continuously take responsibility for it—one must act on that identity by painting, for example, or raising a child. Furthermore, one can actually produce "real" consequences if one becomes responsible for one's identity; while there may not be a way to say with absolute certainty whether or not Edna is an artist. She does, after all, achieve concrete results from this identity—she makes money at her trade. As we read toward the end of the novella, a picture dealer "negotiated with her for some Parisian studies to reach him in time for the holiday trade in December" (137). But Edna comes erroneously to believe that there might be some ultimate freedom beyond all inhabitable identities—that to place herself beyond all available identities would be to finally achieve a freedom beyond constraint. But such a freedom, as the novella implies almost from the beginning, can only be from life, itself.

Edna is a woman who longs for and descends into an identity-less non-space, akin to madness, which has no representative status. In other words, despite the decades of criticism that identifies Edna as an example of the kind of woman who faced the insurmountable challenges of patriarchal sexism, this essay asserts that her status ultimately becomes less and less representative of any kind of woman at all—in her time or ours—and that her most damning or fatal error is the assumption that, in such a non-representative space, she might finally achieve autonomy. Others have suggested that the cause of such a fatal quest on her part is directly related to losing her mother when she was a child. Thus, critics argue that Edna's journey is unconsciously linked to her longing for relationships with lovers or parental figures—specifically, relationships that cannot become actualized.[2] While this essay respects such readings, the central argument here is that the result of such impulses, whatever the cause, is the same: a woman who abandons her various roles— mother, wife, artist, friend, lover—to follow the chimera of an identity-less non-state that promises ultimate freedom. In other words, Edna's most self-damning flaw is her quest to place herself beyond the realm of representation—to place herself emphatically beyond comparison to any person at all, man or woman. I will further suggest that the text demonstrates this kind of confusion—the same kind Edna struggles with—at the level of language, and that this ambivalence or ambiguity, along with Edna's own lack of will to live by or fulfill her desires, mirrors the real cause of her demise. Here, too, we can read her plight as a warning—an example of what can happen if a woman does not actively dedicate herself to and pursue an inhabitable or practical identity.

Let us, for once, take the title and central theme of this novella seriously. That is, let's assume this text involves a woman who undergoes an awakening. Whether this awakening is meant in a darkly ironic or a straightforward way, let us inquire what it is that rouses Edna from sleep. To what, specifically, does she awaken? While there are certainly signs or premonitions of this awakening almost from the novella's beginning, it seems it occurs at the central moment on the evening during which Edna hears Madame Reisz playing the piano and then later swims by herself for the first time. Before Madame Resiz begins playing, we are given the following information about Edna:

> Edna was what she herself called very fond of music. Musical strains, well rendered, had a way of evoking pictures in her mind. She sometimes liked to sit in the room in the mornings when Madame Ratignolle played or practiced. One piece which that lady played Edna had entitled "Solitude".... "When she heard [the piece] there came before her imagination the figure of a man standing beside a desolate rock on the seashore. He was naked. His attitude was one of hopeless resignation as he looked toward a distant bird winging its flight away from him. (33)

This is an interesting passage, not least because of its foreshadowing of the novella's ending—Edna's last moments before plunging, naked, into the sea. But it's also noteworthy for the gender switch. This is a man, and given the restrictions Edna and other women like her faced at this time, restrictions so often brought up in criticism about this work, it's tempting to see part of this imagined scene as a wish-fantasy, because Edna—in terms of social, sexual, artistic freedoms—ultimately wants to be a man. But the fantasy itself is anticlimactic; the freedoms associated with being a man lead not to fulfillment here but to "hopeless resignation," the phrase itself also a foreshadowing of Edna's giving herself up to Fate, a point to which we will be continually returning.

When Madame Reisz plays for Edna on this evening, the narrator explains that "It was not the first time [Edna] had heard an artist at the piano" (33). Nonetheless, the narrator notes, it was "the first time [Edna] was ready, perhaps the first time her being was tempered to take an impress for the abiding truth" (34). Something powerful is happening to Edna, though what that "something" is, we are not told. But there will be attendant consequences. Edna will change her life in certain important ways because of this and the following events. When she later decides to go swimming in the moonlight—"perhaps it was Robert" who persuaded her, the narrator notes—she decides to do so alone, despite the fact that she had only recently been learning how to swim. What this event signifies is best illustrated by the text itself:

> A feeling of exultation overtook her, as if some power of significant import had been given her to control the working of her body and soul. She grew daring and reckless, overestimating her strength. She wanted to swim far out, where no woman had swum before....As she swam she seemed to be reaching out for the unlimited in which to lose herself. (36)

This is powerful, revolutionary language: the prose illuminates a moment of transcendental achievement for Edna in which the physical act of swimming, unaccompanied and for the first time, reflects the infinite potential and power of her inner self. Again, one can safely argue that such a moment ultimately facilitates the other revolutions Edna will eventually enact—taking up a career in art, leaving her husband's house, enjoying sexual love, to name a few. Yet, even on this night, Edna seems conflicted about this event and its significance to her own life.

After the swim, Edna leaves the party to be by herself. Robert catches up to her. At first, she speaks as if to herself about the many different emotions she's feeling on this strange, moonlit night. She then goes to the hammock, Robert assisting her. Edna asks him for a shawl, and says curtly that he may stay "if he wished to" until her husband returns. They sit together in silence, and then we get this nearly unbelievable sentence: "No multitude of words could have been more significant than those moments of silence, or more pregnant with the first-felt throbbing of desire" (40). At the very least, we might call these words problematically ambiguous: "Desire for whom?" we can fairly ask. Edna has just experienced this breakthrough, this moment in which she finally learns to swim—with all of its Emersonian allusions and self-reliant glory—on this romantic moonlit night, romantic in the strictly transcendental sense.

And here, almost without any plausible explanation, the reader confronts the implication of a romantic-amorous connection with Robert. It's as if the moment Edna achieves a practical freedom, she immediately transfers that to this already aborted love—precisely because it cannot be realized or consummated.

This confusion or indecision on Edna's part continues, even after Robert leaves. When her husband returns and tells her to get inside and go to bed, Edna defies him repeatedly. Finally, she decides to go in. Here is the passage: "Edna began to feel like one who awakens gradually out of a dream, a delicious, grotesque, impossible dream, to feel again the realities pressing into her soul" (41). Such a dream is impossible, critics contend because of the social demands and restrictions placed on a woman like Edna: she cannot stop being a wife and mother—with all that these identities entail.[3] Yet, Edna proves that if this alone is the dream—freedom, if not total, then a significant amount of it, from motherhood and her marriage—she *does* achieve it. It is not impossible. The point here, despite what the narrator *appears* to imply, is that it is only Edna's belief that her experiences in the water (and their consequences on her sense of self) constitute a mere dream; the text makes it clear that these possibilities are not a mere dream. Since the point of view here, though in third person, is significantly limited to Edna, when it comes to characters' inner thoughts, we are tempted receive that view as if it were the novel's.

Late that same night, Edna has restless sleep and awakes with "an impression upon her half-awakened sense of something unattainable" (42). What that is—new social freedoms? A love affair with or marriage to Robert?—is not made clear. If both, then the problem will be the same she's had with Léonce; she will belong to someone else. If the former, then it's not clear why she immediately goes to spend the day with Robert in this newly awakened freedom. The narrator then states, "However, [Edna] was not seeking refreshment or help from any source, either external or from within. She was blindly following whatever impulse moved her, as if she had placed herself in alien hands for direction, and freed her soul of responsibility" (42). This is one of the most telling signs that Edna will ultimately refuse to take up her fictitious selves—whichever they may be, however real the consequences—or dedicate herself to them in such a way as to navigate the very patriarchal pressures she must certainly face as a woman.

Edna spends the day after these monumental scenes of a personal, apparently autonomy-inspiring awakening with another person—Robert. And in yet another telling moment, when she meets him later, and he offers her a light breakfast of coffee and a croissant, Edna admits that she had not thought about having breakfast. The narrator states, "[Robert] told [Edna] he had often noticed that she lacked forethought" (43). The two spend the day together in a kind of unreal, fantasy space. At one point, they discuss the prospect of finding pirate treasure. Edna tells Robert, "Pirate gold isn't a thing to be hoarded or utilized. It is something to squander and throw to the four winds, for the fun of seeing the golden specks fly" (46). This serves as a kind of allusion to their own stolen treasure— their private time together, their burgeoning and, on some levels, illicit relationship. But if so, this quote also implies that Edna is perfectly content to enjoy his time without making further claims on it. If she's not really in love with Robert, the legitimate, ultimately unanswered question returns: what is Edna after? The problem is not that the answer is not available to her and all women like her. Rather, the problem is that Edna refrains from actively deciding on a set of answers she could then attempt to actualize in order to give her life meaning. Over and over, she retreats into safe—precisely because they are unattainable—fantasies, leaving nothing left to live for. Put another way, Edna consistently runs *from* but never *toward* anything—at least not for very long, and not with great conviction. Or, as Madame Ratignolle tells Edna, "In some way, you seem to me like a child, Edna. You seem to act without a certain amount of reflection which is necessary in this life" (127).

And so she cultivates and lingers in this non-space, the day's fantasy. When Edna awakes from a nap in the bed a kind stranger offers her, she playfully constructs and enlarges the belief that she and Robert are alive on a strange planet, many, many years after she has gone to sleep: "How many years have I slept?...The whole island seems changed. A new race of beings must have sprung up, leaving only you and me as past relics. How many ages ago did Madame Antoine and Tonie die? And when did our people from Grand Isle disappear from the earth?" (49). Before they leave the island, Madame Antoine tells them about local legends. At this point, narration itself also turns fantastic. The point of view is third-person, limited to Edna, yet here, too, the line is blurred between reality and fantasy—much as it is with Edna. This blurring for Edna is fatal, as we'll see: "Edna could hear the whispering voices of dead men and the click of muffled gold. When she and Robert stepped into Tonie's boat…misty spirit forms were prowling in the shadows and among the reeds, and upon the water were phantom ships, speeding to cover" (51).

Many critics have focused on *The Awakening*'s ending, some going so far as to suggest that Edna's suicide represents a kind of triumph in the high romantic mode, a meta-textual victory, in which the protagonist ascends through suicide into myth, a kind of modern Venus.[4] I'm not going to spend time analyzing the novella's ending except to note that here such a reading not only falsely reads Edna's actions as an achievement of autonomy, but perpetuates the kind of fantasy Edna fatally clings to, precisely the kinds of fiction, which lead to her despair in the first place.

Let us take a moment to distinguish between two kinds of fictions I've alluded to so far. First, there is the inhabitable fiction of identity, in which a person believes, and by which she lives, a fiction that involves dedication as well as responsibility, in order for it to have substance. And second, the fantastic kind, which seems to represent an escape from reality, but which ultimately robs the person indulging it of the very means of engaging with and navigating the otherwise merciless and deadly aspects of an all-too real existence. Consider Hawthorne's Hester Prynne, for example, who lives by her own beliefs, who dedicates herself to an identity that is initially no less fictitious than the one assigned to her by her community—symbolized by the A on her chest—in such a way that, by her very actions, she changes the meaning of that letter from "adulteress" to "angel." This would be an example of the power of an inhabitable fiction. Such an identity would, of course, accommodate the terms of existence and even allow for room, if the person chose to extend its boundaries, to change some of its conventions—as, for example, Madame Ratignolle inhabits, yet willfully manipulates, and pushes the boundaries of her "mother-woman" role. The kind of fiction Edna engages in with Robert, on the other hand, offers absolutely no respite from the very reality she wishes to escape. Robert knows how fantastic their day together has been; he must be aware of the fact that Edna is unwilling to commit herself to a relationship with him in the so-called real world. This is made clear when Edna explains to him why she's hurt that he is going away: "But can't you understand? I've grown used to seeing you, to having you with me all the time, and your action [leaving for Mexico] seems unfriendly, even unkind" (58–59). Robert is going there on a business venture, to make his living. Besides seeming remarkably selfish and self-absorbed, Edna's comments here are noteworthy for their lack of declarative passion, their lack of intentionality—not, "I love you," nor even "I care deeply for you," but "I've grown used to seeing you."

This lack of dedication—a recurring pattern in Edna's life—is made more clear by the narrator right after Robert leaves Edna:

> For the first time she recognized the symptoms of infatuation which she felt incipiently as a child, as a girl in her earliest teens, and later as a young woman. The recognition did not lessen the reality, the poignancy of that revelation by any suggestion or promise of instability [i.e. she is older now and *should* know what such childish infatuation without commitment might lead to]. The past was nothing to her; offered no lesson which she was willing to heed. The future was a mystery which she never attempted to penetrate. The present alone was significant; was hers, to torture her as it was doing then with the biting conviction that she had lost that which she had held, that she had been denied that which her impassioned, newly awakened being demanded. (59)

It's not clear when she makes manifest such a demand. To say one has "grown used to seeing" someone is hardly to demand their presence in one's life. Here the "awakening" the narrator alludes to seems neither renewing nor affirming but destructive, an avenue toward despair.

As part of my title suggests, I am reading the line "casting aside her fictitious self" in an unconventional way. The line comes from the narrator commenting on Léonce's feelings about his wife's actions. Here is the passage:

> It sometimes entered Mr. Pontellier's mind to wonder if his wife were not growing a little unbalanced mentally. He could plainly see that she was not herself. That is, he could not see that she was becoming herself and daily casting aside that fictitious self which we assume like a garment with which to appear before the world. (75)

It's tempting to read this as the narrator's (and, ultimately, the novel's) implication that in freeing herself from some previous "fictitious self"—wife and mother, presumably—Edna is becoming some truer, and therefore freer, self. The problem with this reading, however, is that it ignores the extent to which Edna's movement from fictitious to truer self, her awakening, only and ultimately leads to despair. However, it is, at the same time, always accompanied by less and less conscious, intentional, willful decision-making on her part—as if one simply cannot negotiate the terms of existence without doing so within socially constructed (and therefore fictitious) identities, the conscious and willful execution of which, on the other hand, need not be absolutely circumscribed.[5] Against such a definition of identity, I want to examine Edna's approach to defining herself in the second half of the novella.

After Edna confesses to Madame Reisz that she loves Robert, in fact in the very next chapter—chapter twenty-seven—she sees and is ultimately seduced by Arobin. The next chapter— chapter twenty-eight—begins with the following passage:

> Edna cried a little bit that night after Arobin left her....There was with her an overwhelming feeling of irresponsibility....There was Robert's reproach making itself felt by a quicker, fiercer, more overpowering love, which had awakened within her toward him. Above all, there

was understanding. She felt as if a mist had been lifted from her eyes, enabling her to look upon and comprehend the significance of life, that monster made up of beauty and brutality. (111)

This is a challenging description of Edna's emotional, psychological state. But it's important to focus on the narrator's assertion that Edna felt overwhelmed by a "feeling of irresponsibility"; this is in keeping with the pattern the novella has drawn for us concerning Edna's reactions to people with whom she believes cannot or will not consummate a relationship beyond the stage of infatuation. It is the reiteration of her belief that she is helpless before, and thus surrenders herself to, fate. And this conflict, this confusion, is mirrored in the narrator's descriptions as well: in Edna's current state of being sexually awakened by Arobin, and amorously awakened by Robert, she feels no control over her life, a life which nonetheless has now become clear with her new understanding. But such clarity does not, on the other hand, give her any sense of control over her *own* life.

In the next chapter, we read, immediately following these descriptions, "Without even waiting for an answer from her husband regarding his opinion or wishes in the matter, Edna hastened her preparations for quitting her home on Esplanade Street and moving into the little house around the block" (111). When her husband hears the news that she has left his house, he reacts by telling her of his disapproval of her actions, but mostly, as the narrator states, because of "what people would say" (123). To cover over this potential damage to his investments, he creates a subterfuge in the form of an announcement that he and his wife are away while their house is having additions made to it. Thus, Léonce only enables Edna's move. As the narrator states, "Mr. Pontellier had saved appearances!" (124). Even if we applaud Edna's actions here, her flight to autonomy, we aren't given the sense of an *insurmountable* patriarchy in this particular case: Edna leaves without asking or even consulting her husband first. He does not stop her. He will even, Edna implies, foot the bill for the celebration. He grumbles that she has left the house, but then fixes the situation without preventing Edna from leaving and living in her own house. This is not to say that Edna doesn't face other patriarchal pressures; it's that she seems far freer than most women, even middle class white women in similar situations.

The affair with Arobin seems to encourage her in this new venture toward selfhood, and yet the language used to describe her feelings does not support the idea that she is taking charge of her destiny. "There was with her an overwhelming feeling of irresponsibility" (111). The party itself, furthermore, proves anticlimactic for Edna, reiterating again the sense that her movement toward a less fictitious self only brings about despair and a longing to indulge in fantasy: "But as she sat there among amid her guests, she felt the old ennui overtaking her....[t]he acute longing which always summoned into her spiritual vision the presence *of the beloved one, overpowering her with a sense of the unattainable*" (emphasis added 118). Freedom is terrifying, and Edna's vulnerability here to indulging herself in this longing for what she cannot attain is understandable. She does not believe she can achieve a meaningful life—alone or with Robert—and thus she nurtures the fiction, however unfulfilling, that requires far less dedication.

After she moves into her own house, we get again these lines, reiterating the sense that for Edna, freedom is not the ability to choose a place or identity to live through but an escape from all restrictions and identity:

> The pigeon house pleased her....There was with her a feeling of having descended in the social scale, with a corresponding sense of having risen in the spiritual. *Every step which she took toward relieving herself from obligations added to her strength and expansion as an individual.* She began to look with her own eyes, to see and to apprehend the deeper undercurrents of life. No longer was she content to 'feed upon opinion' [whose?] when her own soul invited her. (emphasis added, 124)

Is it class that oppresses her? If so, how easily she has cast it off. And what do we make of this sense of expanding as an individual when obligations are lifted? Edna does not seem to apprehend that a meaningful life requires some set of obligations; the point is the ability to personally choose them without having them applied from without. This, Edna fails to see.

Toward the end of the novella, Edna's belief—fatalistic and fatal—that she cannot control her own life becomes absolute: "She answered her husband with friendly evasiveness...all sense of reality had gone out of her life; she had abandoned herself to Fate, and awaited the consequences with indifference" (137). Note the voice—active. Not "she was abandoned by fate," nor yet "she felt as if in the hands of fate," but "she [herself] abandoned herself to fate." This, arguably, is the fatal mistake Edna makes—that she believes, even as the novella suggests otherwise, that she cannot combine motherhood and personhood.

In conclusion, consider the passage, in which Madame Reisz speaks to Edna. The pianist reminds Edna of the dedication required to be an artist, the constant need to consciously, willfully dare and defy. Madame Reisz's final words in this scene take on added weight when we read this novella for the second time: "Be careful; the stairs and landings are dark; don't stumble" (85). In allegorical terms, Madame Reisz seems to be warning Edna that to *begin* an endeavor, in art or love, requires far less courage, dedication, and care than to actively and diligently *pursue* it. What freedoms Edna has worked to achieve in order to pursue various identities—artist or lover—can only bring her fulfillment to the extent that she actively dedicates herself, consciously and with effort, *to* those pursuits. As with Adèle's subtle advice to Edna, these admonitions go unnoticed by Edna, and, arguably, by most readers. In this case, the novella, through the character of Madame Resiz, seems to imply that unlike Edna, whose last name means "to bridge" in French, women like her might conceivably begin with an ideal and nevertheless make the necessary leap of practically inhabiting and sustaining it.

Given the trends in the critical reception and positioning of Chopin's novella in the last forty years—the legitimate and highly political task of rescuing this once over-looked work and rightfully pacing it in the canon—it's sometimes easy to forget that *The Awakening* is a work of literature and not merely a socio-political call to action. It's unfair to reduce the text to a simple moral. On the other hand, perhaps the very contentious quality of criticism over *The Awakening*, the fact that this work has resisted any single, totalizing critical reading over these many decades, reaffirms just how alive, how scintillating it continues to be.

Notes

1. As William Bartley notes, summing up the most popular (and apparently mutually exclusive) critical responses to *The Awakening*:

> At one pole of critical consensus, then, is the judgment that Edna's suicide is the despairing act of a spiritually exhausted woman, defeated in her confrontation with patriarchal constraint....This response, or rather family of responses, is flatly contradicted by another: that Edna's suicidal swim is a heroic moment of self-creation and self-possession, even of mythic apotheosis in the high romantic mode." ("Imagining the Future..." 724)

2. In a fascinating article, Rosemary Franklin reminds us that many critics have taken this psychoanalytic approach—connecting Edna's early loss of her mother with her pathology of becoming infatuated with people or modes of existence that cannot become realized. Taking up and modifying this argument, Franklin states:

> In a search for a psychoanalytic and explanatory model for motherlessness in *The Awakening* and Edna's ensuing depression and death, we need to examine a pre-oedipal theory that stresses the relationship with the mother, whom the infant fantasizes as an unconditionally loving Maternal Presence who fulfills all needs. Julia Kristeva, a psychoanalyst and linguist, demonstrates the inevitability of separation from the Maternal Presence and the developing self....She takes a linguistic approach to infant development and the acquisition of language, with an emphasis on the baby's relationship to the mother. The infant thus begins to acquire a self when it learns to speak, and thus enters the "Symbolic" realm. The pre-oedipal experience, which cannot be described because it has no language, becomes the unconscious when the speaking subject enters the "Symbolic." Kristeva calls this pre-oedipal space the "Semiotic," which makes itself known in literary texts by gaps, rhythm, discontinuities, ambiguity, inarticulate voices, and many other non-verbal and non-linear "pulsions." According to Kristeva, all creative pieces balance the Semiotic and the Symbolic. ("Chopin's 'The Awakening'")

> While I agree with this reading, I want to insist that it takes us away from the more enduring feminist reading which would assert that Edna is an everywoman of her time, who is not permitted to combine motherhood and

personhood. Franklin's analysis instead makes an exceptional case study of Edna as a woman whose early motherless-ness inflicts psychological trauma on her for the rest of her life.

3. As Joyce Dyer argues, "Society, as well as the conscience of Edna herself, offers no relief....Motherhood and selfhood were incompatible in Edna's century" (*The Awakening...* 103).

4. Sandra Gilbert's often-cited article "The Second Coming of Aphrodite" proclaims, "Defeated, even crucified, by the 'reality' of nineteenth-century New Orleans, Chopin's resurrected Venus is returning to Cyprus or Cythera" (58). But as William Bartley reminds us, such a farfetched post-narrative assertion "*cannot* have taken place in *The Awakening*—the text simply will not permit it" ("Imagining the Future..." 729).

5. This argument is mirrored by Marta Caminero-Santangelo's claim, referring to the relationship between madness in women and patriarchal societies: "insanity is the final surrender to such [dominant, patriarchal] discourses, precisely because it is characterized by the (dis)ability to produce meaning—that is, to produce representations recognizable as meaningful within society" (*The Madwoman* 11).

Works Cited

Bartley, William. "Imagining the Future in *The Awakening*." *College English* 62.6 (2000): 719–46.

Caminero-Santangelo, Marta. *The Madwoman Can't Speak: Or Why Insanity Is Not Subversive*. Ithaca: Cornell UP, 1998.

Chopin, Kate. *The Awakening*. 1899. Reprint. Intro. Marilynne Robinson. New York: Bantam Books, 1988.

Dyer, Joyce. *The Awakening: A Novel of Beginnings*. New York: Twayne Publishers, 1993.

Gilbert, Sandra M. "The Second Coming of Aphrodite: Kate Chopin's Fantasy of Desire." *The Kenyon Review* 5.3 (1983): 44–66.

Franklin, Rosemary F. "Chopin's 'The Awakening': A Semiotic Novel." *PSYART: A Hyperlink Journal for the Psychological Study of the Arts*. 15 Dec. 2009. Web. 30 Oct 2013. <http://www.psyartjournal.com/article/show/franklin-chopins_the_awakening_a_semiotic-novel>.

Ramos, Peter "Unbearable Realism: Freedom, Ethics and Identity in *The Awakening*." *College Literature*, 37.4 (2010): 145–165.

"The Subtle Quivering Life": Reading *The Awakening* Through Kate Chopin

David Z. Wehner

> Religion and science are the two most powerful forces in the world today, especially in the United States.
>
> —Edward O. Wilson

If one accepts an invitation to a party, one should not go to the party and complain about the food, the décor of the host's home, or the guest list; if one accepts the invitation, one should go and be a polite guest. Therefore, because I accepted an invitation to submit an article to this collection devoted to Kate Chopin's *TheAwakening*, perhaps it represents bad manners to begin the essay saying that we, Chopin's critical community, focus too much on this one novel to the exclusion of her other work, and such an exclusive focus gives us a skewed reading of this novel and of Kate Chopin. For example, in the introductory essay of his collection analyzing Kate Chopin, Harold Bloom gives a nod to Chopin's entire body of work, but then spends his essay dissecting *The Awakening*. If we focus juston this one novel, we tend toward a feminist reading of Chopin, as this text easily lends itself to such an interpretation: Edna Pontellier awakens to the fact that she lives in a patriarchal culture hostile to her true self, and her new consciousness leads her out of her marriage and into the Gulf of Mexico. But then one has Chopin's short story "Athénaïse," where the protagonist has an awakening triggered by her discovery that she is pregnant, and her new consciousness leads her *back* into her marriage.

If we only focus on *The Awakening*, we tend to read Chopin's work as a critique of Christianity because, after all, when Edna goes with Robert to Our Lady of Lourdes Church, "her one thought was to quit the stifling atmosphere of the church" (34–35).[1] But then one has "A Sentimental Soul," where Mamzelle Fleurette loves the married Lacodie. During confession, her priest tells her to stop pursuing this affair, but the story ends with Fleurette hanging a picture of her illicit love on the wall beside her crucifix; that is, she does not rip her crucifix from the wall but instead reconciles the dictates of her heart with those of her faith.

If we focus onlyon *The Awakening*, we tend to have a grim vision of Chopin's work, what Bert Bender calls an extended and "darkening" meditation on post-Darwinian humanity ("Teeth" 459). *The Complete Works of Kate Chopin* contains ninety-six short stories and two novels. Of those ninety-eight works, only two end with the protagonist committing suicide: *The Awakening* and "Her Letters." That is, ninety-six of her ninety-eight works do not end with the "final bleak awakening" of this novel (Bender "Teeth" 464). We read *The Awakening* as Chopin's definitive work, through which we can view her *oeuvre*, but nothing in her fiction or letters or papers suggests that she saw this novel as her defining or even her best work. Therefore, if we place *The Awakening* within her entire body of work, if we look at this novel as only one part of a larger corpus, a different picture emerges. From 1889 until 1904, Chopin articulated a consistent, idiosyncratic religious vision informed, in part, by the Catholicism of the first half of her life and, in part, by her reading of Charles Darwin in the second half. Her work continually comes back to an image of a life that quivers, pulsates, palpitates—frequent words in her writing—and her characters must recognize this life, embrace it, or suffer the consequences. The conflict in much of her fiction lies in whatever entity takes one away from this life force, whether an inherited religious tradition or a scientific intellectual mindset. We can then read *The Awakening* as but one iteration within this larger set of abiding concerns.

Literary scholars tend to be drawn to firsts: the first published volume of poetry written by a New World resident? Anne Bradstreet's *The Tenth Muse, Lately Sprung Up in America* of 1650. Beginning of the black American literary tradition? Phillis Wheatley's *Poems on Various Subjects, Religious and Moral* of 1773. First writer in the American canon to fully depict a fictional Catholic world? Kate Chopin. That is, we talk about Chopin as a regionalist writer producing local color, forgetting that Catholicism constitutes a large part of that local color. Born in 1850, Chopin grew up in a Catholic family in St. Louis, where she attended the Academy of the Sacred Heart from the ages of five until eighteen. Per Seyersted states that Kate Chopin "lived in a milieu which was devoutly Catholic and expected her to be the same" and that from 1879–84, when she lived in Cloutierville, Louisiana—the setting for much of her fiction—she went to church "fairly regularly" (*Biography* 29, 45). By no accident, then, Christian references fill her work. Of her ninety-six short stories, four take place at Easter, five at Christmas. Religious diction runs throughout her stories: Almighty God, "the litany of the Blessed Virgin," awakening, transfiguration, hope, mercy, rapture, ecstasy, Christ, the Holy Ghost, and Assumption (*CompleteWorks* 600). *The Awakening* begins on a Sunday with most of the Grand Isle guests attending Mass, and it contains Adèle Ratignolle, the "faultless Madonna" (11). In the writer's fiction, characters enter and leave convents, enter and leave monasteries, go to confession at one church and then switch to another. Chopin's world is decidedly a Catholic world.

Per Seyersted and Sandra Gilbert see the 1880s as the point in Chopin's life when she left the Catholicism of her early adulthood due to Darwin's influence. In 1883, when Chopin resided in Natchitoches, Louisiana, her husband, Oscar, died, and the writer moved back to St. Louis a year later. In 1885, her mother died, and Chopin befriended Dr. Kolbenheyer, a "determined agnostic," who persuaded her to read Darwin, Thomas Huxley, and Herbert Spencer (Seyersted, *Biography* 49). We know from her diary that she actually read Darwin, as the diary records a visit from a Mr. and Mrs. Schuyler one evening. William Schuyler had agreed to write a sketch of her, which appeared in August 1894 in *The Writer*, and in the sketch, Schuyler writes that after Oscar's death, "The works of Darwin, Huxley, and Spencer were her daily companions" (Chopin, *Miscellany* 117). Following the long-held tension between religion and science, we might read this chronology as supporting a view that Chopin left religion for science. A colleague of mine, a former nun who isnow a professor, once told me, "You can take the girl out of the church, but you can't take the church out of the girl." Put another way, Carlos Fuentes writes that the renowned filmmaker Luis Buñuel represents "one of the most compelling, if uncategorizable, intellectual tendencies of the twentieth century: that of religious temperament without religious faith" (21). By the time Chopin began publishing in 1889, her religious faith may have faded, but a religious temperament, greatly inflected by Darwin, remained.

Traditionally, we have Darwin stand as a metonym for the clash between evolution and creationism, science and religion. Chopin found in Darwin, however, a conception of life replicating itself over millions of years; of life becoming almost an entity in itself, transcending its material conditions, reproducing itself, procreating, pushing forward over incomprehensible expanses of time. Despite its reputation, Darwin's writing contains a nuanced stance toward the question of religion, and at points he seems less the determined rationalist and more an uncertain Victorian man who finds in nature what one might call the scientific sublime. For example, he ends *The Origin of Species*—459 pages of small print, dense theory, and overwhelming evidence—with this elegant sentence:

> There is grandeur in this view of life, with its several powers, having been originally breathed by the Creator into a few forms or into one; and that, whilst this planet has gone cycling on according to the fixed law of gravity, from so simple a beginning endless forms most beautiful and most wonderful have, and are being evolved. (459)

His writings contain a sense that in Natural Selection he found what Sandra Gilbert calls—in speaking of Edna Pontellier—"the imagination's desire for amplitude and awe" (25). Darwin comes back again and again to one word in describing plants and animals in both *Origin* and *Descent of Man*: "wonderful." Throughout *Origin* and *Descent*, Darwin describes the flora and fauna as "wonderful," "beautiful," "wondrous," "wonderfully beautiful," "gorgeous," "marvelous," and "magnificent" (*Origin* 131, 74, 126; *Descent* 442, 321, 172, 474).

This Darwinian conception of a "wonderful," "gorgeous" life force permeates Chopin's stories. In "After the Winter," on Easter eve, "the whole earth seemed teeming with new, green, vigorous life everywhere" (182). In "Alexandre's Wonderful Experience," the title character "rejoiced to be alive and to feel himself again one of the multitude," while in "A Reflection," the first story Chopin wrote after *The Awakening*, the narrator longs to be part of "that moving procession of human energy; greater than the palpitating earth and the things growing thereon" (*Private* 266, *Complete* 622). "Palpitate" means to pulsate, to throb and comes from the Latin *palpare*, meaning "to touch." In *The Awakening*, Dr. Mandelet describes Edna as "palpitant with the forces of life"; "palpitant" means palpitating, quivering (67). In "A Morning Walk," Archibald gazes at the "shadows of quivering leaves" playing upon the window casement, and in "Tante Cat'rinette," the narrator tells us that the night was "pregnant with the subtle quivering life of early spring" (568, 340). Standing behind, running throughout Chopin's world, then, one finds this life, energy, palpitating, pulsating, throbbing, quivering; and this life force forms the conflict of many of her stories: her characters recognize this force and adjust their lives to it or separate themselves from this life and live with the results.

If Chopin depicts a Catholic world, tellingly, Christian asceticism stands as one of the entities threatening to cut one off from this life force, and we see this concern in *The Awakening* and throughout her work. While at the Academy of the Sacred Heart, Chopin wrote an essay entitled "Christian Art. 1867," in which she argues that Christianity's "superiority lies in the pre-eminence given to spirit over matter" (*Private* 33). Chopin, seventeen when she wrote this, no longer privileged spirit over matter by the time she began publishing in 1889 at thirty-nine years old. In fact, her body of work attempts to articulate her own particular vision of the relationship between the two entities. For example, the Virgin Mary—"the chief Christian ideal of a feminine being"—represents a figure from the Catholicism of Chopin's young adulthood that the writer must resolve with the beliefs outlined above (Seyersted, *Biography* 148). The doctrine of the Immaculate Conception of the

Blessed Virgin dates to 1854 and Pius IX, and it claims that, at the moment of Mary's conception, the Holy Spirit intervened, keeping Mary unstained by human sin. In Chopin's time, therefore, the Virgin Mary became an even more exalted figure in the Catholic Church and became a figure the writer had to reconcile with her ideas of the sensuous. She effected such a reconciliation by jettisoning much of the emphasis placed on the Madonna. Chopin's Aunt Boyer once gave her ten-year-old niece an unlined notebook that included a lace-bordered picture of a young girl wearing a garland and gazing up at the Virgin Mary; by the time of *The Awakening*, the "gazing up at the Virgin Mary" has left Chopin's fiction. On the opening page of the novel, we meet the Farival twins playing a duet from "Zampa." When we next meet them in chapter nine, they again play a duet from "Zampa," and the narrative tells us that they always dress "in the Virgin's colors, blue and white, having been dedicated to the Blessed Virgin at their baptism" (23). They always wear blue and white, and, apparently, they always play the duet from "Zampa," which explains why, while they play, the parrot shrieks, "*Allez vous-en! Sapristi!*," which translates "Go away! For God's sake!" (23). The twin's grandfather insists that the bird be removed and "consigned to regions of darkness," but Victor Lebrun objects and the bird stays (23). That is, the text associates the twins with the Virgin Mary, and the portrayal does not flatter them.

The Awakening also gives us Madame Ratignolle—a "faultless Madonna," a "sensuous Madonna" dressed in "pure white"—who serves as Edna Pontellier's foil (11, 12, 15). Ratignolle has been married seven years and about every two years has a baby. She epitomizes a "mother-woman": "They were women who idolized their children, worshiped their husbands, and esteemed it a holy privilege to efface themselves as individuals and grow wings as ministering angels" (9). The language here—worship, holy, angels—elevates the role of mother to a religious role, and thus a mother-woman becomes a Madonna, a holy mother. When Léonce chastises Edna for her inattentiveness to their children—"If it was not a mother's place to look after children, whose on earth was it?"—he chastises her, in part, because she does not act like a mother-woman (7). And though the text describes Ratignolle as a "sensuous Madonna," this does not make her a sexual Madonna, which would contradict the idea of the virgin mother. That is, Chopin's writing does not depict Ratignolle as a sexualized mother as it does Athénaïse, the title character of the story discussed below. Ratignolle may be a sensual Madonna, but she displaces any sexual instincts in herself into maternal ones.

Taking a cue from her friend, Edna continually channels her budding feelings for Robert into her children. In one paragraph, Léonce mentions to his wife that he saw Robert in the city; in the next paragraph, Edna impatiently leads the children out of the sun and scolds the quadroon for her inattention (45). In one moment, Edna admits to Mademoiselle Reisz that she loves Robert; in the next, she sends her children chocolates with a "tender message" and "an abundance of kisses" (78). Ratignolle channels—and Edna tries to channel—her sexual urges into activities considered proper in her day. Seyersted tells us that the Creoles believed that a "woman should be satisfied with her home," and this description fits Ratignolle: she conceives every second year, and her only passions appear to be domestic ones (*Biography* 66). Chopin wanted to conceptualize a role of motherhood outside the one envisioned by the church and the sciences of her day, but also one outside that of some of her contemporary feminists. Charlotte Perkins Gilman, for instance, believed that "woman with her maternal instincts was the great socializing force in human history" (Civello 30). Chopin, however, did not envision mothers automatically as social reformers, nor Virgin Marys, nor desexualized domestic goddesses. She wanted a mode of motherhood and womanhood that placed women in the midst of the fleshy sensuousness of nature.

Ratignolle does not embody such a mode, nor does Mademoiselle Reisz, the pianist; and, indeed, the two women form the Scylla and Charybdis between which Edna must navigate. The text makes clear the opposition of Ratignolle to Reisz when it tells us that Ratignolle "was on the most distant terms with the musician, and preferred to know nothing concerning her" (57). If Adèle Ratignolle embodies the quintessential mother-woman and "faultless Madonna," Reisz objects "to the crying of a baby," and the narrator describes her as "a homely woman, with a small weazened face and body" (25). Reisz represents the artist Edna would like to be, but in order to become that artist, Reisz has had to forfeit "feminine sensuous pleasure" and exist with an "essential sexlessness" (Wolff 15; Bender "Teeth" 470). Both Ratignolle and Reisz, like a nun or a virgin, have foregone sexual pleasure—Ratignolle channels it into her family, Reisz into her art—so if Edna attempts to conceptualize a mode of femininity that includes a relationship to the flesh, she must do so outside of the models offered by these two women.

Asceticism wants to deny certain pleasures of the material world, in order to pursue higher spiritual values, but Chopin, in a sort of displaced sacramentalism, believes one finds the higher spiritual values in the material world. We see this quality even in Chopin's first piece of fiction, "Emancipation: A Life Fable," which tells of an animal born in a cage that one day discovers the door open. At first, he does not leave the cage, but he cannot stay because "the spell of the Unknown was over him" (37). One day, in a mad flight, the animal, hungry and thirsty, runs out of the cage, "seeing, smelling, touching of all things" (37). Though a piece of juvenilia—Chopin wrote it at nineteen years old—"Emancipation" presages many of the themes and images of the author's work. Like this fable, *The Awakening* begins with an animal in a cage, a parrot, and the novel's protagonist, like many of Chopin's characters, hungers and thirsts to see, smell, and touch all things, including the sexual. This novel continually reminds the reader of the sensuous quality of nature, of how nature appeals to the senses. Chapter five ends with the line, "The sun was low in the west and the breeze was soft and warm," while late in the novel, at the dinner just before Edna leaves for the pigeon house, the narrative tells us, "Outside the soft, monotonous splash of a fountain could be heard; the sound penetrated into the room with the heavy odor of jessamine that came through the open windows" (14, 84). Because Edna leaves the windows open, nature can come into the room, and its softness and odor can "penetrate" the diners. On the last page of the text, Edna casts aside "the unpleasant, pricking garments from her, and for the first time in her life she stood naked in the open air, at the mercy of the sun, the breeze that beat upon her, and the waves that invited her" (108). This sentence contrasts the unpleasant "pricking" sensations of Edna's culture with the sensuous quality of nature, and for the first time in the protagonist's life, the sun, the breeze, and the waves can touch "her white body," and she can touch nature (109). In the next moment, Edna swims into the Gulf of Mexico, and the narrator tells us, "The touch of the sea is sensuous, enfolding the body in its soft, close embrace" (109). The novel repeatedly shows us the seductive qualities of the sea, and in this moment, Edna reciprocates the seduction.

The animal in "Emancipation" wants to see, smell, touch, eat and drink—it wants to use and experience its senses. Edna, too, hungers and thirsts. Chopin's fictional and non-fictional writing continually ties this hunger to the material, to the flesh. In her honeymoon diary, Chopin writes about visiting the falls on the Rhine, "So closely did we approach them that the spray fell upon us like rain. Such a delicious, indescribable feeling of moistness" (*Private* 113). Similarly, in her fiction, in "A Shameful Affair," the protagonist thinks of an illicit kiss as "the most delicious thing" of her life, while in "The Kiss," the narrator says of Nathalie, "her lips looked hungry for the kiss which they invited" (134, 381). Here, nature—the spray of the waterfall, the flesh of the body—exists as something delicious to be tasted and savored with satisfaction. When Edna begins to feel desire for Alcée, the text speaks of "her awakening sensuousness," so this awakening to the sensuousness of the material represents part of the awakening of the title. Before her nap on *Chênière Caminada*, Edna removes "the greater part" of her clothes and looks at "the fine, firm quality and texture of her flesh" (36). In Christian theology, one must leave the flesh in order to be reborn in the spirit; in Chopin's world, Edna must become aware of the flesh, must reclaim the very flesh denied by the Church, in order to awaken to the sensuous.

Max Weber writes of the Puritans' "sharp distinction between things divine and things of the flesh," but in Chopin's conception of nature and the quivering life inherent in nature, she wants to blur the lines between the divine and the flesh (110). Critics speak of Edna's "spiritual emancipation" (Radcliff-Umstead 63) and "spiritual liberation" (Gilbert 11), or they speak of Edna's "sexual awakening" (Walker 101); Seyersted accurately combines the two: "Edna's sexual emancipation is so completely interlocked with her spiritual breaking of bonds that she insists on both with equal force" (*Biography* 145). With Chopin, however, one must have a supple definition of sex that goes beyond simple coitus. Freud's *Three Essays on the Theory of Sexuality*, published a year after Chopin's death, drew criticism for its insistence on the sexuality of infants, but the essays make clear that Freud uses *sex* loosely to mean any bodily pleasure. Infants discover that their body can give them pleasure, and they attempt to repeat those sensations, whether sucking their thumb, withholding their feces, or rocking back and forth. Freud terms infants "polymorphously perverse," meaning they have no qualms about gaining pleasure wherever they can find it in their body (100). In this way, infants are sexual, and they will focus this diffuse sexuality on the genitals later in adolescence. To become aware of the sensuous, Chopin's characters must, in Freudian terms, become polymorphously perverse. They must learn to take pleasure from their entire body—not just in the areas, places, and times condoned by society—and to do so has spiritual significance.

Chopin's fiction, then, continually combines the sensuous and the sexual with the spiritual, and we see this quality most prominently in "Athénaïse." The story begins with Athénaïse Miché leaving her new husband, Cazeau, not because he mistreats her, but because she realizes she despises marriage. Cazeau brings her back once, but she leaves a second time, this time going to New Orleans, where she takes a room in a boarding house and tries to puzzle out her feelings surrounding this new marriage. After several weeks, the keeper of the house, Sylvie, realizes that Athénaïse is pregnant and informs her. At first Athénaïse remains silent, but then "her whole being was steeped in a wave of ecstasy. When she finally arose from the chair in which she had been seated, and looked at herself in the mirror, a face met hers which she seemed to see for the first time, so transfigured was it with wonder and rapture" (451). By the language—ecstasy, transfigured, wonder, and rapture—one might think this moment represents the Annunciation, but the next lines tell us that when our protagonist now thinks of her husband, "the first purely sensuous tremor of her life swept over her [. . .] her whole passionate nature was aroused as if by a miracle" (451). Whereas, before this announcement, Athénaïse had been uninterested in her husband sexually, now, when she returns home and kisses her husband, "he felt the yielding of her whole body against him. He felt her lips for the first time respond to the passion of his own" (454). With the Annunciation, Mary was a virgin; with this annunciation, Athénaïse becomes sexual "as if by a miracle." Bender reads this story as Athénaïse accepting "her place as mistress in the Darwinian hierarchy of sex," and therein Bender implies a critique of this story as conservative in that it falls in line with accepted cultural gender norms, as opposed to the more radical *TheAwakening*, which challenges those norms ("Quarrel" 191). One could, however, instead read them as not contradictory, but complementary: both stories combine religion, sex, and the natural world, and in both, women awaken to their animal, and thus sexual, nature—with one character, that desire directs her toward her husband, andwith the other, toward men other than her husband.

The sin, the problem lies for Chopin in whatever entity takes one away from and obscures this continual life force inherent in nature, whether it be the Church or even the scientific rationalism embodied in a figure like Darwin. In *Descent of Man*, the biologist writes, "Man has advanced in his intellectual powers but has retrograded in his instincts" (616). Darwin looks at this retrogression neutrally or even positively—this represents the triumph of the scientific outlook and humankind's evolution; Chopin sees the replacement of instincts with intellect as a de-evolution—such a switch divorces us from nature. "A Morning Walk" demonstrates that a strictly intellectual and scientific approach to the world, too, risks severing one from the very world one proposes to study. Chopin wrote this story in April 1897, and it stands as the last or second-to-last story that she wrote before she began working on *The Awakening* in June. It appeared in the *Criterion*, originally entitled "An Easter Day Conversion."

Therefore, one can see, in the spring and summer of 1897, Chopin working out her thinking about how her characters, male and female, turn around, awaken, and experience rebirth. Chopin sets the story in spring—the time of year Darwin calls "the breeding season" or "season of love"—and it begins with Archibald, our scientific protagonist, taking a walk like an "animal which rebels against an unaccustomed burden" (*Descent* 297, 359; *Complete* 566). On any other Sunday, Archibald would be dissecting insects and observing them "at close range," for he liked to approach nature in a "practical and profitable manner" (567). But this particular Easter Sunday, the spring day speaks to him "in a new, delicious way, while the blood in his veins beat a response" (567). On his walk, Archibald sees Lucy, whom he met before but does not remember. As Lucy heads to Easter services, Archibald offers to carry her flowers, and when he does, "The odor of the flowers was heavy and penetrating, like the fumes of a subtle intoxicant that reached Archibald's brain" (568). While in such an "intoxicated" state, the scientist looks down at Lucy, and "her soft, curved lips made him think of peaches that he had bitten" (568). Next, "He followed her into the church; he did not know why, and for once he did not care to investigate his motives" (568).

Inside the sanctuary, the open stained glass windows allow in the sunlight, the sound of birds, "and the shadows of quivering leaves" (568). When the minister turns to address the congregation, twice he says, "I am the Resurrection and the Life," and as Archibald:

> gathered it into his soul a vision of life came with it; the poet's vision, of the life that is within and the life that is without, pulsing in unison, breathing the harmony of an undivided existence.

> He listened to no further words of the minister. He entered into himself and he preached unto himself a sermon in his own heart, as he gazed from the window through which the song came and where the leafy shadows quivered. (569)

The story ends here, so what we have just seen represents the conversion of the original title. In this story, the asceticism not of the church, but of science cuts Archibald off from this "pulsing" energy inherent in nature, and what brings him back to life lies not entirely outside the church either. That is, Chopin could have had Archibald not follow Lucy into church but continue on his way off into the woods, where he has a conversion experience inspired by his close examination of an insect through a magnifying glass. However, instead he leaves his scientific studies and has his conversion in church, on Easter Sunday, listening to Christ's words, "I am the Resurrection and the Life" (John 11:25). But Archibald's experience does not entirely represent a Christian conversion either in that no sooner does he hear these words than he stops listening to the minister and enters into his own thoughts and preaches his own sermon. "A Morning Walk" and *The Awakening*, then, represent two stories from the spring and summer of 1897, in which the protagonists live a "divided existence" cut off "from the life that is within and the life that is without." Asceticism of different kinds separates them off from this life, and an attending to the senses and hence the sensuousness of existence awakens them to this force—Archibald attends to the spring day, the odor of the flowers, the curve of Lucy's lips, the stained glass, and the quivering leaves; Edna to the texture of her flesh, the odor of jessamine, the soft, warm breeze, and, finally, the touch of the sea on her naked body. Both have a vision of the "harmony of an undivided existence," and both perhaps do not achieve it.

If we remove *The Awakening* from its privileged position in our scholarship on Chopin, if we look at this novel as but one piece of a larger body of work, an image of Chopin emerges as a writer with complicated, quirky, personal religious views and with a nuanced vision of the relation between the flesh and the spirit, the secular and the sacred. She drew a thin line between religion, sex, and nature and allowed these entities frequently to penetrate—an oft-occurring word in her work—each other. She saw in Darwin an image of life—aggressive, awesome, all-encompassing—that has been there pulsing insistently for billions of years, and she imagined an existence "undivided" from this force. "A Morning Walk" describes this "vision of life" as "the poet's vision," but it also represents

Chopin's vision as seen in *The Awakening* and throughout her body of work.

Note

1. When this essay quotes Kate Chopin's fiction, the reader can assume that the text comes from *The Complete Works of Kate Chopin*, edited by Per Seyersted. Quotations from *The Awakening*, however, will come from the edition listed in the Works Cited.

Works Cited

Bender, Bert. "Kate Chopin's Quarrel with Darwin before *The Awakening*." *Journal of American Studies*, 26:2 (1992): 185–204.

_____. "The Teeth of Desire: *The Awakening* and *The Descent of Man*." *American Literature: A Journal of Literary History, Criticism, and Bibliography*, 63:3 (1991): 459–73.

Chopin, Kate. *The Complete Works of Kate Chopin*. Ed. Per Seyersted. Baton Rouge: Louisiana State UP, 1984.

_____. *A Kate Chopin Miscellany*. Eds. Per Seyersted and Emily Toth. Natchitoches, LA: Northwestern State UP, 1979.

_____. *Kate Chopin's Private Papers*. Eds. Emily Toth and Per Seyersted. Bloomington:Indiana UP, 1998.

_____. *The Awakening*. Ed. Margo Culley. New York: Norton, 1994.

Civello, Paul. "Evolutionary Feminism, Popular Romance, and Frank Norris's 'Man's Woman.'" *Studies in American Fiction*, 24:1 (1996): 23–44.

Darwin, Charles. *The Descent of Man*. Amherst, MA: Prometheus, 1998.

_____. *The Origin of Species by Means of Natural Selection or the Preservation of Favoured Races in the Struggle for Life*. New York: Penguin, 1958.

Freud, Sigmund. *Three Essays on the Theory of Sexuality*. Trans. James Strachey. New York: Basic, 2000.

Fuentes, Carlos. *This I Believe: An A to Z of a Life*. New York: Random House, 2005.

Gilbert, Sandra M. "Introduction: The Second Coming of Aphrodite." *The Awakening*. New York: Penguin, 1984.

Radcliff-Umstead, Douglas. "Chopin's *The Awakening*: The Discovery ofEternity." *Zeitschrift für Anglistik und Amerikanistik: A Quarterly of Language, Literature and Culture*, 36:1 (1988): 62–67.

Seyersted, Per. *Kate Chopin: A Critical Biography*. Baton Rouge: Louisiana State UP, 1969.

Walker, Nancy. "Feminist or Naturalist: The Social Context of Kate Chopin's *The Awakening.*" *The Southern Quarterly: A Journal of the Arts in the South*, 17:2 (1979): 95–103.

Weber, Max. *The Protestant Ethic and the Spirit of Capitalism.* Trans. Talcott Parsons. New York: Routledge, 2001.

Wolff, Cynthia Griffin. "Un-Utterable Longing: The Discourse of Feminine Sexuality in *The Awakening.*" *Studies in American Fiction*, 24:1 (1996): 3–22.

Kate Chopin's *The Awakening*: Authenticity and the Artist

Janet Beer

and Helena Goodwyn

The Awakening, published in 1899 and originally entitled "A Solitary Soul," earns its place as a pivotal text in the history of feminist literature and criticism as the realization of Kate Chopin's ambition to present the "inward life" (*Complete Works* 893) of a woman estranged from her external circumstances. It is testament to Chopin's achievement that *The Awakening* has the enduring capacity to open itself to new insights from successive generations of readers and theorists. Analysis of Edna Pontellier's supposed "failure" (*Complete Works* 887) as wife and mother is common in Chopin studies, and the burgeoning of her career as an artist is often deployed to support discussions of her "rebirth."[1] Less usual, however, is a discussion of Edna as a serious and potentially economically independent professional—in that role of artist—in the context of her search for the authentic life. This essay will seek to examine, in some detail, Edna's ultimate refusal to develop her talent as a painter.

Edna Pontellier, when we first encounter her, exists merely in a prolonged imitation of the life of the provincial wife and mother. Chopin signposts her heroine's potential for rebellion against the conventional expectations of such a role early in the narrative, when we meet a scene of domestic disharmony. New readers might find Edna's reaction to Mr. Pontellier's rude awakening of her, upon his return from a night of gambling, disproportionate; but his accusation of her "habitual neglect of the children" produces an "indescribable oppression, which seemed to generate in some unfamiliar part of her consciousness" (*Complete Works* 886). As the reader will eventually discover, it is the awakening of this "unfamiliar part" of Edna's consciousness that sets her adrift from the life she has been leading heretofore.

Near the beginning of the novel, Edna accomplishes her first solitary swim—an achievement, for which all the onlookers give themselves credit. Her "achievement" is curiously described as "unlooked for" but nevertheless it empowers her to feel she would like "to swim far out, where no woman had swum before." (*Complete Works* 908) The elation of her triumph wears off quickly, however, and Edna is left with the enfeebling negative force of her sense of inadequacy: she is "unaccustomed" and "unaided" and so believes she "should have perished out there alone." (*Complete Works* 909) The sharp reversal of her new found self-confidence is intensified by Chopin's repeated use of the reversing prefix "un," which acts throughout the novel as a cruel reminder, by virtue of its proximity to each word it negates, of how close the protagonist comes to achieving authenticity, but finds it, ultimately, "unattainable." (*Complete Works* 913)

One of Chopin's central interests throughout her fiction is in the depiction of the "inward life" (*Complete Works* 893) of women, often through development of a singular incident, which can be seen to encapsulate a whole history (as in "Her Letters" or "The Story of an Hour"). In many of the short stories, and in both her novels, *At Fault* and *The Awakening*, Chopin's writing highlights the predicament of those who do not fit with their era, those who are pushing at, or get pushed towards, the boundaries of the possible or the permissible in terms of class, race, gender, age, and religion. In the story "A No-Account Creole," Euphrasie is young, lower-middle class, and female, yet she is definitively in control and in charge of "the old Santien place," keeping her father and her old and new lovers quietly in thrall to her wisdom and will. (*Complete Works* 82) Hector Santien, in the story "In and Out of Old Natchitoches," exists in a delicately poised state of ambiguity between homo- and heterosexuality, respectability and notoriety, having thrown off the burden of the plantation and its class demarcations for a studiedly alternative life in the city.

Chopin's protagonists often come to grief because they cannot attain a sense of authenticity, as in being true to one's self, or they are forced to relinquish the life they once expected to lead, like

Madame Pélagie. In the story that bears her name, Madame Pélagie's "footsteps [are] forced into the light," although "her soul stayed in the shadows of the ruin" of the house and the life that she led before the Civil War. (*Complete Works* 239) In "Désirée's Baby," Désirée's very existence depends upon her husband's faith in her: his rejection of their baby is therefore a negation of her too, which culminates in her self-destruction in the indiscriminate embrace of the "deep, sluggish bayou." (*Complete Works* 244) La Belle Zoraïde, in the story by the same name, wishes to validate her own caste and color when she rejects the enslavement of an arranged marriage. But instead, she is punished for her attempt at self-determination and driven mad by repeated confutations of her most basic aspirations—to love, to motherhood—and so she turns "her face to the wall." (*Complete Works* 306) In The Awakening, Edna Pontellier casts off her marriage ties and social bonds in order to begin a search for personal authenticity and fulfillment. What she uncovers, however, is a deeper disquiet which leads ultimately to the terminal "soft, close embrace" of the Gulf. (*Complete Works* 1000)

Despite this litany of wasted, unfulfilled lives, in some rare cases, the authentic life arrives unexpectedly, actually against the grain of rebellion, as it does for the eponymous heroine Athénaïse or for Suzanne St. Denys Godolph again in "In and Out of Old Natchitoches"; and that unexpected life is a conventional one. Both these women find eventual fulfillment in marriage and contentment in future motherhood; and some, not least Madame Ratignolle and her fellow "mother-women" in *The Awakening*, find authenticity and are even "delicious in the rôle." (*Complete Works* 888)

As with many of the French realists that Chopin so admired, the "life" that she was drawn to portray was often a life at a point of crisis: a crisis not always evident, obvious or dramatic, and sometimes derives from an event as seemingly trivial as the purchase of two new pairs of shoes in the briefest of short stories, "Boulôt and Boulotte," or a failed liaison that results in a marriage not previously entertained as a possibility in "At the Cadian Ball."

In her book *Unveiling Kate Chopin*, Emily Toth makes the point that Chopin never received sufficient praise for what makes

The Awakening such an enduring and relevant text, that is, that it is a novel about the subject Chopin "had been studying all her life: how women think" (226). In one short novel, Chopin offers us a range of female typologies: the "mother-women [...] delicious in the role" (*Complete Works* 888); the young woman, one of a pair of "lovers"; the adulteress; the widow, a "lady in black...telling her beads" (*Complete Works* 882), and the artist, Mademoiselle Reisz: "self-assertive" with "a disposition to trample upon the rights of others." (*Complete Works* 905) Chopin presents her female characters to us in emphatically defined positions, conscious, as her use of the term "role" indicates, of the fact that these women are performing. The spectacle before us is that of the woman defined by her level of subjugation to a man, showcasing the finite positions women were permitted to occupy in turn-of-the-century Louisiana. The narrowness of definition illustrates just how confined and delimiting the spaces are: courtship, marriage, widowhood, the artist—the latter, apparently, necessarily a spinster and, moreover, a monster— "partially demented [...] extremely disagreeable and unpleasant." (*Complete Works* 966) Edna Pontellier is, from the outset, uncomfortable and awkward with the labels "mother" and "wife." However, they are so deeply institutionalized that to some extent she is able to mimic them without much effort. Thus, she shows herself willing, for the sake of not appearing "unamiable and uninterested" to make "winter night garments" for her children at the height of summer, despite not being able to "see the use of anticipating" (*Complete Works* 889) the inevitable change of season. But, as elsewhere in *The Awakening*, Chopin's use of the prefix "un" acts as a juxtaposing force, drawing the reader's attention to the emotion or act that Edna aims at, but cannot quite authentically experience.

When Edna tries to move away from the bonds of her marriage and motherhood, the gap between her "outward" performance and "inward" self widens. In casting off "that outward existence which conforms," for "the inward life which questions" (*Complete Works* 893), Edna exposes an unguarded narcissism that other characters in the novel, and critics of the text, have likened to the behavior of a child. This unabashed self-interest conflicts with the mask of approved womanliness: Madame Ratignolle tells her "you seem to act without a certain amount of reflection" (*Complete Works* 979) when cautioning her not to be alone with Arobin, and Edna tells Doctor Mandelet "I don't want anything but my own way" (*Complete Works* 996). The problem for Edna is that she cannot have her own way: she will always exist in a world where she is reputationally and socially dependent on others. Mademoiselle Reisz attempts to advise Edna's newly exposed self: "The bird that would soar above the level plain of tradition and prejudice must have strong wings. It is a sad spectacle to see the weaklings bruised, exhausted, fluttering back to earth" (*Complete Works* 966). And yet Edna "only half comprehend[s] her." She cannot think "of any extraordinary flights" because, as with her swim, she does not see in herself the necessary strength of will to fly alone.

Edna's awakening has been widely acknowledged to be an awakening unto the self, and it is because of the disturbing, internal nature of this awakening that Edna suffers several rapid and alarming shifts of consciousness leading to her attempts to define a different life for herself. She is bewildered by the "mother-women," genuinely puzzled by those who "esteemed it a holy privilege to efface themselves as individuals" (*Complete Works* 888), but it does not stop her from trying to engage inauthentically with their ways. Kate Chopin describes the eventual shedding of that inauthenticity when she articulates Monsieur Pontellier's reaction to the changes in Edna's behavior: "He could see plainly that she was not herself. That is, he could not see that she was becoming herself and daily casting aside that fictitious self which we assume like a garment with which to appear before the world" (*Complete Works* 939).

The most fulfilling experience Edna has during her fateful summer at Grand Isle is in direct contrast to that which would be experienced by the mother-women because it is mentally and physically all-consuming and totally egocentric. Edna is inspired by the sea and "the exultation" (*Complete Works* 908) of taking charge of her body in the waves, to the extent that she experiences, for the first time, a recognition of her capacity for an act of pure individuation.

This is not merely the satisfaction of personal achievement: to swim unaided gives her something, which is solely her own, representing, as she comes to understand, a form of freedom. Chopin tells us that Edna spent "much of her time in the water," towards the end of that summer in Grand Isle, once she "had acquired finally the art of swimming" (*Complete Works* 927). This is, however, a necessarily solitary act which, while it validates, also casts doubt. The tests of Edna's strength that Mademoiselle Reisz administers on her return to the city are, additionally, such as to make her doubt her capacity for sustaining the self-belief necessary to nourish a "soul that dares and defies" (*Complete Works* 946).

Chopin paints Edna's own explanation of her young life as a series of unaccounted for and unconnected incidents, which, until the point at which the novel opens, have left her emotionally and intellectually untouched. Her early life is described in the language of detachment: "she was a grown young woman when she was overtaken by what she supposed to be the climax of her fate" and "her marriage to Leonce Pontellier was purely an accident" in which "no trace of passion or excessive and fictitious warmth colored her affection, thereby threatening its dissolution." Edna is "fond of her children in an uneven impulsive way. She would sometimes gather them passionately to her heart; she would sometimes forget them." Chopin's linguistic choices are striking: Edna is "overtaken," her marriage is an "accident," "fate" is responsible for her position (*Complete Works* 898). Because becoming a wife and mother are not self-willed, articulated instead as inadvertent, Edna cannot recognize these roles as authentic to her. But she is not troubled by this simulation, even when it means that she "forgets" the existence of her children. This is because she understands her own incompatibility with the demands of domesticity even if, as yet, she does not see that there is an alternative. The text recounts a "heated argument" between Edna and Madame Ratignolle, in which Edna attempts to express that she would "give up the unessential […] her life for [her] children" but that she wouldn't give herself. (*Complete Works* 929) Edna Pontellier comprehends her own indifference to the identity of Creole wife and mother, but her understanding of her unsuitability does not make her any more capable of discovering the way in which she could achieve an alternative mode of existence. This is principally because her options are constrained by forces she ultimately deems to be larger than the powers of any individual.

When she returns to New Orleans, Edna sets up a studio in the house on Esplanade Street that she shares with her husband and introduces the possible identity of "artist."[2] The progress of Edna's talent is, however, charted so subtly by Chopin that the reader may be guilty of not noticing her originality and growing proficiency. We first learn of Edna's interest in drawing in Grand Isle: "Mrs. Pontellier had brought her sketching materials, which she sometimes dabbled with in an unprofessional way. She liked the dabbling. She felt in it satisfaction of a kind which no other employment afforded her" (*Complete Works* 891). The sketching is accompanied by a similar set of emotions as were provoked by the solitary swim because the activity itself and the expression of its effect are entirely Edna's own. The semantic choices Chopin makes when discussing Edna's burgeoning artistry are telling in their relation to the world of work. The sketching is an "employment." But the significant prefix returns with Edna's designation of her "employment" as "unprofessional." The bracketing of the term "unprofessional" within the somewhat glib embrace of the verb "dabble" draws attention to its incongruity and alerts the reader to the pecuniary potential of Edna's art. Her desire for autonomy develops quickly after she sets up her studio, a move swiftly followed by her decision to establish her own "pigeon-house" (*Complete Works* 968). She is confident about making decisions about her money and her dwelling; she is assertive and clear about her status when mocking Robert for his conventionality: "I am no longer one of Mr. Pontellier's possessions to dispose of or not. I give myself where I choose" (*Complete Works* 992). In talking about her painting, her possible profession, however, Edna is less confident, less assured, and becomes uncertain about what it might mean for her as an individual.

Even when her hard work and application result in a significant achievement and consequent approval from a figure of some authority—"Laidpore is more and more pleased" (*Complete Works*

963)—impartial judgment only produces fleeting self-belief. Having felt such elation—temporarily—the feeling of success gives way to a sensation that she is proficient in her work because of accident or luck. Throughout, Edna experiences a disjunction between the decisions she makes and her ownership of them. Even as she exults in her first swim, it is described "as if some power of significant import had been given her to control the working of her body and her soul" (*Complete Works* 908). Edna's lack of self-belief is so overpowering that the only plausible explanation for her achievement must be that it is a fluke or derives from some invisible force temporarily lent to her because she has a crucial lack of confidence that the desired outcome can be achieved through self-will. Edna has "no interest in anything about her" life (*Complete Works* 935) except her art, figured as "work," and yet, she seeks out the opinion of a "mother-woman" in Madame Ratignolle as to whether or not she might "work again." This opinion, we are informed in advance, will be "next to valueless," and in her pursuit of it, Edna dooms herself to the repercussions of those feelings of narcissistic "complacency" she cannot "control." Chopin describes the longing that Edna is seeking to satisfy: "she sought the words of praise and encouragement that would help her to put heart into her venture"—another telling reference to the implied commercial possibilities of Edna's "work." She needs approval, perhaps even permission, before she can embark upon her change of life. Madame Ratignolle's flattery of Edna's talent as "immense" (*Complete Works* 937) is articulated in the context of Edna as amateur, as dabbler; and it is this permission that Edna gives to Madame Ratignolle and to Léonce to circumscribe her achievements, and her talent, as trifling and that will contribute ultimately to her undoing. The most telling of these exchanges is the one that Edna has with Léonce, when he grants his consent—albeit negatively and aggressively—for her to pursue her work: "'Then in God's name paint! But don't let the family go to the devil. There's Madame Ratignolle; because she keeps up her music, she doesn't let everything else go to chaos. And she's more of a musician than you are a painter'" (*CW* 939). Edna is caught between others' view of her as a woman with an appropriate female accomplishment, whether in music or in painting, and the demands of the authentication of herself as a woman with a profession, even a vocation.

To begin with, "being devoid of ambition" (*Complete Works* 956) Edna has only self-expression and exploration in mind, and yet, she makes a commitment to achieve something in her own right: "she was working with great energy and interest, without accomplishing anything, however, which satisfied her even in the smallest degree" (*Complete Works* 939); as ever, she is her own harshest critic. Edna never articulates anything like satisfaction with her work: "After surveying the sketch critically she drew a broad smudge of paint across its surface, and crumpled the paper between her hands" (*Complete Works* 891–2). This pattern, of creation and negation, is repeated time and time again in the novel.

Edna's commercial success is expressed by her alongside the positive judgments of her teacher: "I am beginning to sell my sketches. Laidpore is more and more pleased with my work; he says it grows in force and individuality. I cannot judge of that myself, but I feel that I have gained in ease and confidence. [...] I have sold a good many through Laidpore" (*Complete Works* 963). When Chopin removes the veil of self-effacement from Edna's speech, we are allowed to discover that Laidpore is "pleased" with her "work," with its "force and individuality," a verdict from which Edna then attempts to distance herself with more self-deprecation: "I cannot judge for myself." But she does at least acknowledge the gain in "ease and confidence," which actually assists her in her resolution "never again to belong to another than herself" (*Complete Works* 963). Such determination and assertiveness indicate that, at this point in the narrative, Edna wishes to prove herself capable of independence, and yet the fragile nature of her self-belief remains a constant threat to her autonomy. That she feels she cannot "judge" for herself, but knows vehemently that she wishes to "belong" to herself, illustrates what might be described as a narcissistic confusion that has actually informed Edna's character from the outset. John Glendening's essay "Evolution, Narcissism, and Maladaptation in Kate Chopin's *The Awakening*" argues that "chance and determinism" is, in fact, a representation of Darwinian theories of "maladaptation, death, and extinction that accompany natural and sexual selection" (41). However, Glendening goes on to acknowledge that theories of evolution and biology do not "adequately address" the psychological aspects of Edna's character and story. Glendening turns to Freud and theories of narcissism stemming from childhood in order to better understand Edna's troubled relationship with herself:

> She displays narcissistic tendencies throughout the novel, and what we learn of her childhood suggests how they originated. At an early age she experienced an abrupt disillusionment about her importance to the external world. Her mother's death prematurely terminated the narcissistic stage of psychic development, universal among young children according to Freud, and the trauma of the disorientation left her fixated on a needy self and on regaining the illusion of total sufficiency.[...] At the core of narcissistic self-involvement is insecurity, specifically a fear of being inconsequential, an empty self or cipher. (56)

Edna's narcissism, as Glendening says, can be glimpsed at intervals throughout the novel, but comes into full force when she throws off her "obligations." Edna's unsteady progress is initially liberating: "relieving herself from obligations added to her strength and expansion as an individual" (*Complete Works* 977-8). This leads to a concomitant growth in physical confidence, walking the streets, watching the world at large: accessing the privileges of the "flaneur," as Helen Taylor has expressed it. But this process of isolation leads to a real lack of equanimity of self, as, ironically, it was those "obligations" which might have kept Edna's re-emergent narcissism in check. We learn that whether or not Edna can "work" on her painting depends almost entirely on the weather. If it is "dark and cloudy" she cannot motivate herself, and, on "rainy" days, "it seemed to her as if life were passing by, leaving its promise broken and unfulfilled" (*Complete Works* 956). On the days when Edna's artistic temperament is met by the sun, however, Chopin also tells us that her work has "reached a stage when she seemed to be no longer feeling her way, working [...] with sureness and ease" (*Complete Works* 956).

The references to her painting that follow on from this accomplished sense of individuation only serve to confirm the significant, externally validated, strength of her talent, now that it is being realized. She completes a canvas—"a young Italian character study [...] without the model" (*Complete Works* 979)—and, on a morning "full of sunlight and hope" she works for "several hours with much spirit" and sees "no one but a picture dealer who asked her if it were true she was going abroad to study in Paris [...] he negotiated with her for some Parisian studies to reach him in time for the holiday trade in December" (*Complete Works* 987-8). This revelation is astonishing; and yet, the narrative changes direction so suddenly we are apt to miss it. Not only is Edna's work marketable, we discover, but it is in such demand that an art dealer wants to arrange to have her works shipped from Paris. This is a serious indication of Edna's present and future commercial success, and yet, it is also the last mention of her painting until the final words of the novel when Mademoiselle Reisz's mockery rings in Edna's ears, as she swims to her death: "'And you call yourself an artist! What pretensions, Madame! The artist must possess the courageous soul that dares and defies'" (*Complete Works* 1000).

Soon after her relocation to the pigeon house, Edna goes to visit her children in Iberville. This visit and its affirmation of her dislocation from the role of mother-woman is a positive step in the direction of her redefinition as an artist: she "looked into" her children's "faces with hungry eyes that could not be satisfied with looking" (*Complete Works* 978). Her maternal feelings are sporadic, she is "fond of her children in an uneven way," and "their absence" is a "relief," which she feels "free[s] her of the responsibility which she had blindly assumed and for which Fate had not fitted her" (*Complete Works* 899). What is arresting about Chopin's employment of the word "Fate" here is that it is used in order to describe a misalignment, a mistake and is, in some ways, a justification for Edna's lack of maternal feelings. Edna here uses "Fate" in order to shed guilt; that her children seem to be healthy, inquisitive and happy in spite of what others would see as her neglect gives her no cause for concern. The children are a condition of an existence that she has not actively chosen, in which she feels no agency. It does not trouble her that, by the time she has returned to the city and is away from them, she has already begun to doubt the real and innate devotion she felt at the "touch of their cheeks" and the "sound of their voices" and is therefore once "again alone" (*Complete Works* 978). What does trouble her, however, is the self-doubt she feels about her art, the desire for perfection that is not a feature of any other part of her way of life. The anxiety and guilt, which might be expected to result from her abandonment of the family home, her husband's comforts, and the daily care of her children, never feature as serious concerns for Edna. What troubles her, finally, is the inevitability of the scandal that will haunt her family, contaminating her future if she leads the life she wants to, and cutting off any path back to the life she has cast off, if her bid for independence proves unsuccessful. Her witnessing of Adèle Ratignole's labor triggers her final realization of the incompatibility of her recent choices with the expectations with which society freights motherhood. Talking to Doctor Mandelet, Edna appears incoherent, unable to decide for herself what she wants; she has just witnessed "the scene [of] torture" that is childbirth, and it has broken the last vestige of a connection with a known reality. She is disturbed by Adèle's imploring exclamation to "Think of the children!" and taken off guard by Doctor Mandelet's innocent inquiry as to whether she will go "abroad" for her painting. Edna now casts all actors her world as oppressors—including those connected to her art before she trails off into incoherence:

> "Perhaps—no, I am not going. I'm not going to be forced into doing things. I don't want to go abroad. I want to be let alone. Nobody has any right—except children, perhaps—and even then, it seems to me—or it did seem –" (*Complete Works* 995)

Ultimately, she cannot believe in the possibility that she could be a successful artist, with a self-worth that is generated internally, and so she falters, instead of taking courage from the opinion of the professionals—the art teacher, the art dealer. She does think of the children, or at least, "children" in some abstract way that seems to threaten her. The "inward life which questions" (*Complete Works* 893) might have saved Edna from the misery of an inauthentic existence, but Adèle Ratignole's command "think of the children" perforates Edna's soul "like a death wound" (*Complete Works* 997). In the last scene, upon Edna's return to the beach, "the children appeared before her like antagonists, who had overcome her." It seems that in the battle between Edna's authentic self (which includes the recasting of herself as an artist) and the inauthentic role of mother, figured here as "the soul's slavery," Edna decides she cannot triumph and so can only attempt to escape or "elude." (*Complete Works* 999)

The point at which Edna's awakening is arrested, by the trauma of witnessing Adèle Ratignole's labor, is still early in the realization of "her position in the universe as a human being [with] relations as an individual to the world within and about her" (*Complete Works* 893). This is necessarily a negative phase, in which Edna is preoccupied with what she is not, or rather, what she no longer wants to be. Before recasting herself as an artist, Edna has been attempting to shake off the "chains" (*Complete Works* 915) of her current existence. The reader learns that she is emphatically not a submissive wife, not a faithful lover, and not a "mother-woman," but, progress arrested, Edna looks about herself and finds only that series of negations—including the most crushing negation of all: that she is not yet an artist. Mademoiselle Reisz's cutting rebuff of her attempt to redefine herself haunts Edna in her last moments: "And you call yourself an artist! What pretensions, Madame!" (*Complete Works* 1000) Finally, the only thing Edna seems to excel at is "not being": an absolute negation of the self solves the problem of having to be defined by a role she ultimately declines to choose. She refuses to commit to anything, and it is because of this that her death is particularly difficult to read.

When Edna eventually learns to swim, it is not because of the "instruction" she receives from any man or woman. Rather, it is alone, and like a "child" filled with "over-confidence," that she finally "lifted her body to the surface of the water." But, as with so many aspects of her life, Edna was not able to feel an authentic connection to the achievement, and so it was "as if some power of significant import had been given her to control the working of her body and her soul" (*Complete Works* 908).

When Edna returns to the scene of her exultant first act of individuation, she recalls the "old terror" of not being able to reach land, but instead she swims "on and on" and does not "look back." Without a purpose to return to, she is indifferent to the "flame" of that "terror" that connected her to the land, and so she is blinded to the fact that she has strength enough to reclaim the shore. Succumbing to the "sensuous, enfolding [...] close embrace" of the sea is ultimately preferable to the knowledge that there is no authentic life awaiting her on the shore. (*Complete Works* 1000).

Notes

1. Carole Stone ("The Female Artist..." 23) and Suzanne Wolkenfeld ("Edna's Suicide..." 223) both see Edna's painting as part of her "rebirth."

2. "I am becoming an artist. Think of it!" (*Complete Works* 946)

Works Cited

Chopin, Kate. *The Awakening*. Ed. Margot Culley. 2nd ed. New York: Norton, 1994.

_____. *Complete Works*. Ed. Per Seyersted. 2 vols. Baton Rouge: Lousiana State UP, 1969.

Glendening, John. "Evolution, Narcissism, and Maladaptation in Kate Chopin's *The Awakening*." *American Literary Realism* 43.1 (2010): 41–73.

Stone, Carole. "The Female Artist in Kate Chopin's *The Awakening*: Birth and Creativity," *Women's Studies* 13 (1986): 23–32.

Taylor, Helen. "Walking Through New Orleans: Kate Chopin and the Female Flaneur." *The Awakening: A Sourcebook*. Ed. by Janet Beer and Elizabeth Nolan. London: Routledge, 2004. 78–82.

Toth, Emily. *Unveiling Kate Chopin*. Jackson: UP of Mississippi, 1999.

Wolkenfeld, Suzanne. "Edna's Suicide: The Problem of the One and the Many." *A Norton Critical Edition: Kate Chopin; The Awakening*. Ed. Margo Culley. New York: W.W. Norton, 1994.

RESOURCES

1850   Katherine O'Flaherty is born on February 8 in St. Louis,
        Missouri. Her father is Thomas O'Flaherty, a successful
        businessman who emigrated from Ireland in the 1820s. Her
        mother is Elizabeth Faris, whose family roots are in French-
        speaking Louisiana. Kate's relationship with her middle-
        aged father is especially close. Several slaves live in the
        family home.

1855   Kate takes up residence as a student at the local Sacred
        Heart Academy. On November 1, her father is killed when
        a newly-built railroad bridge collapses under the weight
        of the first train, which is full of prominent local people.
        Kate's mother, suddenly a wealthy widow, is now more
        independent than she could ever have been as a wife.

        Kate is withdrawn from the academy later that month. Her
        maternal great-grandmother, Victoire Verdon Charleville,
        begins to home-school her and has a major and lively impact
        on the girl's intellectual development. At this time, Kate
        begins developing a strong interest in music—an interest
        that will last her whole life.

1860   The census this year—the year in which the Civil War
        begins—records that Kate's mother owns six slaves. Opinion
        about slavery is sharply divided in St. Louis.

1861   Kate is confirmed in the Catholic Church. Her older half-
        brother, George, volunteers for military service on the
        Confederacy's side during the Civil War. St. Louis, at this
        point, is occupied by Union troops.

1862	George is captured and imprisoned by Union forces but is later released. Young Kate rips down a Union flag that had been hung at her home without permission and is threatened with arrest. She avoids this fate thanks to the intervention of a pro-Union neighbor. She is now sometimes called St. Louis's "littlest Rebel."
1863	Kate's early tutor, her great-grandmother, dies on January 16. Her Confederate half-brother, George, dies of typhoid fever on February 17. After a significant Confederate defeat that summer, Union troops in St. Louis, who threaten to burn down the O'Flaherty home, force Kate's family to raise a Union flag over their house. Eventually, the family's slaves depart.
1865	Kate attends the Academy of the Visitation this year but then returns to Sacred Heart Academy.
1866	On November 21, Kate is inducted into the "Children of Mary" at Sacred Heart Academy after being selected for this distinct honor by her teachers and fellow students. Kate is one of only five members elected from her class.
1868	On June 29, Kate graduates from Sacred Heart Academy, where she had been a popular and talented student. During her time there she reads widely and after the graduation her reading intensifies and expands to include contemporary writers.
1868-1870	Kate is active (somewhat reluctantly) on the St. Louis social scene, which emphasizes parties, dancing, and behavior Kate regards as superficial and boring.
1869	Kate meets her future husband at a party. From March to May, Kate visits New Orleans. She enjoys her stay there and admires the city. Kate writes her first (unpublished)

short story, "Emancipation: A Life Fable," a very brief work exploring themes of confinement and liberty.

1870	On June 9 in St. Louis, Kate marries Oscar Chopin, who grew up in Louisiana and had lived for several years in France during the Civil War. From June to September, they honeymoon, arriving in continental Europe on July 7. Kate keeps a honeymoon diary. The honeymoon is abbreviated when war breaks out between Prussia and France. In October, Kate and Oscar settle in New Orleans, where they live in the non-French section of the city, thus annoying Oscar's hot-tempered father, who had emigrated from France and loved all things French. Kate explores New Orleans, often on long walks, and Oscar admires her free spirit.
1871	Oscar begins a successful career in the cotton business. Jean Baptiste, a son and the first of six children, is born on May 22 in New Orleans and is baptized in St. Louis in August. The Chopins have servants, including at least one of color, who becomes the "mammy" of the Chopins' infant son.
1872	Kate possibly meets the famous French impressionist painter Edgar Degas, some of whose stories may have influenced *The Awakening*, her later novel.
1873	Oscar Chopin, Jr. is born in St. Louis on September 24, 1873 and is baptized there. On December 27, Thomas O'Flaherty (Kate's brother) dies in an accident while buggy-racing in St. Louis.
1874	During the spring, the Chopins visit St. Louis and, for the second time, visit Grand Isle (near New Orleans) in the summer. On September 14, Oscar, a member of the "White League," participates in the "Battle of Liberty Place" to preserve and enhance the power of whites. The effort is

only briefly successful. On October 28, a third son, George Francis, is born in St. Louis and is baptized there. The Chopins move to the Garden District of New Orleans.

1876	A fourth son, Frederick, is born in New Orleans on January 26.
1878	A fifth son, Felix Andrew, is born in New Orleans on January 8. Oscar's cotton business begins to suffer because of poor harvests.
1879	Oscar's business as a cotton-broker fails, and the Chopins move from New Orleans to the small town of Cloutierville (pronounced "Cloochy-ville") in northwest Louisiana, where Oscar had been raised and where Kate also had relatives on her mother's side. While there, they employ two servants of color. Oscar supervises several small plantations and opens a general store. On December 31, Marie Laiza ("Lélia"), their sixth child and first and only daughter, is born.
1880	In this year's census, Kate misreports her age to make herself seem three years younger than she is.
1881	Oscar, in poor health, goes to Hot Springs, Arkansas, hoping his condition will improve.
1882	In the fall, Oscar becomes sick with malaria and dies on December 10, heavily in debt.
1883-1884	Rather than seeking the help of a male relative, Kate tries to run Oscar's businesses herself, especially the general store. This experience is later reflected in her first novel. Kate becomes involved with a married man named Albert Sampite.

1884	Kate returns to St. Louis and moves in with her mother, who had urged her to leave Louisiana.
1885	Her mother dies on June 28 of "sarcoma." Encouraged by her mother's doctor, who praises her writing, Kate begins to become involved in liberal intellectual circles in St. Louis.
1887	In May, Kate visits Cloutierville for the first time since Oscar's death.
1888	Kate writes her first poem; begins a story titled "Euphraisie"; publishes a polka; and reads and admires stories by the French writer Guy de Maupassant, a major influence on her own later work. Kate is also at work on a text she lists in her notebook as "Unfinished Story – Grand Isle."
1889	"If It Might Be" (a poem) is published, as are two stories, "Wiser than a God" and "A Point at Issue." In April, Oscar's body is moved from Louisiana to St. Louis for reburial.
1890	In April, Kate completes her first novel, *At Fault*, which is set in Louisiana. After it is rejected for publication, Kate pays to have a thousand copies published. Reviews are reasonably positive.

Kate begins work on a second novel, *Young Dr. Gosse and Théo*, which she finishes in November. Kate becomes an original member of the "Wednesday Club," a women's group founded by the mother of T. S. Eliot. Chopin, however, she soon dislikes the organization and resigns after two years. In December, she publishes the first of many stories for children. |
| 1891 | Her second novel, *Young Dr. Gosse and Théo*, is rejected and is subsequently rejected nine more times. Kate declines to pay for its publication. She now turns her attention mainly to writing short stories, including the first of many set in |

Louisiana. She writes nine such stories in eight weeks, and all are accepted for publication. She also writes a play, the only such work of hers to survive.

1893

"Désirée's Baby" (one of her most popular stories) is published in *Vogue*, which will eventually publish nearly a score of her tales. In May, Chopin travels to New York and Boston to meet with editors and publishers in order to promote her career, without many positive results. She remains less successful in her attempts to publish poems than in her efforts to publish stories. The publishing firm of Houghton Mifflin accepts for publication a collection of twenty-three short stories (*Bayou Folk*).

An October hurricane decimates Grand Isle, the Louisiana resort that is a central setting for Chopin's later novel, *The Awakening*. Because of her responsibilities to her beloved children, Chopin cannot write as much or as often as she may have wished. When she does write, however, the children surround her.

1894

Kate begins keeping a diary for two years. On March 24, Houghton Mifflin publishes *Bayou Folk*. By midsummer, the book has attracted more than one hundred published notices, but most of them strike Kate as superficial. She begins translating eight mostly gloomy stories by Maupassant. In June, she attends a writers' conference but finds the experience dissatisfying and later publicly criticizes the conventional forms of writing encouraged there. Her criticism is met with various angry reactions.

In June, Kate is profiled in a local publication and in August is profiled, for the first time, in a national magazine for writers. She continues to publish her own stories in many important venues. Kate destroys her copy of *Young Dr. Gosse and Théo* after that novel has been again rejected by various publishers. She publishes one of her most famous stories, "The Dream of an Hour" (which is later retitled "The Story of an Hour").

1895	In March, Kate submits a collection of translated Maupassant stories to Houghton Mifflin, which rejects them.
1897	A collection of original stories is rejected by Houghton Mifflin. Kate publishes six essays and works on *A Solitary Soul* (original title of *The Awakening*). In November, she publishes her second collection of short stories, *A Night in Acadie*.
1898	Kate completes her new novel, now called *The Awakening*; both the novel and a planned collection of short stories (*A Vocation and a Voice*) are accepted by the same publisher.
1899	*The Awakening* is published on April 22. Many reviews are negative. In July, Kate publishes an ambiguously worded commentary on *The Awakening* in which she *seems* critical of Edna, the novel's main character.
1900	Kate is included in the very first *Who's Who in America*. The publisher of *The Awakening* decides *not* to publish her third short story collection, *A Vocation and a Voice*. A St. Louis newspaper profiles Kate.
1902	On June 4, Kate's son Jean marries. A month later, Chopin's last story is published.
1903	Kate moves to a home closer to Jean and his wife, who dies in July while giving birth.
1904	Kate enthusiastically attends the St. Louis World's Fair for several days, including on August 20; later that day, she has a cerebral hemorrhage. Kate dies on August 22 and is buried on August 24 in Calvary Cemetery in St. Louis (where her

mother is buried) under a headstone listing only her name and dates.

For the many facts and figures cited in this chronology, special thanks are due to Emily Toth, whose two superb biographies of Chopin—*Kate Chopin* (New York, Morrow, 1990) and *Unveiling Kate Chopin* (Jackson: University Press of Mississippi, 1999)— are crucial to anyone seeking information on Chopin's life. The chronology in the Library of America edition of Chopin's writings (ed. Sandra M. Gilbert; New York: Library of America, 2002) clearly draws on Toth's work and is itself a model of its kind. Also especially thorough is the chronology in Joyce Dyer's *The Awakening: A Novel of Beginnings* (New York: Twayne, 1993). And, of course, all students of Chopin are indebted to the pioneering biographical work of Daniel Rankin and Per Seyersted.

Works by Kate Chopin

Long Fiction
At Fault, 1890
The Awakening, 1899

Short Fiction
Bayou Folk, 1894
A Night in Acadie, 1897
A Vocation and a Voice, ed. Emily Toth, 1991
The Kate Chopin Companion, ed. Thomas Bonner, Jr., 1988

Miscellaneous
The Complete Works of Kate Chopin, ed. Per Seyersted, 1969
A Kate Chopin Miscellany, ed. Per Seyersted and Emily Toth, 1979
Kate Chopin's Private Papers, ed. Emily Toth and Per Seyersted, 1998

Anastasopoulou, Maria. "Rites of Passage in Kate Chopin's *The Awakening*." *Southern Literary Journal* 23.2 (1991): 19–30.

Arms, George. "Kate Chopin's *The Awakening* in the Perspective of Her Literary Career." *Essays on American Literature in Honor of Jay B. Hubbell*. Ed. Clarence Gohdes. Durham: Duke UP, 1967. 215–28.

Arner, Robert. "Kate Chopin." *Louisiana Studies* 14.1 (1975): 11–139.

Barrish, Phillip. "*The Awakening*'s Signifying 'Mexicanist' Presence." *Studies in American Fiction* 28.1 (2000): 65–76.

Batten, Wayne. "Illusion and Archetype: The Curious Story of Edna Pontellier." *Southern Literary Journal* 18.1 (1985): 73–88.

Beer, Janet, ed. *The Cambridge Companion to Kate Chopin*. Cambridge, England: Cambridge UP, 2008.

_____ and Elizabeth Nolan, eds. *The Awakening: A Sourcebook*. New York: Routledge, 2004.

Bender, Bert. "The Teeth of Desire: *The Awakening* and the Descent of Man." *American Literature* 63.3 (1991): 459–73.

Biggs, Mary. "'Si Tu Savais': The Gay/Transgendered Sensibility of Kate Chopin's *The Awakening*." *Women's Studies: An Interdisciplinary Journal* 33.2 (2004): 145–81.

Bloom, Harold, ed. *Kate Chopin*. New York: Chelsea House, 1987.

Bonner, Thomas. *The Kate Chopin Companion, with Chopin's Translations from French Fiction*. New York: Greenwood, 1988.

Boren, Lynda S., Sara deSaussure Davis, and Cathy N. Davidson, eds. *Kate Chopin Reconsidered: Beyond the Bayou*. Baton Rouge: Louisiana State UP, 1992.

Bryfonski, Dedria, ed. *Women's Issues in Kate Chopin's The Awakening*. Farmington Hills, MI: Greenhaven, 2012.

Bunch, Dianne. "Dangerous Spending Habits: The Epistemology of Edna Pontellier's Extravagant Expenditures in *The Awakening*." *Mississippi Quarterly* 55.1 (2001): 43–61.

Casale, Ottavio Mark. "Beyond Sex: The Dark Romanticism of Kate Chopin's *The Awakening*." *Ball State University Forum* 19.1 (1978): 76–80.

Chopin, Kate. *Complete Novels and Stories: At Fault; Bayou Folk; A Night in Acadie; The Awakening; Uncollected Stories*. Ed. Sandra M. Gilbert. New York, NY: Library of America, 2002.

Clark, Zoila. "The Bird That Came out of the Cage: A Foucauldian Feminist Approach to Kate Chopin's *The Awakening*." *Journal for Cultural Research* 12.4 (2008): 335–47.

Collins, Robert. "The Dismantling of Edna Pontellier: Garment Imagery in Kate Chopin's *The Awakening*." *Southern Studies* 23.2 (1984): 176–97.

Craft, Brigette Wilds. "Imaginative Limits: Ideology and *The Awakening*." *Southern Studies* 4.2 (1993): 131–39.

Daigrepont, Lloyd M. "Edna Pontellier and the Myth of Passion." *New Orleans Review* 18.3 (1991): 5–13.

Dawson, Hugh J. "Kate Chopin's *The Awakening*: A Dissenting Opinion." *American Literary Realism* 26.2 (1994): 1–18.

Dawson, Melanie. "Edna and the Tradition of Listening: The Role of Romantic Music in *The Awakening*." *Southern Studies* 3.2 (1992): 87–98.

Disheroon-Green, Suzanne. "Whither Thou Goest, We Will Go: Lovers and Ladies in *The Awakening*." *Southern Quarterly* 40.4 (2002): 83–96.

Dyer, Joyce. *The Awakening: A Novel of Beginnings*. New York: Twayne, 1993.

_____. "Reading *The Awakening* with Toni Morrison." *Southern Literary Journal* 35.1 (2002): 138–54.

_____. "Lafcadio Hearn's *Chita* and Kate Chopin's *The Awakening*: Two Naturalistic Tales of the Gulf Islands." *Southern Studies* 23.4 (1984): 412–26.

Eble, Kenneth. "A Forgotten Novel: Kate Chopin's *The Awakening*." *Western Humanities Review* 10 (1956): 261–69.

Elfenbein, Anna Shannon. "Kate Chopin's *The Awakening*: An Assault on American Racial and Sexual Mythology." *Southern Studies* 26.4 (1987): 304–12.

_____. *Women on the Color Line: Evolving Stereotypes and the Writings of George Washington Cable, Grace King, Kate Chopin*. Charlottesville: UP of Virginia, 1994.

Ewell, Barbara C. *Kate Chopin*. New York: Ungar, 1986.

_____. "Unlinking Race and Gender: *The Awakening* as a Southern Novel." *Southern Quarterly* 37.3–4 (1999): 30–37.

_____ and Pamela Glenn Menke. "*The Awakening* and the Great October Storm of 1893." *Southern Literary Journal* 42.2 (2010): 1–11.

Foata, Anne. "Aphrodite Redux: Edna Pontellier's Dilemma in *The Awakening* by Kate Chopin." *The Southern Quarterly* 33.1 (1994): 27–31.

Fox-Genovese, Elizabeth. "Kate Chopin's Awakening." *Southern Studies* 18 (1979): 261–90.

Franklin, Rosemary F. "*The Awakening* and the Failure of Psyche." *American Literature* 56.4 (1984): 510–16.

_____. "Poe and *The Awakening.*" *Mississippi Quarterly: The Journal of Southern Culture* 47 1 (1993): 47–57.

Frye, Katie Berry. "Edna Pontellier, Adèle Ratignolle, and the Unnamed Nurse: A Triptych of Maternity in *The Awakening.*" *Southern Studies* 13.3-4 (2006): 45–66.

Gale, Robert L. *Characters and Plots in the Fiction of Kate Chopin.* Jefferson, NC: McFarland, 2009.

Gartner, Carol B. "Three Ednas." *Kate Chopin Newsletter* 1.3 (1975): 11–20.

Gaskill, Nicholas M. "'The Light Which, Showing the Way, Forbids It': Reconstructing Aesthetics in *The Awakening.*" *Studies in American Fiction* 34.2 (2006): 161–88.

Gentry, Deborah S. *The Art of Dying: Suicide in the Works of Kate Chopin and Sylvia Plath.* New York: Peter Lang, 2006.

Gilbert, Sandra M. "The Second Coming of Aphrodite: Kate Chopin's Fantasy of Desire." *Kenyon Review* 5.3 (1983): 42–66.

Glendening, John. "Evolution, Narcissism, and Maladaptation in Kate Chopin's *The Awakening.*" *American Literary Realism* 43.1 (2010): 41–73.

Gray, Jennifer B. "The Escape of the 'Sea': Ideology and *The Awakening.*" *Southern Literary Journal* 37 1 (2004): 53–73.

Green, Suzanne Disheroon, David J. Caudle, and Emily Toth. *Kate Chopin: An Annotated Bibliography of Critical Works.* Westport, CT: Greenwood, 1999.

Gremillion, Michelle. "Edna's Awakening: A Return to Childhood." *Perspectives on Kate Chopin: Proceedings from the Kate Chopin International Conference, April 6, 7, 8, 1989.* Eds. Grady Ballenger, et al. Natchitoches, LA: Northwestern State Univ., 1992. 169–76.

Hailey-Gregory, Angela. "'Into Realms of the Semi-Celestials': From Mortal to Mythic in *The Awakening.*" *Mississippi Quarterly* 59.1-2 (2005): 295–312.

Harmon, Charles. "'Abysses of Solitude': Acting Naturally in *Vogue* and *The Awakening.*" *College Literature* 25.3 (1998): 52–66.

Hoder-Salmon, Marilyn. *Kate Chopin's The Awakening: Screenplay as Interpretation.* Gainesville: U of Florida P, 1992.

House, Elizabeth Balkman. "*The Awakening*: Kate Chopin's 'Endlessly Rocking' Cycle." *Ball State University Forum* 20 2 (1979): 53–58.

Jasenas, Elaine. "The French Influence in Kate Chopin's *The Awakening.*" *Nineteenth-Century French Studies* 4 (1976): 312–22.

Jones, Suzanne W. "Place, Perception and Identity in *The Awakening.*" *The Southern Quarterly* 25.2 (1987): 108–19.

Justus, James H. "The Unawakening of Edna Pontellier." *Southern Literary Journal* 10 2 (1978): 107–22.

Kaur, Iqbal, ed. *Kate Chopin's* The Awakening: *Critical Essays*. New Delhi: Deep & Deep, 1995.

Kearns, Katherine. "The Nullification of Edna Pontellier." *American Literature* 63.1 (1991): 62–88.

Kelley, Lori Duin. "Continence and Excessive Amativeness: The Medical Background of Dr. Mandalet's Diagnosis of Edna Pontellier's Awakening." *Southern Studies* 5.3-4 (1994): 125–32.

Killeen, Jarlath. "Mother and Child: Realism, Maternity, and Catholicism in Kate Chopin's *The Awakening*." *Religion and the Arts* 7.4 (2003): 413–38.

Koloski, Bernard, ed. *KateChopin.org*. The Kate Chopin International Society. Web. <http://www.katechopin.org/>.

_____, ed. *Approaches to Teaching Chopin's* The Awakening. New York: Modern. Language Association of America, 1988.

_____. "The Antholigized Chopin: Kate Chopin's Short Stories in Yesterday's and Today's Anthologies." *Louisiana Literature: A Review of Literature and Humanities* 11.1 (1994): 18–30.

_____, ed. *Awakenings: The Story of the Kate Chopin Revival*. Baton Rouge, LA: Louisiana State UP, 2009.

Lant, Kathleen Margaret. "The Siren of Grand Isle: Adèle's Role in *The Awakening*." *Southern Studies* 23.2 (1984): 167–75.

Leary, Lewis. "Kate Chopin, Liberationist?" *Southern Literary Journal* 3 (1970): 138-44.

LeBlanc, Elizabeth. "The Metaphorical Lesbian: Edna Pontellier in *The Awakening*." *Tulsa Studies in Women's Literature* 15.2 (1996): 289–307.

Leder, Priscilla. "An American Dilemma: Cultural Conflict in Kate Chopin's *The Awakening*." *Southern Studies* 22.1 (1983): 97–104.

Levine, Robert S. "Circadian Rhythms and Rebellion in Kate Chopin's *The Awakening*." *Studies in American Fiction* 10.1 (1982): 71–81.

Lewis, Jenene. "Women as Commodity: Confronting Female Sexuality in *Quicksand* and *The Awakening*." *MAWA Review* 12.2 (1997): 51–62.

Linkin, Harriet Kramer. "'Call the Roller of Big Cigars': Smoking out the Patriarchy in *The Awakening*." *Legacy: A Journal of American Women Writers* 11.2 (1994): 130–42.

LoShiavo, David. "A Matter of Salvation Versus Freedom: Understanding Edna's Conflict through Hebrew Metaphor in *The Awakening*." *Southern Studies* 8.1–2 (1997): 83–90.

Mahon, Robert Lee. "Beyond the Love Triangle: *Trios in The Awakening.*" *Midwest Quarterly: A Journal of Contemporary Thought* 39.2 (1998): 228–34.

Mainland, Catherine. "Chopin's Bildungsroman: Male Role Models in *The Awakening.*" *Mississippi Quarterly* 64.1–2 (2011): 75–85.

Malzahn, Manfred. "The Strange Demise of Edna Pontellier." *Southern Literary Journal* 23.2 (1991): 31–39.

Margraf, Erik. "Kate Chopin's *The Awakening* as a Naturalistic Novel." *American Literary Realism* 37.2 (2005): 93–116.

Martin, Wendy, ed. *New Essays on* The Awakening. New York: Cambridge UP, 1988.

Mathews, Carolyn L. "Fashioning the Hybrid Woman in Kate Chopin's *The Awakening.*" *Mosaic: A Journal for the Interdisciplinary Study of Literature* 35.3 (2002): 127–49.

May, John R. "Local Color in *The Awakening.*" *Southern Review* 6 (1970): 1031–40.

McGee, Diane. "The Structure of Dinners in Kate Chopin's *The Awakening.*" *Proteus: A Journal of Ideas* 17.1 (2000): 47–51.

Mikolchak, Maria. "Kate Chopin's *The Awakening* as Part of the Nineteenth-Century American Literary Tradition." *Interdisciplinary Literary Studies* 5.2 (2004): 29–49.

Morton, Mary L. "The Semiotics of Food in *The Awakening.*" *Southern Studies* 8.1–2 (1997): 65–72.

Muirhead, Marion. "Articulation and Artistry: A Conversational Analysis of *The Awakening.*" *Southern Literary Journal* 33.1 (2000): 42–54.

Nelles, William. "Edna Pontellier's Revolt against Nature." *American Literary Realism* 32.1 (1999): 43–50.

O'Brien, Sharon. "The Limits of Passion: Willa Cather's Review of *The Awakening.*" *Women & Literature* 3.2 (1975): 10–20.

Ostman, Heather, ed. *Kate Chopin in the Twenty-First Century: New Critical Essays.* Newcastle upon Tyne, England: Cambridge Scholars, 2008.

Papke, Mary Elizabeth. *Verging on the Abyss: The Social Fiction of Kate Chopin and Edith Wharton.* New York: Greenwood, 1990.

_____. "Taking the Waters: The Summer Place and Women's Health in Kate Chopin's *The Awakening.*" *American Literary Realism* 39.1 (2006): 1–19.

Parvulescu, Anca. "To Die Laughing and to Laugh at Dying: Revisiting *The Awakening.*" *New Literary History: A Journal of Theory and Interpretation* 36.3 (2005): 477–95.

Perspectives on Kate Chopin: Proceedings from the Kate Chopin International Conference, April 6, 7, 8, 1989, Northwestern State University, Natchitoches, Louisiana. Natchitoches, LA: Northwestern State UP, 1990.

Petry, Alice Hall, ed. *Critical Essays on Kate Chopin.* New York: G. K. Hall, 1996.

Pizer, Donald. "A Note on Kate Chopin's *The Awakening* as Naturalistic Fiction." *Southern Literary Journal* 33.2 (2001): 5–13.

Portales, Marco A. "The Characterization of Edna Pontellier and the Conclusion of Kate Chopin's *The Awakening.*" *Southern Studies* 20.4 (1981): 427–36.

Potter, Richard H. "Kate Chopin and Her Critics: An Annotated Checklist." *Missouri Historical Society Bulletin* 26 (1970): 306–17.

Radcliff-Umstead, Douglas. "Literature of Deliverance: Images of Nature in *The Awakening.*" *Southern Studies* 1.2 (1990): 127–47.

Ramos, Peter. "Unbearable Realism: Freedom, Ethics and Identity in *The Awakening.*" *College Literature* 37.4 (2010): 145–65.

Rich, Charlotte. "Reconsidering *The Awakening*: The Literary Sisterhood of Kate Chopin and George Egerton." *Southern Quarterly* 41.3 (2003): 121–36.

Ringe, Donald A. "Romantic Imagery in Kate Chopin's *The Awakening.*" *American Literature* 43.4 (1972): 580–88.

Roscher, Marina L. "The Suicide of Edna Pontellier: An Ambiguous Ending?" *Southern Studies* 23.3 (1984): 289–97.

Rosowski, Susan J. "The Novel of Awakening." *Genre* 12 (1979): 313–32.

Ryan, Steven T. "Depression and Chopin's *The Awakening.*" *Mississippi Quarterly* 5.1 2 (1998): 253–73.

Schweitzer, Ivy. "Maternal Discourse and the Romance of Self-Possession in Kate Chopin's *The Awakening.*" *Boundary 2: An International Journal of Literature and Culture* 17.1 (1990): 158-86.

Seidel, Kathryn. "Art Is an Unnatural Act: Mademoiselle Reisz in *The Awakening.*" *Mississippi Quarterly* 46.2 (1993): 199–214.

Seyersted, Per. *Kate Chopin: A Critical Biography.* Baton Rouge: Louisiana State UP, 1969.

_____ and Emily Toth. *A Kate Chopin Miscellany.* Natchitoches: Northwestern State UP, 1979.

_____, ed. *The Complete Works of Kate Chopin.* Baton Rouge: Louisiana State UP, 1969.

Shaw, Pat. "Putting Audience in Its Place: Psychosexuality and Prospective Shifts in *The Awakening.*" *American Literary Realism* 23.1 (1990): 61–69.

_____. "Shifting Focus in Kate Chopin's *The Awakening.*" *Southern Studies* 1.3 (1990): 211–23.

Skaggs, Peggy. "Three Tragic Figures in Kate Chopin's *The Awakening*." *Louisiana Studies* 13 (1974): 34–64.

_____. *Kate Chopin*. Boston, MA: Twayne, 1985.

Spangler, George M. "Kate Chopin's *The Awakening*: A Partial Dissent." *Novel: A Forum on Fiction* 3.3 (1970): 249–55.

Springer, Marlene. *Edith Wharton and Kate Chopin: A Reference Guide*. Boston: Hall, 1976.

Stange, Margit. "Personal Property: Exchange Value and the Female Self in *The Awakening*." *Genders* 5 (1989): 106–19.

Stone, Carole. "The Female Artist in Kate Chopin's *The Awakening*: Birth and Creativity." *Women's Studies: An Interdisciplinary Journal* 13.1–2 (1986): 23–32.

Sullivan, Ruth and Stewart Smith. "Narrative Stance in Kate Chopin's *The Awakening*." *Studies in American Fiction* 1 (1973): 62–75.

Taylor, Helen. "Walking through New Orleans: Kate Chopin and the Female *Flaneur*." *Southern Quarterly* 37.3–4 (1999): 21–29.

Thornton, Lawrence. "*The Awakening*: A Political Romance." *American Literature* 52.1 (1980): 50–66.

Tompkins, Jane P. "*The Awakening*: An Evaluation." *Feminist Studies* 3.3–4 (1976): 22–29.

Toth, Emily. "Kate Chopin on Divine Love and Suicide: Two Rediscovered Articles." *American Literature* 63.1 (1991): 115–21.

_____ and Per Seyersted, eds. *Kate Chopin's Private Papers*. Bloomington: Indiana UP, 1998.

_____. "Kate Chopin's Secret, Slippery Life Story." *Southern Quarterly* 37.3–4 (1999): 45–50.

_____. "Kate Chopin's Unvarnished Life Story." *Southern Studies* 8.1–2 (1997): 111–19.

_____. "Kate Chopin's *The Awakening* as Feminist Criticism." *Louisiana Studies* 15 (1976): 241–51.

_____. "The Shadow of the First Biographer: The Case of Kate Chopin." *The Southern Review* 26.2 (1990): 285–92.

_____. *Unveiling Kate Chopin*. Jackson, MS: UP of Mississippi, 1999.

Treu, Robert. "Surviving Edna: A Reading of the Ending of *The Awakening*." *College Literature* 27.2 (2000): 21–36.

Urgo, Joseph R. *The Southern Literary Journal* 20.1 (1987): 22-32. *JSTOR*. Web. 10 Dec. 2013.

Wade, Carol A. "Conformity, Resistance, and the Search for Selfhood in Kate Chopin's *The Awakening*." *Southern Quarterly* 37. 2 (1999): 92–104.

Walker, Nancy. "Feminist or Naturalist: The Social Context of Kate Chopin's *The Awakening.*" *Southern Quarterly* 17.2 (1979): 95–103.

_____. "Women Drifting: Drabble's *The Waterfall* and Chopin's *The Awakening.*" *Denver Quarterly* 17.4 (1983): 88–96.

White, Robert. "Inner and Outer Space in *The Awakening.*" *Mosaic: A Journal for the Interdisciplinary Study of Literature* 17.1 (1984): 97–109.

Windolph, Christopher. "Dr. Mandelet's Discovery and Edna's Suicide in Kate Chopin's *The Awakening.*" *Southern Studies* 8.1–2 (1997): 53–63.

Witherow, Jean. "Flaubert's Vision and Chopin's Naturalistic Revision: A Comparison of *Madame Bovary* and *The Awakening.*" *Southern Studies* 8.1–2 (1997): 27–36.

_____. "'To Love a Little and Then to Die!': Chopin Awakens Emma Bovary." *Southern Studies* 14. 2 (2007): 29–48.

Wolff, Cynthia G. "Thanatos and Eros: Kate Chopin's *The Awakening.*" *American Quarterly* 25 (1973): 449–71.

_____. "Un-Utterable Longing: The Discourse of Feminine Sexuality in *The Awakening.*" *Studies in American Fiction* 24.1 (1996): 3–22.

Yaeger, Patricia S. "'A Language Which Nobody Understood': Emancipatory Strategies in *The Awakening.*" *Novel: A Forum on Fiction* 20.3 (1987): 197–219.

Robert C. Evans is I. B. Young Professor of English at Auburn University at Montgomery (AUM), where he has taught since 1982. In 1984, he received his PhD from Princeton University, where he held Weaver and Whiting fellowships as well as a University fellowship. In later years, his research was supported by fellowships from the Newberry Library, the American Council of Learned Societies, the Folger Shakespeare Library, The Andrew W. Mellon Foundation, The Huntington Library, the National Endowment for the Humanities, the American Philosophical Society, and the UCLA Center for Medieval and Renaissance Studies.

In 1982, he was awarded the G. E. Bentley Prize and, in 1989, was selected Professor of the Year for Alabama by the Council for the Advancement and Support of Education. At AUM, he received the Faculty Excellence Award and has been named Distinguished Research Professor, Distinguished Teacher Professor, and University Alumni Professor. Most recently, he was named Professor of the Year by the South Atlantic Association of Departments of English. He is one of three editors of the *Ben Jonson Journal* and is a contributing editor to the *John Donne Variorum Edition*.

Evans is the author or editor of nearly 30 books on such topics as Ben Jonson, Martha Moulsworth, Kate Chopin, John Donne, Frank O'Connor, Brian Friel, Ambrose Bierce, Amy Tan, early modern women writers, pluralist literary theory, literary criticism, twentieth-century American writers, American novelists, Shakespeare, seventeenth-century English literature, and the poetry of World War I. He is also the author of roughly three hundred essays or notes on a variety of topics, especially dealing with Renaissance literature, critical theory, women writers, short fiction, and literature of the nineteenth and twentieth centuries. His work on Kate Chopin includes a critical companion to her short fiction and a forthcoming annotated critical edition of *The Awakening*.

Robert D. Arner is professor of English and Comparative Literature at the University of Cincinnati and the author of the first American dissertation on Chopin (*Kate Chopin, Music from a Farther Room: A Study of the Fiction of Kate Chopin* [1970]), which was subsequently revised and published as a special "Kate Chopin" issue of *Louisiana Studies*. He has also published several additional pieces on Kate Chopin's stories, as well as numerous articles and notes on other American writers, including Ernest Hemingway, Nathaniel Hawthorne, Edward Taylor, Charles Brockden Brown, Benjamin Franklin, and others. His books and monographs include *Dobson's Encyclopaedia: The Publisher, Text, and Publication of America's First Britannica, 1789-1803* (University of Pennsylvania Press, 1991), *James Thurber* (Ohio Authors Series, 1979), and *The Lost Colony in Literature* (North Carolina Department of Natural Resources, 1985).

Janet Beer is the vice-chancellor of Oxford Brookes University. She is the author of *Edith Wharton: Traveller in the Land of Letters* (1990), *Kate Chopin, Charlotte Perkins Gilman, Edith Wharton: Studies in Short Fiction* (1997), *Edith Wharton*, (2002), and editor of *The Cambridge Companion to Kate Chopin*, (2008). She is the co-editor of *Special Relationships: Anglo-American Antagonisms and Affinities, 1854-1936* (2002), *American Feminism: Key Source Documents 1848-1920* (2002), *The Awakening: A Sourcebook* (2004), *Lives of Victorian Literary Figures IV: Edith Wharton* (2006), and *Edith Wharton's 'The House of Mirth'* (2007). In 2011, she published *Edith Wharton: Sex, Satire and the Older Woman*, co-authored with Avril Horner.

Thomas Bonner, Jr. is professor emeritus at Xavier University of Louisiana, where, until recently, he was W. K. Kellogg Professor and Chair of English. He has twice served as Distinguished Visiting Professor at the United States Air Force Academy. In addition to *The Kate Chopin Companion with Chopin's Translations from French Fiction*, he has published books and monographs on William Faulkner, Edgar Allan Poe, Southern fiction, and Southern poetry. For twenty years, he served as editor of *Xavier Review* and Xavier Review Press. He has published and spoken on Kate Chopin and her writing since 1969.

Stephen Paul Bray is completing a master's degree at Auburn University at Montgomery, where he has won a number of awards. He is the co-author of a recent essay on Elie Wiesel's *Night* and is doing his master's thesis on the poet George Herbert.

Joyce Dyer has published many essays on Kate Chopin as well as a full-length book on *The Awakening*. She is the author of three memoirs (*In a Tangled Wood*, *Gum-Dipped*, and *Goosetown*) and the editor of *Bloodroot: Reflections on Place by Appalachian Women Writers*. She has published essays in newspapers and magazines, such as *North American Review, The New York Times, Writer's Chronicle, cream city review,* and *Southern Literary Journal*. She teaches creative writing at Hiram College, Ohio and currently lives in Hudson, Ohio, where she's working on a book about her town's most famous citizen—John Brown.

Sarah Fredericks is a doctoral student at the University of Arizona. She has a particular interest in Southern Literature, nineteenth- and twentieth-century American female writers, Mark Twain, and Kate Chopin. Her essay "The Profane Twain: His Personal and Literary Cursing" appeared in *The Mark Twain Journal* (49.1-2 [2011]: 9-66).

Helena Goodwyn is currently completing her PhD thesis: 'The Americanisation of W. T. Stead', at Queen Mary, University of London. In 2012, she was awarded the Gale Dissertation Research Fellowship in Nineteenth-Century Media by the Research Society for Victorian Periodicals. Her research focuses on reassessing Stead's career as a newspaper man and proponent of "new journalism" in order to establish his work as being one of the first truly transatlantic collections of British writing. She holds a BA in English Language and Literature from the University of Leeds and an MA from King's College London.

Bernard Koloski is editor of KateChopin.org, the website of the Kate Chopin International Society. He has edited and written five books and several articles about Chopin.

Courtney Lane Rottgering holds a BA in English from the University of Mississippi and is nearing completion of her master's degree at Auburn University at Montgomery. She works in the University of Texas system at its San Antonio campus.

Jeffrey Melton holds a PhD from the University of South Carolina and is an associate professor of American Studies at the University of Alabama. He is the author of *Mark Twain, Travel Books, and Tourism: The Tide of a Great Popular Movement* (University of Alabama Press, 2002, rpt. 2009) and co-editor of *Mark Twain on the Move: A Travel Reader* (University of Alabama Press, 2009). He has published on travel literature, tourism, and humor, including articles in *South Atlantic Review*, *Papers on Language and Literature*, *Studies in American Humor*, and *Popular Culture Review*. He has also contributed essays to *A Companion to Mark Twain* (Blackwell) and *The Cinema of Terry Gilliam* (Columbia/Wallflower).

Mary E. Papke is professor of English at the University of Tennessee. She is the author of *Verging on the Abyss: the Social Fiction of Kate Chopin and Edith Wharton* and *Susan Glaspell: A Research and Production Sourcebook*. She is also editor of *Twisted from the Ordinary: Essays on American Literary Naturalism*. In addition, she has published essays on feminist theory, postmodern women writers, the unpublished drama of Evelyn Scott, the political theatre of Sean O'Casey, and Marxist literary criticism in early twentieth-century America, among other topics. All of these projects have focused significantly on issues of gender and class ideologies as well as the process of ethical and aesthetic evaluation.

Peter J. Ramos has criticism featured in *MELUS*, *College Literature*, *The Faulkner Journal*, *The CEA Critic*, *Mandorla*, *Pleiades*, *Poetry Daily*, and *The Other Latin@: Writing Against a Singular Identity* (Eds. Blas Falconer and Lorraine M. López, University of Arizona Press, 2011). His poems have appeared in *Colorado Review*, *Puerto Del Sol*, *Painted Bride Quarterly*, *Indiana Review*, *Verse*, *Mississippi Review* (online) and other journals. He is the author of one book of poetry, *Please Do Not Feed the Ghost* (BlazeVox Books, 2008). He is associate professor of English at Buffalo State College, where he offers courses in nineteenth- and twentieth-century American literatures within a cross-cultural context.

Julieann Veronica Ulin joined Florida Atlantic University as an assistant professor of British and American Modernism in 2009. She received her PhD in English from the University of Notre Dame, where she was the Edward Sorin Postdoctoral Fellow in the Humanities from 2007-2009. She holds an MA in English from Fordham University and a BA in English from Washington and Lee University. Her scholarship has appeared in *American Literature*, *Critical*

Insights: Southern Gothic (Salem Press) and *Richard Wright: New Readings for the 21st Century* (Palgrave Macmillan). She is the editor of *Race and Immigration in the New Ireland* (University of Notre Dame Press) and the author of *Medieval Invasions in Modern Irish Literature* (Palgrave Macmillan).

David Z. Wehner is associate professor at Mount St. Mary's University in Emmitsburg, Maryland, where he teaches nineteenth- and twentieth-century American literature and specializes in the history, theory, and literature of secularization. He has published work on Kate Chopin, Flannery O'Connor, and Toni Morrison in journals, such as *American Literary Realism*, *Mississippi Quarterly*, and the *Flannery O'Connor Review*.

Index _____